THE FLAG

The story of Revd David Railton MC and
the Tomb of the Unknown Warrior

ANDREW RICHARDS

CASEM   LE

Oxford & Philadelphia

First published in Great Britain and the United States of America in 2017.
Reprinted as a paperback in 2019 by
CASEMATE PUBLISHERS
The Old Music Hall, 106–108 Cowley Road, Oxford OX4 1JE, UK
and
1950 Lawrence Road, Havertown, PA 19083, US

Copyright 2017 © Andrew Richards
Reprinted in paperback 2019

Paperback Edition: ISBN 978-1-61200-749-6
Digital Edition: ISBN 978-1-61200-448-8

A CIP record for this book is available from the Library of Congress and the British Library

Printed in the United Kingdom by TJ International
Typeset in India by Lapiz Digital Services, Chennai

For a complete list of Casemate titles, please contact:

CASEMATE PUBLISHERS (US)
Telephone (610) 853-9131
Fax (610) 853-9146
Email: casemate@casematepublishers.com
www.casematepublishers.com

CASEMATE PUBLISHERS (UK)
Telephone (01865) 241249
Email: casemate-uk@casematepublishers.co.uk
www.casematepublishers.co.uk

This book is dedicated to my brothers in arms who have left us during or after serving their country and to those that survived and live with the consequences and aftermath today.

Contents

Foreword: *From the Dean of Westminster*   vi
Preface   viii
Acknowledgements   x
Prologue   xii

1	Sleepless Nights	1
2	Early Days in France	22
3	Vimy Ridge	42
4	Graveyards	57
5	Military Cross	80
6	Winter of Death	93
7	Private Denis Blakemore	113
8	Kaiserschlacht	134
9	Back to Blighty	150
10	Now or Never	163
11	The Unknown Warrior	173
12	Hanging the Flag	201
13	Going Home	221

Epilogue   249
Appendix: Countries that Adopted the Idea of the Unknown Warrior   251
Notes   253
Bibliography   280
Index   285

From the Dean of Westminster

The Grave of the Unknown Warrior is just one of 3,300 graves, tombs or memorials in Westminster Abbey. Kings and queens are buried there, from Edward the Confessor in 1065 to George II in 1760 and including Henry V, Henry VII and Elizabeth I; scientists include Isaac Newton and Charles Darwin; politicians and statesmen include Wilberforce and Gladstone; musicians, writers, poets and actors, amongst them Purcell and Handel, Dickens and Kipling, Chaucer and Tennyson, Garrick and Olivier; a cardinal and archbishops, abbots and monks, deans and canons; soldiers, sailors and airmen; explorers and adventurers; courtiers, charity workers and campaigners; the list goes on. Many of the tombs are fine and the monuments elaborate, even magnificent. But none compares in dignity with the Grave of the Unknown Warrior.

Many of the burial places and memorials in the Abbey have their moment of prominence. Annually on a birthday at some memorials, or at others to mark a centenary, flowers are laid or a wreath by descendants or by a society celebrating a poet's power or a statesman's skill, and prayers are said. But the Unknown Warrior's is the only grave over which no one ever walks, surrounded usually by poppies, though on a recent occasion marking the centenary of the Commonwealth War Graves Commission by fresh flowers and herbs, and the only grave regularly to receive a wreath laid by a king or queen or president on a state visit to Her Majesty the Queen or by a head of government.

And each November, while the Field of Remembrance is laid in St Margaret's Churchyard to the north of the Abbey, the Grave of the Unknown Warrior is honoured with countless poppies laid down by the relatives or comrades of service men and women fallen in battle and those who have gone to their rest. The Grave remains for countless people a profoundly moving symbol of service and sacrifice.

This account of the life and ministry of the Reverend David Railton, army chaplain and parish priest, whose idea it was to bury an Unknown Warrior in Westminster Abbey, at the heart of our nation and Commonwealth, an idea that continues to resonate so strongly, published as we commemorate the centenary of the First World War, serves not only to enhance our understanding of his motivation and his commitment but also, I hope, to inspire and encourage us to spend our lives in the service of almighty God and of our fellow men and women.

The Very Reverend Dr John Hall
Dean of Westminster
7th June 2017

Preface

Shortly after I began my early research for this book, it became apparent to me that the story of Reverend David Railton, MC, had to be told. Living through times of great change, being tested by history and circumstance, he held on to his love of God, country, and fellow man. He advocated for religious pluralism while some sections of society were rife with sectarian division. He remained a patriot even when he disagreed with some of his country's actions. And he championed the cause and rights of ordinary soldiers with whom he had shared trenches.

Based on my research, reading his correspondence, and interviewing his family, I have no doubt that David was deeply affected by his wartime experiences. Family members, friends, parishioners, and his own words demonstrate that despite his stoicism, he was a man deeply troubled and scarred. Like most soldiers when they returned home, David did not talk much about the war. His son, Andrew Scott Railton said David never talked about his time in the trenches.[1] That is not surprising. It is generally accepted that soldiers traumatised by conflict rarely talk about it. David Railton Q.C., grandson of Revd David Railton, said the same of his own father, Andrew, who had a distinguished service record during the Second World War.[2] Although modern medicine identifies unwillingness to talk and social withdrawal as symptoms of Post-Traumatic Stress Disorder (PTSD), during that era, being reticent about your war record was more of an accepted British social norm. It was not considered polite or good manners to talk about what 'one got up to' during the war, even though this abstention often exacerbated their problems.

Despite silently carrying this burden and at times being extremely distressed, David always relied on his faith in God and the love of a strong family to help him through. Stories told locally of his night-time walks around Margate were well known. Although some residents may have found this habit a little strange, modern research on PTSD pinpoints insomnia as another symptom. Although medical professionals probably would not recommend walking alone at night, it was David's way of coping – and he helped others along the way.

This story of Reverend David Railton, M.C., his flag, and the Tomb of the Unknown Warrior is based on factual evidence, but on occasion, some creative licence has been taken to create scenes as I imagined them. With regards to dialogue, although all places and people are factually correct, if there is no footnote, then the same creative licence has been used.

David's First World War letters to his wife, Ruby, were donated to the Imperial War Museum in the 1990s by his son, Andrew. The letters were typed under Ruby's supervision sometime after David's death in 1955. A lot of the contents (presumably, anything of a personal nature) were removed.[3] There is no record of any letters written by David between 28 April and 12 July 1916, whilst he was at Vimy Ridge. As that was his first experience under German attack, it is likely that he simply did not have time. The reason why his wife did not offer up any letters after 31 May 1917, when he became Senior Chaplain 19th Division, is unknown, but is dealt with during the book.

David's divine gift as an orator inspired soldiers, airmen, and civilians throughout two world wars and over a forty-year span. He was able to inspire all who heard him speak, and he led by example. Almost a hundred years after he returned from the Western Front, the example he set, the values he held high, and his humility are timeless and resonate with me today.

I am saddened by the thought that throughout his life, David did not receive the recognition he deserved. His link to the Tomb of the Unknown Warrior remained untold for years, being consigned to the archives of a few newspapers and magazines despite the fact that it inspired similar memorials to be established all around the world. Sixty-two years after his death, this book elaborates on that link and tells the tale of a remarkable man, his experiences on the Western Front, and the flag he carried with him.

Acknowledgements

My grateful thanks to Mrs Margaret Railton and her son, Mr David Railton QC. Thank you for having the courage to allow a simple soldier like me access to your precious family archive. I will never be able to thank you enough for the faith and trust you have shown me.

I am also thankful to the following individuals and organisations: Ancestry.com; Ms Annie Barnes, britaininfocus.org.uk; Mr David Blake AMA, Army Museum of Chaplaincy; Mr Shaun Blanchard, Marquette University; Mr James Brazier; the British Museum; Mrs Brenda Brown; Mr Robert Butterworth, Kilflynn Church Preservation Society; Mr Robin Colyer; Major (Retd) Jasper Dalgliesh, JPD Photography; Mr Ian Dickie, Margate Museum; The Very Revd Canon Dr J. J. W. Edmondson; Mr Charles Fair; Ms Tara Freeman, St Lawrence University; Mr Phillip Green; Chris Harper and family of the Harper Partnership; Dr James E. Hawdon, Virginia Polytechnic Institute and State University; Headquarters, London District; the Household Cavalry Museum; Pastor Bruce R. Johnson; Margate Historical Society; Margate Library; WO1(GSM) (Retd) W. Mott, Welsh Guards; Ms Sara Moule; the National Archives, Kew; Revd Dr John R. H. Railton; Ms Christine Reynolds, Westminster Abbey Archive; Mr Peter Rowden; the Salvation Army Heritage Centre; Dr Brett L. Shadle, Virginia Polytechnic Institute and State University; the *Times* Archive; Miss Fawn Walters, Canterbury Cathedral Archive; Captain Grant Webster, Joint Service Mountain Training Centre (Scotland).

Special thanks to my mother, Mrs C. E. Richards, for helping me with many clerical questions, and to my brother and sister-in-law, Mr Gary and Mrs Alison Richards, for the many trips to various archives and museums. Also, special thanks to Ruth Sheppard and everyone at Casemate Publishers.

And finally, a very special thank you to my wife, Mrs Melissa Farmer Richards, for the hours spent editing, reading and supporting me throughout. I could not have done this without you.

Prologue

Thursday, 26 April 1923, London, England

Crowds had started to gather outside 17 Bruton Street, hours before the horse-drawn state carriage arrived. Despite the cold spring weather and gloomy post-war economy hanging over their heads, Londoners packed the streets to see the future Duchess of York. Offices and businesses all across London closed for the day, with thousands of people jostling and pushing, trying to secure the best vantage points.

At just after eleven o'clock, Lady Elizabeth Angela Marguerite Bowes-Lyon stepped out of her family's London residence and into the public eye; everyone strained their necks and stood as high as they could to catch a glimpse. Her father, Claude George Bowes-Lyon, 14th Earl of Strathmore and Kinghorne, wearing the uniform of the Lord Lieutenant of Angus, looked more nervous than his daughter. Her ladies-in-waiting, who held her train and bouquet of flowers, helped Lady Elizabeth into the carriage. Footmen, wearing their distinctive livery and medals earned during the war, stood to attention with their backs to the black iron railings at the entrance to the house. The large crowd, held back by police, gasped in delight at the sight of her, and most men instinctively removed their hats.

This was the first time the son of a reigning British monarch had not taken a bride of equal royal lineage from another royal family of Europe. A commoner was leaving the front door of a house on a London street to marry a prince, second in line to the throne, at Westminster

Abbey. The people of London stood and cheered, waving their hand-kerchiefs in the air.

News of the engagement of the Duke of York to Lady Elizabeth Bowes-Lyon had come as a surprise. The second son of the king marrying before his elder brother was unusual, but that the Bowes-Lyons were not from another European royal family – even though they were descendants of ancient Scottish nobility – was a break from recent royal protocol. Concerned about public opinion, as well as casting off the Germanic family name of Saxe-Coburg and Gotha, replacing it with the very English name of Windsor in July 1917, the King decided his children would be free to marry into British families if they so wished.

Following the engagement announcement,[1] the papers were filled with news of the couple. Leading up to the wedding, stories introduced Lady Elizabeth to their readers. They read about her father converting their Scottish family home, Glamis Castle, into a hospital for soldiers recuperating from wounds received in France and Belgium. They learned of the terrible price the Bowes-Lyon family, like many thousands of other families all over Britain, had paid during the war.

Even so, the jury of public opinion was still out, as the country waited for her to step into the spotlight. The nation struggled in the aftermath of the war – much had changed. Despite victory, Britain was racked with social upheaval and industrial unrest, the popularity of the ruling classes at an all-time low. Many worried the revolutions that had torn apart some European countries in 1919 could do the same to Britain.

So it wasn't the best time for another member of the entitled elite, such as Lady Elizabeth Bowes-Lyon, to be introduced to the British public. But from the moment she stepped onto the street on that cold spring morning, the people took her into their hearts. The dress she wore was a decadent deep ivory-coloured chiffon moiré with pearls and silver thread, from the top fashion house of Madame Handley Seymour; however, she looked like one of the people. There was a simple elegance about her, which everyone instantly warmed to. Her dress, her smile – everything about her seemed to take away the cold, even if just for a moment. It was on this London street that a love affair between the British public and Elizabeth Bowes-Lyon began, and it would last another eight decades.

As soon as Lady Elizabeth and her father were safe inside the carriage, it moved off past cheering onlookers towards Berkeley Square. Not entitled to a ceremonial escort from the Household Cavalry because of their status as commoners, despite Lord Strathmore having previously served as an officer in the Second Life Guards,[2] he and his daughter were escorted to Westminster Abbey from their home by eight mounted policemen on white horses. The route down Berkeley Street, west along Piccadilly and around Hyde Park Corner, was packed, and the crowds grew bigger and louder along Constitution Hill, all down the Mall, and across Horse Guards Parade. Only on Whitehall near the Cenotaph were the crowds more subdued. The five-year-old national shrine to Britain's war dead was a place of great reverence for a nation still grieving. Some onlookers did not feel it appropriate to cheer and wave at what was now considered the country's most solemn monument.

The carriage came around Parliament Square, passing hundreds of soldiers and sailors lining the streets, stood to attention with their rifles presented in front of them. Two divisions of Household Cavalry, fresh from escorting the royal family, now lined up to wait for the newlyweds to reappear from the Abbey. Arriving as Lady Elizabeth Bowes-Lyons, she would leave as the Duchess of York.

When the state Landau carriage pulled up in front of the West Entrance, two footmen on the rear climbed down, lowered the steps and opened the doors. Lord Strathmore stepped out first, then helped his daughter. Once they were ready and everything was in place, they moved through the Great West door and into the Abbey. Further ahead, someone had fainted, bringing the procession to a halt.

Set into the stone floor just inside the Abbey lay an engraved slab of black marble from Namur in Belgium, covering the remains of a British soldier from the Great War, buried with full military honours just three years earlier. While they waited, Lady Elizabeth moved forward and approached the grave. She carefully knelt down and laid her bouquet of white roses, lilies of the valley and heather[3] onto the marble slab. Slowly she rose and took a pace backwards, pausing for a moment. The congregation were curious at this departure from protocol. Those close enough could clearly see that despite this being her wedding day, there was immense sadness in her eyes. Some speculated afterwards that once the procession had stopped, she suddenly thought of her brother Fergus who died in 1915 at the Battle of Loos. His body had not been found.

After a few seconds of stillness and sad reflection, she looked up at the Padre's Flag – a battle-scarred Union Jack hanging off a pillar to the left of the grave. The sadness quickly disappeared; a half smile returned to her face as she turned back towards her father. Bridesmaids straightened the train of the dress while Lady Elizabeth and Lord Strathmore waited for the procession to re-form. The signal came, the choir sang 'Lead Us Heavenly Father', and the bride's procession walked past the grave where her flowers now lay, towards Lady Elizabeth's future husband and members of the royal family, who were waiting at the altar.

CHAPTER I

Sleepless Nights

'Not for ourselves alone are we born.'

CICERO

Monday, 10 January 1921, Margate, England

The rain had stopped earlier in the night. The Revd David Railton MC put on his coat, hat, scarf and gloves, then left the vicarage through the front door. His leather-soled shoes crunched on the gravel driveway as he headed towards the road. He'd been awake for about an hour. Sleepless nights were a regular occurrence since his return from France. He found that once he was awake he couldn't just lie there in bed waiting for sleep to return. He'd tried staring at shards of light from outside as they danced on the ceiling, or he'd listen to the metronomic ticking of the clock in the hallway, hoping it might have a hypnotic effect upon him. He'd even tried sitting by the fire, wrapped up in a blanket in front of the dying embers, staring at its ever-changing colours, praying that sleep might return. But over the past two years he'd discovered that the only thing that helped his nerves and kept his mind calm once he was awake was to walk.

In the dead of night, walking through the town, along the rail-tracks or on the promenade seemed to help. The exercise and fresh sea air cleared his mind. He spent the time thinking about sermons and speeches, even starting to compose a letter or two in his head. The more he thought of everyday tasks, the less time he had to think of the war. But try as he might, like most soldiers who had returned from the horrors of trench warfare, there was always something – a name, a place, or perhaps even a smell – something would bring it back. The air was sharp and crisp after the rain had passed; the clearing sky meant they might get a late frost before the sun rose. He pulled his scarf up over his mouth, then crossed the bridge over the rail-line and headed along St Peters Road.

By the early 1920s, expansion of Margate's urban areas had pushed down to the rail-line next to College Road. In time, development would spill over into the countryside, eventually surrounding the vicarage with housing estates and a new hospital built in 1930. But at this time the vicarage sat on the edge of town, straddling the line between advancing urban sprawl and the Kent countryside.

Lit by white gas street lamps spaced about 50 yards apart, staggered on either side of St Peters Road, the darkened houses and narrow passageways that separated them cast a gloom that may have seemed a little forbidding to some. Street lighting had improved in the town, but because of its location on the coast during the war, restrictions had been in place. The 'Defence of the Realm Act' prohibited lights from the sea and bright lights in other parts of the town.[1] Consequently, Margate was still badly lit after the sun went down. But David had spent many nights alone in total darkness trying to find his way back from the trenches. Margate's darkened streets held no fear for him.

★★★

The year 1921 was a defining one for David Railton. It was the year when his pre-war life clashed with traumatic experiences in the trenches and shaped his future. In a letter to his wife, written from the harsh and bitter cold of a trench on the Ypres Salient in January 1917, he made a promise: 'If God spares me I shall spend half my life in getting their rights for the men who fought out here.'[2]

Although he did this – arguably spending more than 'half his life' fighting for them – by the end of 1921, it looked like he was about to embark on a personal crusade to help all those in society who were not able to fend for themselves, not just those who'd fought in France.

At first glance it looks like he had already achieved much. His idea to bring home an unknown comrade from France to be buried in Westminster Abbey had been achieved. The public reaction and outpouring of support was far more than he, the Dean of Westminster, the Prime Minister and even King George V could have expected. But outside the parish, despite being mentioned by *The Times* on 13 November 1920 as the 'originator of the idea',[3] very few people knew of Railton or of the flag that was draped upon the coffin and now lying at the foot of the grave of the Unknown Warrior.

The year would start with a cold reality check for David and fellow Anglican clergymen up and down the country. The first Sunday service of the New Year was usually a time when congregations swelled with parishioners looking to start anew with a confirmed resolve of worship, wanting to see the New Year in with their family in their parish church. But the number of people sitting in the pews of churches up and down the length and breadth of Britain was low. Before the war, there had been a steady rise in numbers regularly attending Anglican churches. During the war, this trend continued. But after the Armistice in 1918, that rise had turned into a sharp decline. In 1914, two-parent families and their children lined up to hear a vicar's weekly sermon, ready to sing their hearts out in praise of the Lord. Just a few years later, however, everything had changed. There were so many families with no males, the sons, husbands, and brothers all cut down in their prime. Some found solace in prayer, but for those left behind, times were hard. Without the returning men, many families had no bread-winner. Children were placed into orphanages while their mothers were forced to seek employment any way they could. Many ended up on the streets. For a soldier returning from the war who had managed to survive the slaughter, the Prime Minister's 'country fit for heroes to live in' had quickly turned into a hell on Earth.

Discontent was everywhere; people seemed to no longer trust those in authority. Their generals had led them to victory, but at what cost? The government's provision of pensions for families of soldiers killed was nowhere near adequate, and there wasn't enough work for the hundreds of thousands of ex-servicemen who had given so much for their country. Against this backdrop David Railton was trusted, his Military Cross a testament to his dedication and bravery. His great oratorical skills meant there would 'always be a queue when he preached'.[4] But the widespread downturn in attendees across Britain was a clear sign that people had abandoned their church *en masse*.

Of all denominations, it seemed especially bad for Anglican Chaplains to the Forces (CF). It would be some years before the publication of Robert Graves' *Goodbye to All That* and Guy Chapman's *A Passionate Prodigality* would leave a lasting stain on the reputation of Anglican chaplains; however, articles and controversial stories had already started to appear in local and national magazines and newspapers. Reports of churchmen in uniform doing anything to stay away from the front line, and soldiers hearing that padres had returned to England the day after their yearlong contracts ended, spread through the ranks of returning soldiers. The reputation of most Anglican clergymen – the minority who went to France and most who stayed within the safety of their parishes – had not gone untarnished.

David knew that time was a great healer, but it appeared to him that something integral which bound British society together had been lost, and it would take a great effort to get it back. The total destruction and wholesale slaughter of many hundreds of thousands of men had ripped open a wound so deep that David had found it difficult to heal – within the church, amongst his parishioners and, sometimes, even within himself. The losses brought about by war and parishioners' unwillingness to attend church made him feel that throughout the country and within the Church of England, the country's faith was starting to fail.

As if the war had not been bad enough, towards the end of the conflict in the spring of 1918 and throughout the first winter after the Armistice was signed, influenza killed millions of people across the globe. Now known to be the H1N1 flu virus, starting in birds then mutating through pigs kept close to the front line in Europe, it was believed to have spread from France. It eventually would claim 50–100 million lives worldwide. After losing sons in the trenches, parents were now losing their daughters at home. Many soldiers who had survived the slaughter of war were returning home to find their homes empty (repossessed by landlords) and their loved ones buried in the town's graveyards. Even devout Christians must have wondered whether their God had forsaken them.

David had only been appointed vicar of the parish church of St John the Baptist in Margate three months earlier, so he was still very new to the job. At the end of the war, he returned as curate of St Mary and St Eanswythe Church in Folkestone in January 1919, the position he'd occupied before departing for France. But his war record, his association with the Unknown Warrior, and his previous work in Folkestone under a very influential clergyman, Canon P. F. Tindall, had brought his name into prominence within the Anglican Church.

He was inducted as vicar of Margate on 25 September 1920.[5] Having previously lived in Margate on Gordon Road with his mother, younger brother and sister, he knew the town and was keen to return to it as vicar of St John's when the Bishop offered him the position. He might have passed his mother's three-story terraced house on one of his nocturnal wanderings, remembering his childhood there. His mother, who now lived just a short distance away in Broadstairs, left Margate when David's youngest brother, Nathaniel, known to all as Gerry, had been ordained into the Church of England. David's mother and sister would move back to Margate later that year, but living in Broadstairs she had already been close enough to help him through some very difficult times after he returned home. In a 1972 letter to Andrew Scott Railton, Mrs Kathleen Lockyer, a friend of the family, described what a huge support David's mother was to him: 'When David came back from France, his eyes damaged by gas and his mind in a turmoil, to take up the demanding parish of Margate, his mother grasped his state of mind and was able to soothe and strengthen him.'[6]

Apart from a string of debilitating illnesses that seemed to inflict the Railton children from time to time,[7] Margate seems to have been a happy place for David as a child. He went to the Stanley House School[8] and in the warmer months walked the short distance from the end of Gordon Road to the Queen's Promenade and beach. He would spend hours playing with his younger brother and sister in the sand during the summer holidays, watching the fishing vessels come and go. These years filled him with happy memories. The only dark cloud in the blue sky of his childhood seemed to be the prolonged absence of his father.

George Scott Railton, the son of a Scottish Wesleyan Methodist minister and missionary, was one of the leading lights in the early days and first Commissioner of The Salvation Army. At the age of 15, after both of his parents died of cholera, he found himself jobless and homeless.

His older brother, Lancelot, who also was a Methodist minister, found him work as a clerk at a London shipping firm. But his unwillingness to write lies on behalf of the company, even if they were just 'white lies', soon had him out of work again.

George's upbringing was strict,[9] so it is no surprise that at an early age teaching the gospel would run deep in his blood. After spending time in Morocco, he met William Booth and joined The Christian Mission, soon to be renamed The Salvation Army. After rising to the rank of General Secretary, then becoming The Salvation Army's first Commissioner, he spent the rest of his life travelling around the world spreading the reach of The Salvation Army until his death in Germany in 1913 at age 64.

Even though Commissioner Railton had strongly objected to both David and his brother studying at Oxford and being ordained into the Anglican Church,[10] they both loved their father. Despite his prolonged absence abroad and views on the way he wanted David and his brother to conduct their lives after they finished school, David respected him and his commitment to the poor. In a radio broadcast to the United States, sometime between 1935 and 1942, David said this of his father: 'Let me say in all sincerity as his elder son, that he was the finest man I have ever known.'[11]

David's mother, Marianne Parkyn, took the lead role in shaping his life while his father spread the Salvationist message across the globe. She was a Salvation Army sergeant and the daughter of a Free Church minister in Torquay, Devon. Her father, a rather strict, stern man of some considerable means and elevated social station in Torquay, strongly disapproved of her association with The Salvation Army. His angst increased tenfold when his daughter announced she was in love with one of The Salvation Army's leaders. At first Mr Parkyn refused Commissioner Railton entry to his house and fought his daughter's wishes to marry, but eventually he relented after he met Railton in person, later describing him as a 'gentleman'.[12] After long consideration and several pleas for his future son-in-law to quit The Salvation Army, including promises of considerable financial support for his wife and family, Mr Parkyn relented and allowed the marriage to go ahead. They were married in London at Exeter Hall on 17 January 1884, in what was more of a public spectacle than a wedding, presided over by William Booth, founder of The Salvation Army.

For the first year of their marriage, Marianne followed her husband from meeting to meeting up and down the length of Britain. Then, on 13 November, that same year, she gave birth to a son, David, in London.[13] Just two months later, on New Year's Day 1885, distressed and reluctant to leave her baby, Marianne dutifully set sail for South Africa with her husband. After a gruelling nine months of long, arduous journeys and prolonged periods nursing her sick husband, they returned to England. Marianne left the ship in Plymouth, frail from constant seasickness on the voyage home and anxious to see her son at her parent's house in Torquay. Meanwhile, her husband continued on to London. Marianne had tried being a 'true Salvation lassie'[14] in support of her dedicated husband but now concentrated on making a home for her children.

With financial support from her father, she bought a house in London and lived there with her son and two other children when they arrived – Nathaniel in 1886[15] and Esther in 1887.[16] Staying in London would have been preferred because it meant the least amount of travel for the Commissioner when he returned to England. But living in London exacerbated the children's illnesses. After a short stay in Davos, Switzerland, they eventually moved to the south coast, taking up residence at 42 Gordon Road.[17] It is not known why the family chose Margate. Many families were trying to escape the pollution that was blighting London, and with the illnesses afflicting the children, they may have been one of those families fortunate enough to do so. The Royal Seabathing Hospital was located in Margate. It is where, according to Mr Ian Dickie of the Margate Museum, 'London's children came to be treated for 2'6" a week... Most children treated there soon got better because the foul London air had actually laid them low with what we know today as asthma and bronchitis.'[18]

★★★

David came to the end of St Peters Road at the corner of Frog Hill. The clouds that brought the rain earlier in the night had cleared completely; stars studded the sky, and David savoured the sight. He looked across the road towards the graveyard of the church, his vision obscured for a moment by the thick fog caused by his breath.

St John the Baptist Church in its current form dated back to 1875, when the architect Ewan Christian restored the roof and spire as part of a Victorian church restoration project that was taking place in England at the time. But the land on which the early English Gothic church now stood had been a place of worship for almost nine centuries. The monks of St Mary's minster had built a chapel for travellers in 1050, with the church growing bigger after several Norman-built extensions throughout the 12th century. After the turmoil of the Reformation in the 16th century, the church separated from the minister of St Mary's, even having its shrines and altars removed. The church had several revisions and extensions; however, up until the Victorian restoration work, it was in a poor state of repair. David had many plans for this ancient house of God – changes that he hoped would help the surrounding community and bring the parishioners back.

Although lighting around the church was poor, he thought he saw someone or something move around the back of the church. He took out a torch, crossed over the road and opened a gate that led through the graveyard to the rear of the church. The habit of carrying a torch everywhere was one he had acquired from his time in the trenches. During the war, he'd conducted many services under torchlight or in complete darkness. Now he never went anywhere at night without one.

As he came around the south side of the church to where he thought he saw movement, he called out.

'Hello, is there anyone there?'

He spoke clearly but with a little hesitation in his voice. He wasn't sure what he was walking into. As he came around the corner, he heard the sound of someone running around the opposite side of the church, across the graveyard towards Church Square. David walked quickly and just caught sight of the man running through the headstones.

'There's no need to run away!' he shouted. 'You're not in any trouble.'

But he knew the man probably hadn't heard him; the sound of his boots on the cobbled path drowned out his voice.

David stopped and looked down at the ground to the rear of the church. The man had propped some wood and cardboard against the church wall; he'd obviously been trying to stay dry and warm. He'd bolted immediately and did not leave anything notable behind.

David walked around towards the vestry door and turned the handle. The door was locked. He then went around to the front of the church and found the large wooden doors were locked too. He groaned. He had left instructions that the church was to be left unlocked, especially on nights as cold and wet as this one.

David turned around again underneath the oak trees and looked back in the direction where the man had run. He stood and thought for a moment.

If he was out sleeping rough in this weather, then he was clearly in need of help…

He decided on a course of action, walked down the main entrance steps and turned left on Church Alley. He moved faster now, a much brisker pace than he usually maintained during his nocturnal strolls. Just a short distance down the narrow and dark alley he turned right on Six Bells Lane and right again on the High Street by the Six Bells Inn.

The area of Margate around St John's, upper parts of the High Street, Church Square and Charlotte Place was much different than the modern housing opposite the church on Churchfields today. In 1921, the narrow street tenements and brick buildings, which dated back as far as the mid-17th century, were known as 'seedy' parts of town. Although cock-fighting had been outlawed years before, the courtyards and narrow passages still held a reputation as places of dubious activities.

David walked quickly down the High Street, the gradient now falling away as the road headed towards the sea front. As he walked by Buller's Yard, he looked across to the arch and peered into the gloom. Over 200 years old and quickly falling into disrepair, Buller's Yard was known to most local residents as the Parish Yard,[19] somewhere the poor and homeless might take refuge. He looked again as he came level and was startled when he heard a voice from the other side of the street.

'Morning, vicar.'

David stopped in his tracks.

'Oh, constable, you gave me such a fright,' he said, catching his breath.

'I'm sorry, sir. I was just wondering why someone would be up and about at this hour and heading down the High Street in such a hurry? I heard you coming right up by the church.'

The constable walked under the arch and crossed the road to where David was composing himself.

'I was just heading to the station to report that I saw someone around the back of St John's. If they are sleeping rough by the church, then I'd like to get them some help if I can.'

'How many did you see, sir?' asked the constable.

'Just the one, I believe,' he replied. 'Constable Freeborn, isn't it?' he enquired.

'That's correct, sir. You head down to the station, and Sergeant Palmer will take a statement if he thinks it's needed. I'll go take a look and head back down in a short while.'

'Thank you, constable. I don't want to make a fuss; I don't think he was causing any trouble. I'd just like to help him if I can.'

'Yes, of course, sir. There's plenty of folks struggling and sleeping rough right now. If I do find him, sir, do you want me to bring him down to the station or take him to Hawley Square?'

David thought for a moment.

'You could encourage him to come to the station. I'll probably be there for a while. I can take him to the Church House myself. But please tell him that he's not done anything wrong. I just want to help," he replied.

"Right you are, sir," the constable acknowledged.

David thanked the constable and continued down the High Street.

The town police had gotten to know their new vicar and become accustomed to his nighttime walks. He called into the police station most nights and joined them for a cup of tea or hot cocoa; for them it whiled away the time, making the hours until their shift ended go just a little bit faster. And as he had done in the trenches with soldiers, David earned a reputation amongst Margate's policemen as being a good listener and someone they could talk to.

★★★

David knew the police had a difficult job to do and was understanding of the way they did it, sometimes under very difficult circumstances. Law and order had to be maintained – all law-abiding citizens understood this. Although policemen were disliked in some areas of the country,[20] in small Kent towns like Margate, the local 'bobby' was generally well respected and liked. But all this changed after the war. Like the Anglican Church, attitudes towards the police were not the same. Amongst soldiers returning home, there was a general hatred of the 'Redcaps' (Corps of Military Police). Because of the way they treated soldiers in the rear areas in Belgium and France, this hatred seemed to transfer to the civil police when they arrived back home.

After the Armistice in 1918, the disastrous system of de-mobilisation known as Pivotalism[21] caused widespread unrest and anger amongst soldiers desperate to go home. The system allowed men with guarantees of employment, such as miners and policemen, to be de-mobbed first, ahead of some men who had fought throughout the entire war. During the scheme, many men agreed to become policemen with the promise of an earlier release, which did nothing to enhance the reputation of anyone in a policeman's uniform. The government and ruling classes were worried about increasing industrial and social unrest, so they intentionally bolstered police numbers at home as quickly as they could.

Earlier in the year, just after David had arrived in the parish, Mr Albert Lawton approached him on behalf of a self-appointed committee of six local philanthropists who were concerned about 'the plight of the distressed in Margate'.[22] He asked if the church would be willing to open the doors of its Church House on Hawley Square, allowing the committee to help provide food and shelter. They had money and volunteers, so all they needed was a suitable building. After consulting with his churchwardens and church council members, the St John's Church House, 55 Hawley Square, was handed over to the committee.

Despite feeding and providing comfort to over a thousand people per week, there soon was mounting resistance from members of the town council. Some of this resistance seems to have been politically motivated. As well as being a local philanthropist, Mr Lawton served as Honorary Secretary of the local branch of the Labour Party. Local civic and business leaders described him as 'a paid agitator'.[23]

To this point David always tried to stay impartial where politics was concerned, but his pathos towards the poor meant he was often drawn to the efforts of the Labour Party throughout his life. In this instance he was the voice of reason when some of the town's employers (through the mayor) at a town council meeting said, 'The unemployed organisation at St John's Church House should now close down.' David intervened by proclaiming that while there was still a need, 'it would be a sin to close it'.[24]

***

Within a few minutes of leaving Constable Freeborn at Buller's Yard, David had walked down the High Street. He heard the waves breaking on the sandy beach just one street over on Marine Drive, turned right, then walked around the far side of the town hall buildings, stepping into the police station at No. 5 Market Street.

The second oldest structure in Margate's town centre, the police station and town hall were two separate buildings connected by a walkway used to move between the buildings above the cobbled street below. The police station was on one side, with the magistrates' court and town hall's meeting room above. On the other side were offices of the Crime Investigation Department (CID) and the town sergeant, with the Mayor's Parlour, Committee Room and offices of the Chief Inspector and Chief Clerk. The outside walls of both buildings were painted a dirty cream colour, with architectural embellishments around the corners, windows and doors, which were painted white. The prevailing weather conditions that often brought sea-salt in the air had quickly attacked the iron guttering, pipes and bars on the police station windows. This added to the weather-beaten look of the building, as rust stains ran down most of the walls. The entrance to the police station was located on the far side of the building and had a blue shaded police lamp above the door.

Hearing the door handle creak and the large, bolt-reinforced door pushed open, the sergeant on duty looked up from the reception desk.

'Good morning, vicar. Two lumps, sir?' he asked, knowing how David took his tea.

'Good morning, Sergeant Palmer. Yes, please,' David said, taking off his scarf and hat.

The sergeant looked over at a constable who sat at the next desk by the telephone and nodded. The constable, who was obviously well accustomed to his sergeant's silent commands, stood up and headed off to the muster room without a word spoken between them.

'Sergeant, I've just bumped into Constable Freeborn up by Buller's Court. I told him I saw someone hanging around the back of the church as I passed.'

The sergeant had a puzzled look on his face and got up from the reception desk. 'You saw someone hanging around, you say?' He picked up a pencil and started taking notes. 'And about what time was this, sir?'

'Not 10 minutes ago,' David replied. Both he and the sergeant looked at the big clock on the wall in the corridor opposite the reception area.

'What was he doing, exactly?'

'Well, nothing really, I suppose. I saw some movement in the shadows, so I walked over to see who it was. Then he ran off towards Church Square,' David explained.

'Was anything missing? What do you think he was up to?'

The sergeant wasn't sure where this was going.

'Well, he left some cardboard and wood, which I think he was using as a shelter by the church walls. I checked the doors, and they haven't been forced. I do like them to be left unlocked when it is cold like this, but the churchwardens must have forgotten. I just wanted to see if we could find him and get him over to the Church House. It's really cold out now, and he must have been soaked from last night's rain.'

David took off his coat and placed it on a chair at the front counter.

'Just another homeless vagrant then?' the sergeant asked.

'Yes, it looks like it, I'm afraid,' replied David.

'We've already taken in two of our regulars tonight,' he said, pointing to the cells with his thumb.

'You come around this side of the desk, sir. When Fleet comes back with the tea, we'll go to my office and wait to see if Freeborn finds anyone.'

A few minutes later, the constable came back from the muster room with a tray holding a pot of steaming tea, three cups and saucers, plus containers of milk and sugar.

'There you go, sir.'

The constable stirred the pot, placed the lid back on, and poured the first cup for the vicar.

'Thank you, constable,' David responded.

'Thank you,' said the sergeant as he took a loud slurp from his cup. 'Hold the fort, constable. I'll be in my office if you need me,' Palmer added.

Carrying his cup and saucer he led David down the corridor past the cells and into the sergeant's office.

'So, how's things at the vicarage, sir? You and your family settling in nicely, I hope?' Palmer asked after he'd sat down.

The Railtons had moved into the newly refurbished vicarage on St Peter's Road, in November 1920. They had lived in temporary accommodation in Sussex Avenue while it was being renovated.[25]

'And is it four – no five – children you have, sir?' the sergeant enquired politely.

'Four girls and a boy,' David smiled, very proud of his large family.

Constable Thompson stuck his head around the sergeant's door.

'It's just as well they gave you that big old house down by Drapers Farm, sir.'

The sergeant gave the young constable a dark look.

'Good morning, sir,' Thompson said. 'I thought I heard you come in.'

'Morning, Constable.' David smiled.

David knew Constable Ernest Thompson from the church. He and his family were active members of the congregation. He'd helped the Railtons move into the vicarage. They'd also spoken on several occasions regarding his time during the war as a drill instructor at the Royal East Kent Regiment (The Buffs) training depot in Canterbury. They had mutual friends in the 19th (Western) Division when David was Senior Chaplain.

'What do you need, constable?' the sergeant asked, cutting short his pleasantries with the vicar.

'I'm about to head out, Sarge. Do you want me to take one of the new probationers with me?'

'Yes, good idea. The more time they are out there the quicker we can get back up to strength.'

Thompson smiled, nodded to the vicar and left the sergeant's office.

★★★

During the war, 444 Margate men lost their lives.[26] In 1914 Margate's population was less than 10,000, which was further reduced because the town lay in a restricted area; travel in and out was carefully monitored. The percentage of soldiers lost per capita for the United Kingdom in the war is thought to be around two per cent; for Margate it was more than four per cent. This high percentage of men who never returned had a huge effect upon the town. Thirteen Margate Borough policemen joined up from a mere strength of two inspectors, six sergeants and 46 constables.[27] Many were support troops, but PC Joseph Start and PC Archibald Jones were amongst the men who never returned.[28]

With that many policemen joining up, it fell upon the special constables (volunteer policemen) to take up the slack. As well as reduced numbers, the force took on many extra responsibilities after war was declared. The police had to enforce other Home Office and War Office mandates as well as patrol the streets of the town while it was forced to be in darkness. According to the 1915 Chief Constable's report:

> An Emergency Act was passed ... making it compulsory for aliens to register, prohibiting alien enemies from residing in districts and towns on the coast... The total number of persons who registered was 1,552 and the number of persons coming under the designation of alien enemies who were expelled from the borough was 278.[29]

The Watch Committee, who oversaw Margate Borough Police Force, made an appeal for more special constables – they had over 500 applicants.[30] Despite this, the police were short-handed throughout the war, and the force was still trying to get back to its full strength more than two years later.

★★★

'That is a big brood, sir. What ages are they?' Sergeant Palmer asked after Thompson had left.

David had to think about it for a moment before reeling off the names of his five children in the correct order.

'Mary is eight, then there's Ruth, aged five; Jean is two now, and the twins Andrew and Freda are just five months old,' he said.

The telephone rang, interrupting the conversation.

Constable Fleet answered the call at the reception desk. David and the sergeant continued talking, but they stopped when they heard the constable walking down the corridor.

'It's Scotland Yard, Sergeant,' Fleet announced.

'Thank you, constable. I'll come back to the front desk.'

He got up and walked down the corridor. David picked up his cup and saucer and followed him.

'Sergeant Palmer,' he said, after he'd picked up the telephone.

He listened for several minutes before politely acknowledging the caller and then hung up the receiver on its hook.

'Right, constable, could you bring me the log please?'

The constable picked up the large buff-coloured logbook from the front desk and passed it to the sergeant. Constable Fleet turned to the vicar.

'More tea, sir?'

'No, thank you, constable. I think I'll be on my way now. I don't want to be getting under your feet.'

The sergeant waved his hand.

'No, sir, have another cup. I'll tell you what's going on once I've made this entry. I just need to do it now otherwise I'm likely to forget.'

The constable poured the remaining tea into David's cup. He stood in the corridor looking at some of the notices and pictures on the walls and waited for the sergeant to finish.

About five minutes later, Palmer closed the logbook.

'That was Scotland Yard,' he said. 'A sergeant and three constables from the Metropolitan Police who have been helping at the station in Ramsgate since all the trouble in August are now heading back to London. For some reason, trains out of Ramsgate are not running this morning so they'll be getting the six o' clock from here. We've been asked to look after them for a few hours.'

He looked across at Constable Fleet and smiled.

'You'd best keep that tea coming, lad.'

★★★

Margate was not considered a town that had much crime. There were a handful of burglaries and very few cases of violence. In the 1915 'Report to the Watch Committee' by the Chief Constable, 'simple larceny' was the most significant offence.[31] With 72 public houses in the borough, there was always a fight or two at closing time. But the clamp down by the government on drinking during the war by raising taxes on alcohol had made drinking a pastime most could not afford. Generally, the streets of Margate were safe, but like most towns and cities throughout Britain, times were hard. The war was over but social unrest was rampant, even in towns like Margate, and especially its neighbouring town, Ramsgate.

On 13 August 1920, a German steamer called the *Hever* had arrived in Ramsgate to transport coke from the town's gas works to Denmark. Coke, a by-product of coal after the gas is extracted, was used to make iron in blast furnaces and sometimes exported. The *Hever* arrived in the harbour flying a German flag. Unfortunately, war resentment and the air raids on east Kent by the Zeppelins and German aircraft were still well remembered. Dockside labourers began loading the coke until word spread through the town about the presence of a ship flying a German flag. Once an angry mob started to assemble on the dockside, the captain was told to move his ship to the West Pier and not show the German flag again. Anger at the sight of a German flag in the harbour, fuelled by the summer heat, was all it took to start some of the worse rioting and public disorder since the Armistice was signed.[32]

Police were brought in from across southern England, with 50 Metropolitan Police officers from London. Several Ramsgate officers were hurt, one seriously, so Scotland Yard allowed four London policemen to stay in Ramsgate while the injured officers recovered. The rioting continued for three days and nights before order was fully restored. A British-flagged ship was tasked to deliver the coke to Denmark, while the *Hever* slipped out of Ramsgate under the cover of darkness.

Ironically, the trade with Denmark was actually benefitting the local economy. Coke was sold locally for two pounds and nine shillings per ton. The Danish government paid seven pounds and 15 shillings. The riots showed a deep resentment smouldering within the working classes – resentment towards Germany, but an even deeper resentment towards any authority at home, too. Six men and one woman were given sentences ranging from four days' to six months' imprisonment.

★★★

About an hour passed before Constable Freeborn came back into the station. David was sat in the muster room talking to several of the other constables on duty.

'No sign of him, sir,' Constable Freeborn said as he walked into the muster room rubbing his hands together to get them warm again. 'I looked all through Churchfields and around Church Square. I even checked behind the Six Bells Inn and in Mummery's Yard. I didn't see a soul, I'm afraid.'

The constable moved over to the table in the corner and put his hand on the teapot to see if it was still hot.

'Is this fresh, Bruce?' he asked Constable Fleet who had followed behind him.

'About 10 minutes ago,' came the reply.

'Oh good, I could murder a cup right now,' he said as he poured himself some tea.

'I've told Constable Thompson and the new lad to keep an eye out for him, sir. But I don't fancy their chances much. Most people out on the streets these days just run a mile as soon as they see a copper,' Freeborn said, slurping his tea mid-sentence.

'That's a shame. I just wish we could get them to understand that there is a hot meal and possibly a bed at the Church House,' David replied.

'Some are just plum out of luck, sir,' Constable Fleet said. 'Those two are probably the luckiest down-and-outs in the town right now,' he continued, pointing back at the cells on the other side of the main corridor. 'At least they're warm and dry and will get some breakfast before they see the magistrate in the morning.'

'The magistrate? What did they do wrong?' David enquired.

'Nothing really, sir. One of the lads picked them up for begging and sleeping out. It's the second time this week. We wouldn't normally charge them but it's a new directive that if they are arrested, then they have to see the magistrate. I reckon they don't want the station turning into a doss house.'

'It's the dilemma we're faced with right now, sir.' Constable Freeborn spoke as Fleet headed back to the reception desk. 'If we leave them out there on a night like tonight, then there is a distinct possibility that they could freeze to death. But if we bring them in, we have to charge them and take them upstairs.'

'Do you know if they were taken over to the Church House?' David asked.

'I'll tell you straight, sir.'

Sergeant Palmer had now stepped into the doorway and spoke before the constable could respond.

'Some of those poor boys who came back from France are in a terrible state. One of the lads in there right now doesn't stop trembling and twitching all the time, and he's mumbling so bad he can hardly string a sentence together. The other one told me he had been looking for a job for over a year, ever since he came back from France. But he's not had a single day of work – not one,' the sergeant said. 'And when they are sent over to Hawley Square, they'll take the food that Mr Lawton and the others are providing. But because it's the church, most won't stay,' he added slightly apologetically. 'Even if you have a bed for them, it doesn't solve the problem of them getting work. Until the government and local authorities realise how bad the unemployment situation is, especially for those poor lads who fought during the war, nothing is going to change.'

After the sergeant had gone back to the reception desk, the muster room became quieter as the constables got ready to go out on their respective patrols. David sat and thought about what he had just heard. He knew the situation was bad, but he hadn't understood to what extent. It was clear to him that for anyone without a job or a roof over their head, the future looked bleak. After he had been deep in thought for some time, he started to become very sleepy. He put on his coat, hat, scarf, and gloves, then started to make his way to the reception desk where he wanted to thank Sergeant Palmer and Constable Fleet for their hospitality. As David approached the desk, the main entrance door opened. In walked the four Metropolitan Police officers who had been stationed in Ramsgate.

'Good morning,' said Sergeant Palmer.

He opened the reception desk door and shook the Met police sergeant's hand. He introduced himself then showed the four men to the muster room where he invited them to rest before catching their train to London.

'Good morning.' David greeted them as they passed him in the corridor.

The final policeman looked twice at David as if he had recognised him. When he got to the end of the corridor, he turned around.

'Padre Railton?' he asked, sounding uncertain.

'Yes.'

The policeman moved forward with a smile on his face, more confident now that he had remembered David's name correctly.

'Sir, forgive me. I thought it was you. I was with the 47th Division in 1916 when you were chaplain to the 19th Londoners on the Ypres Salient.'

'Oh yes.' David paused. 'I can't say I can place your name though.'

'Oh, you won't remember me, sir. But I remember you and a couple of the services you gave. I also remember that flag you used. Someone told me that it was your flag that was on top of the coffin of the Unknown Warrior last November on Armistice Day. Is that true, sir?' he asked.

'Yes, it is, and the flag is still there at the foot of the grave.'

'Well, I'll be sure to go and pay my respects when I get back to London. You can count on that, sir,' the policeman stated.

'How did you end up as a policeman?' David enquired.

'I started out with the 19th but became a trench policeman under the division's Provost Marshal. After the war, I was offered a job in the Met, which I took. So here I am,' he said, smiling.

He saw that the padre was looking tired.

'Well, sir, I hope you don't mind, but I had to say hello. Your services that I attended were a great help to me and all the other lads, too.'

He touched the front of his helmet and turned to join his colleagues in the muster room.

'Thank you, constable, thank you.'

David turned and walked towards the door, then stopped and thanked Sergeant Palmer and Constable Fleet once again before he stepped out into the cold.

★★★

David was just coming back up to the church when he saw the early morning light of a winter dawn starting to fill the eastern sky. He paused for a moment and watched the sky's colour slowly change from dark to lighter hues. He was standing on the kerb looking towards the spire of St John's thinking about the plight of ex-servicemen when something occurred to him. He had listened to what the police officers had said about the two men in their cells and particularly remembered something Sergeant Palmer had said: *Until the government and local authorities realise how bad the unemployment situation is, nothing is going to change.*

He also remembered something that he had written shortly after he'd arrived in Margate: 'There are many problems that cannot be solved in a hurry … amongst them are factors as to the present status of our ex-servicemen and the needs of relatives of those who died for us.'[33]

David now knew what had to be done. He would go home, wait for Ruby to wake up then talk to her about his idea.

CHAPTER 2

Early Days in France

'A Great European war under modern conditions would be a catastrophe for which previous wars afforded no precedent.'

SIR EDWARD GREY

Monday, 26 April 1916, Bouvigny Woods, France

For the first time since joining the 47th (2nd London) Division, David was able to sit down on his straw-stuffed mattress in the relative calm of his flea-infested hut and think about writing to his wife. Situated behind the division's front-line positions with the reserve units and amongst the divisional transport and wagon lines, David's billet was in the woods, close to the village of Bouvigny. This was where most of the 47th Division padres had been housed since the division had assumed responsibility for the Souchez-Carency sector of the front line at Vimy Ridge. From time to time, David would hear complaints about the huts, especially if someone had been bitten by something crawling on the floor or hiding in their mattress. But he didn't like to hear padres grousing about their perceived poor living conditions and discomfort. He was well aware what the men of the battalions at the front line endured. He had already seen and experienced much worse.

For once, David was alone in the hut, which he shared with several other padres and staff officers, most of whom were assigned to posts within 47th Division Headquarters (HQ). Finding a peaceful moment to write to his wife had been difficult as of late. Any quiet time up to this point had been taken up writing to relatives of soldiers over whose burials he had presided. Also, the door to the wooden hut was constantly opening and closing as men came and went all hours of the day and night. Padres were on call 24 hours a day, but with most burials conducted under the cover of darkness, the call to proceed to the front line, almost five miles away, usually came late in the day, with most movement only permitted after dark.

He had not arrived back at his billet until the early hours of the morning, but it was now mid-afternoon, and he felt well rested. For the moment all was quiet. Even the gunners a few hundred yards away seemed to have the afternoon off. So, before being called back to duty, David took out his writing pad and an envelope from the pack in which he kept all his personal belongings, pulled up a makeshift table built by a previous occupant of the billet, and started to write to his wife: 'The brigade moves today; another one takes our place in the trenches. It is my duty to remain here, and go up to the cemetery tonight, in case there are any casualties for me.'[1] David paused for a moment, thinking about what had taken place the previous night before continuing.

★★★

David Railton and Ruby Marion Willson were married at St Cuthbert's Church in Kirklinton, Cumberland, in the late summer of 1910.[2] Just a mile from the church was the summer residence of her late father, Walter De Lancey Willson, who was buried in the grounds of St Cuthbert's in 1907. Willson was the owner of a chain of north-east grocer's shops, Walter Willson Ltd. For many years, Willson and his family spent their summers at Kirklinton Park, a sprawling red brick house set in many acres of Cumberland countryside. Inheritance of the Walter Willson 'empire' passed to his eldest daughter, Alice Mary Willson, and because of archaic inheritance laws still in place at the time, this fortune passed to her husband, Sir Stephen Harry Aitchison. Despite this, the other Willson children were by no means poor. They were well looked after in his will and by their mother, who was also financially independent.[3]

Despite Ruby's financial stability, David was well aware of the struggle back in Folkestone. Shortages of food and fuel were already starting to hit home, and with German air raids on the Kent coast increasing, David might have wished that he'd moved his family away from the English Channel before he left. Ruby lived with their two daughters – Mary, who was three, and Ruth, who was born just a month before David left for France – in a Victorian three-story terraced house at 16 Millfield.[4] Any guilt David felt for leaving his family at such a time was countered by his sense of duty to King and Country. He also was comforted knowing they were being looked after thanks to Ruby's family's finances. Three domestic servants lived with the family. Mrs Murdock, the housemaid, had moved from Gateshead to Ashford (and then to Folkestone) with them after Ruby and David were married.[5] Mabel Cost had been hired in Ashford as a cook and had also moved to Folkestone with the family.[6] Ruby also hired a nanny who lived with them throughout the war.

David and Ruby met in Liverpool in 1908 while David was serving as curate of St Dunstan's. Ruby was involved with social and charitable work for the poor of the city.[7] After graduating from Keble College, Oxford, David studied at the Bishop's Hostel in Liverpool, where he was ordained into the Church of England. The Bishop of Liverpool, whom David greatly admired, would make a huge impression upon the young cleric and influence the way he conducted himself throughout his life.

When Francis Chavasse was enthroned as Bishop, on 31 May 1900,[8] the City of Liverpool was immersed in religious factionalism; there was very little cooperation or even contact between Anglicans, Catholics and Non-Conformists. The Bishop's call to bring together all creeds and religions became central to David's own core beliefs; it was something that had started to take root in him several years before while he was at Oxford, but it was the Bishop's influence that convinced him. The Bishop had four sons and two daughters. David became friends with twins Christopher and Noel Chavasse. Christopher, the elder by 20 minutes, also was ordained into the Anglican Church. Noel practised medicine. Both twins were accomplished athletes, playing rugby at Oxford and gaining 'Blues' for running against Cambridge. They both would go on to represent Great Britain in athletics at the 1908 Olympic Games.

During his time at Oxford, David served as a private soldier in the 1st (Oxford University) Volunteer Battalion.[9] The Oxford Volunteers organisation was the forerunner to the University Officers' Training Corps (UOTC), put in place in 1908 by Secretary of State for War Richard Haldene, as part of the Haldene reforms in the Territorial and Reserve Forces Act 1907. David left the Oxford Volunteers a day before the formation of the new UOTC. He took with him a Master of Arts Degree and several years of service as a part-time soldier. When he arrived in Liverpool, as well as studying to be ordained, he immediately joined another Territorial unit, the 10th (Scottish) Battalion, the King's Liverpool Regiment (Liverpool Scottish) as a soldier, not a padre. For the next two years he spent many weekends exercising with the regiment in Scotland, which did nothing except enhance his love for his father's country of birth. Noel Chavasse also was posted to the Liverpool Scottish after being commissioned into the RAMC in 1913.

★★★

Once David finished the letter, he folded it and addressed the envelope. Then he reached for his pack and put his writing equipment away. He'd learned the hard way about always having his pack close to him with everything put away inside. It contained all he needed to conduct services should he need to leave in a hurry, which had happened several times since he'd arrived on the continent. On one such occasion, he found himself arriving at the front-line trenches in the dark without his pack, and he was unable to retrieve it for several days. *Never let your pack out of your sight,* he'd said to himself many times since then. With the items he needed to conduct a service, such as a small wooden cross and two candlesticks, he had enough room for a few personal belongings, including his writing pad and envelopes, and items he could not be without for a day or two. Also in this pack (which had the name 'D. Railton' written on the flap in bold black letters), folded tight and neat, was a large Union Jack flag.

Soon after arriving in France, David was asked by his mother-in-law, Mrs Mary De Lancey Willson (known to all close family members as 'Dubby'),[10] if there was anything he needed. He requested a few personal items, but he also asked her to try to acquire a large Union Jack that he could use as an altar cloth. Ever since he'd left England, whilst conducting services he had felt the need for 'a symbol of our national life and radiant colour in the midst of all the horrors in France'.[11] In the drab colourless landscape of a million khaki uniforms, he knew the bright red, white and blue colours would be popular with the troops.

British Army regiments had taken their regimental colours and standards to war for hundreds of years. During campaigns like the Napoleonic Wars a century before, they were used as rallying points. But modern warfare and the abandonment of antiquated linear battle tactics had made this use irrelevant. Also, the chance that they may be lost or captured had become much more of a concern. During the Zulu War at Isandlwana in 1879, colours of the 24th Regiment of Foot were captured after nearly 1,300 men were killed. At Laing's Nek in 1881, the Boers came very close to taking the regimental colours of the 58th (Rutlandshire) Regiment of Foot, who would be the last British Army regiment to carry its colours into battle. Although military commanders and politicians in Whitehall may have denied it, the thought of British regimental colours being paraded in Berlin, the way Wellington's victorious army did after Waterloo with captured French colours, was unthinkable to them. Throughout the war, regimental colours would not follow the troops across the English Channel to the continent. David thought it was a mistake that 'no regimental colours were allowed in any sector even for a space of a week'.[12] It was one of the reasons he had asked for a flag to be sent.

The flag arrived just two weeks after David had landed in France. It was large (some of his fellow officers said it was *too* large), but even at 8½ by 4¼ feet, it folded up quite small and fitted comfortably into his pack. David saw it less as a symbol of any regimental loyalty; instead it reminded him and his soldiers of their homeland and why they were there. He received some odd comments at first, but the longer the war went on, the more the men who attended his services appreciated the presence of his flag; it was the bond that kept everyone and everything together through some very tough times.

David wasn't the first padre to have thought of using a Union Jack for services in France and Belgium. The Revd Ernest Crosse, chaplain to the 8th and 9th Battalions of the Devonshire Regiment, had been in the trenches since 1915. He used his Union Jack as a shroud when he buried 163 members of his regiment after the opening day of the Battle of the Somme.

The solitude of his billet still undisturbed, David decided to make some tea and relax while he could. He knew tonight would probably be another long one. After the tea had steeped for a while, he sat down and looked out across the cleared area of the woods. Spring flowers had started to appear, and fresh buds were showing signs of life on the trees undamaged by shelling. He started to think about all that had happened during the few short months he'd been in France. Much had changed in such a brief time. Gone was the bravado that he and the rest of his battalion had brought with them across the Channel. The patriotism was still there, no doubt. But it was now tempered with a more pragmatic and realistic view of how the war was going. As the casualties started to mount up, every soldier, at some stage, thought about his own mortality and wondered if he would ever see his homeland again. But no matter how bad things got, David would always be thankful. 'God has been good to me... No honour of this life will ever compare with the honour of serving with the Northumberland Fusiliers and the London Division. God has preserved my life',[13] he wrote in a letter to his wife.

***

Just after he married, David was appointed curate of St Mary's Church in Ashford, Kent. Ashford was a well-renowned parish that had thrived since Canon Peter Francis Tindall had been appointed there in 1888. It became known as 'one of those places where the best Curates served their title – [where] those destined for great things within the church' were sent.[14] Despite being fully committed to his new parish, David wanted to continue his military service in some capacity, so as soon as he arrived in Kent, he applied to become a Chaplain to the Forces. On 11 December 1911 he was appointed Fourth Class Chaplain to the Territorial Forces, ranking as Captain.[15] He then was attached to 2nd (Home Counties) Field Ambulance (Fd Amb), Royal Army Medical Corps (RAMC), whose drill hall was in Ashford.[16] At least one night a week, he put on his uniform and paraded with his men. Although they were not a fighting force as the Liverpool Scottish had been, David knew that should the country ever go to war, he would be needed at a field ambulance.

In 1914, at the outbreak of war, David followed Canon Tindall when he left Ashford to become vicar of Folkestone parish church.[17] Because of the distance to Ashford and his commitments in Folkestone, David was no longer able to stay involved with his unit in Ashford, so he had to resign his commission. He fully expected to be allowed to rejoin automatically once the first volunteers were sent abroad. But despite completing a 'Declaration by a Candidate for a Commission', Army Form W 3075 on 4 January 1915,[18] he would have to wait a year before he was selected for service abroad in January 1916.

***

Folkestone soon became the major embarkation port for British soldiers heading to war on the European continent – many thousands would not return, while many thousands more returned wounded. Houses were turned into makeshift hospitals, and the green, carefully manicured lawns of 'The Leas' were turned over by the boots of men and the hooves of horses. Folkestone and Shorncliffe camp had become one massive military encampment.

Within a short walking distance of both his home and the church of St Mary and St Eanswythe, David would spend most of his time helping out in the hospitals and tending to those recovering or in need of pastoral guidance. He also tried to be at the top of Slope Road by Albion Gardens 'to wave Godspeed to every draft of soldiers who marched down the "Slope" to the embarkation pier'.[19] The cry of 'Step Short' would be heard at the top of the road (re-named 'Remembrance Road' in the 1920s) many times, as thousands of men headed down to the docks for embarkation on a boat that would take them to France.

By 1916 it was clear that the war was not going to be over anytime soon. The zeal and enthusiasm that had exploded across Europe with the outbreak of war had long since vanished. The realisation that there would be no swift victory for either side really became apparent during the winter of 1914–15. For the Germans, the Schlieffen Plan had not produced the predicted early victory over France so it could then look east towards Russia, decisive in its overall strategy for winning the war. It failed mainly due to the indecisive leadership of some of its generals, whose lack of belief in and a conviction to carry out the Schlieffen Plan led to defeat at the Marne. And for the British and French, the counter-attack known as the 'Miracle of the Marne' and subsequent 'Race for the Sea' brought no decisive breakthrough either. Germany was forced to fight on two fronts, but any Allied victory was limited as a tactical success; the German Army still occupied large tracts of France and most of Belgium. By the end of 1914, the war of movement had ended, with both sides digging in once winter was upon them. Trench warfare had begun, and despite several attempts from Allies and Axis to break the stalemate at Neuve Chapelle, Ypres, Aubers, Festubert, and Loos in 1915, by the time David went for his interview and medical at the War Office on 4 January 1916,[20] the front line had hardly moved in 14 months.

***

With the stalemate and terrible loss of life, the formation of new divisions and regiments was accelerated. Still recruited on a voluntary basis until the Military Service Act became law in March 1916, the new divisions included many 'Pals battalions', recruited from relatively small and localised areas, with large groups of friends encouraged to join up together. And it was to one of these battalions that David was sent when he left the War Office on that cold January afternoon.

The C1 Chaplains' Branch (later to become the Royal Army Chaplains' Department) had sworn in David Railton that afternoon and then posted him to the 18th (Tyneside Pioneers) Battalion, The Northumberland Fusiliers, who were due to leave for France in just 72 hours. The Army provided a grant of 10 pounds for every officer to have his uniform made. Several tailors in London had been making officers' uniforms at short notice since the start of the war, so David's rush was not unusual for them. But 72 hours was cutting it fine, even for them. He had just one day at home with his family to get everything together before leaving on another train along the south coast to meet his new battalion.

He arrived in Southampton on Friday, 7 January, with just enough time to get through embarkation, meet his new Commanding Officer (CO), Lieutenant-Colonel John Shakespeare, and board the 290-foot Thames excursion paddle steamer, the *Golden Eagle*. Then, with life-jackets donned and with a torpedo boat and a minesweeper as escorts, they set sail for France.

Stories of increasing losses had come back to England from the continent, but most soldiers on the *Golden Eagle* that night knew nothing of the full horror that awaited them. They sang and joked about the Germans as if they hadn't a care in the world. They were amongst friends and finally getting the chance to go and kick the Kaiser's backside. David knew many people from the north-east – their housekeeper, Mrs Murdock, was from Gateshead – but even he struggled to understand some of the men's broad Geordie dialect. Just before dark, a young officer started singing. Then, for several hours, many different songs drifted out across the waves of the English Channel. But when the wind picked up, several men got seasick as the flat-bottomed paddle steamer pitched and rolled in the building swell. David narrowly avoided being ill and was very happy when, in the early morning light, the port of Le Havre was visible over the bow. Writing to his wife after they arrived on French soil, he said this of the crossing: 'Many fellows ill. DR nearly so but cold wind kept me secure.'[21] Once the battalion disembarked and was back on dry land, they marched up the hill from the port to a transit camp and were fed in a Salvation Army hut.

***

Stood there, eating a bowl of lukewarm stew, talking to Salvation Army officers, David must have thought of his father. Commissioner Railton had died on the continent in Cologne, Germany, three years earlier. David hoped his father would have been proud of his son embarking on this great crusade despite whom they were fighting against. He knew that his father's views were complicated and that he might have been torn and conflicted when war broke out. The irony of both his sons coming to help fight Germany (a country his father greatly admired), where he had been trying to recruit Salvation Army soldiers, was not lost on David.

His mother had also wondered what her husband would have thought of it all. In a letter she wrote, 'I often think how keenly interested "R" would have been in the terrible experiences of all the lands of Europe just now.'[22] Commissioner Railton, aged 64, was travelling to Switzerland from Germany when he had a heart attack and died. He was rushing to meet a connecting train whilst carrying a heavy suitcase. All the years of travel and ill health had caught up with him; his heart could take no more. He was buried in Abney Park Cemetery, London, next to William Booth.

Looking out over the windswept English Channel, David remembered his father with great admiration. He had a strict devotion to prayer, even though he and his younger brother were 'tested' somewhat by its severity at times. It was the Commissioner's custom to strictly observe the daily prayer hour.[23] No matter where they were, at the appointed time, he would drop to his knees and pray aloud. In 1920, David recalled to his father's biographers that he and his brother had a unique way of dealing with it:

> At any rate, it taught us to shut our eyes in order that we might not see the surprised expression of the children and grown-ups passing by. But nothing he ever did of this kind seemed 'professional' or a form; it was part of the walk and most natural. One minute he would talk with us or to one of our school friends, and the next minute to his Father in Heaven.[24]

In 1903, from his dormitory room at the Grammar School in Macclesfield, David showed his true affection and admiration for his father when he wrote a poem for him:

> On Father's return from Ireland I dedicate these feeble verses to him…
> I greet you grand old warrior with a warm clasp of the hand,
> I pray that God the Father will ever by you stand.
> He has for many years long gone because he knows your heart,
> He will for still more years to come divinely take your part.
> And when the battle's roar doth cease and Jesus calls you home,
> You'll realise what is perfect peace around his glorious throne.[25]

★★★

Early next morning, the battalion was loaded onto a train, and for the next 24 hours it made a slow journey to Blendecques, just south of

St Omer. The 18th Northumberland Fusiliers came under the command of the 34th Division, which was scattered over a wide area east of St Omer and for the moment being held in reserve. After arriving at the station, the battalion dismounted from the train, was fed some food, found all its equipment, and then set off to march to its billets at the village of Staple, a distance of 11 miles.

The battalion was to be billeted in Staple for about two weeks, most of its time spent route marching. David was billeted in a small farmhouse on the edge of the village on the main road towards Bailleul. The front line was 25–30 miles away, but with the wind in the right direction, he could hear the guns. The time spent in Staple was quiet and pleasant, and the hospitality shown by the occupants of the village was without fault. But David could tell that the officers and men were eager to get to the front. Talk was about nothing other than what the men would do to the Hun once they got there.

David held his first church service to the entire battalion in a factory yard on Sunday, 16 January. He thought the hymns he chose were well received, and despite this being a mandatory parade, even for the non-believers he noted that 'the men sang well'.[26] This would have been the first time he had preached a sermon as a military chaplain in France.

His pathos for the men under his care was not limited to those who attended church services. David Railton cared for all his men, even those who had fallen foul of military law. His first experience of how British Army justice was meted out to offenders in wartime came when two privates in the battalion got drunk one night shortly after they had arrived in France. In peacetime they would have been sentenced to 14–28 days' detention. But because there were no cells available, they were sentenced to Field Punishment No. 1. As well as carrying out menial tasks such as cleaning the kitchens and performing hard labour during daylight hours, each night for two hours they were chained (standing up) to the wheels of gun-carriages by their feet and wrists outside battalion HQ. It was forbidden to speak to the men while field punishment was being carried out, but David was prepared to risk admonishment. In a letter to his wife, he explained that the men looked bitterly cold and that he thought the worst prison in England was nothing compared to field punishment. As he walked by them, he looked around to check that he wasn't being watched.

'Cheer up, old sons, come and see me directly you are out of this,' he said quietly, before walking off into the dark.[27]

Although Field Punishment was not meant to physically harm soldiers, it was open to abuse, especially by units that were officially 'in transit', meaning the punishment was administered by individual battalions and not by the respective division's Provost Marshal as prescribed by the *Manual of Military Law*. Field Punishment was abolished in 1923.

As soon as he arrived in France, David started to hear that he might not be staying with the battalion much longer. Unlike other battalions, the 18th Northumberland Fusiliers was raised to be the divisional pioneer troops rather than a front-line infantry battalion. This meant that once they were deployed, companies and even platoons might be spread over a large area, attached to other battalions. As the number of padres in France and Belgium was quickly being outstripped by the number of new infantry battalions, a decision was made for padres from pioneer battalions to move to infantry battalions and brigades, where it was felt they would be of more use. New establishment figures published in 1915 effectively doubled the number of padres with front-line units, but it took some time for the number of padres on the ground to come anywhere close to what was required. Once the battalion started to spread throughout the division as they deployed along the front line, David began working more with the 103rd Brigade, one of the three brigades within the 34th Division.

On 19 January, the battalion was ordered to march to a designated location where the entire division lined up along a countryside road to be inspected by General Joseph Joffre, overall commander of all French and British forces, and General Sir Douglas Haig, Commander-in-Chief, British Expeditionary Force (BEF). Although it was a mainly dry day with just intermittent showers, previous rain and snow had left the roads and tracks deep in mud. The conditions were good on the feet, especially for those recovering from blisters, but not great for a review. In good old British Army tradition, the division was lined up at least an hour before the designated time. While they were waiting, the wind picked up and it started to rain. Word came just as the rain stopped to put on their cloaks. Five minutes later, just before Generals Joffre and Haig were due to arrive, the order came down the line to take them off again. With frozen and numb fingers and bayonets fixed in place, soldiers were fumbling trying to put their cloaks away whilst keeping their rifles out of the mud and not impaling themselves on the bayonet. Just moments later, the two staff cars drove by slowly. Then, covered in mud, the soldiers marched the 10 miles back to their billets. The men joked about it, but for David it seemed the most 'un-martial parade' he'd ever seen.[28] The Commanding Officer sarcastically said of the inspection, 'Troops having marched 20 miles to be gazed at for about 20 seconds would be none the worse for a pat on the back.'[29]

After two weeks in Staple, the battalion was suddenly ordered to march the short distance to Les Ciseaux, a village that was closer to the front line. David had arranged several church services that day, only to be told that they were moving so the services were cancelled. The next day, the General Officer Commanding (GOC) III Corps, Lieutenant-General Sir William Pulteney, inspected the division. Based on David's letter to his wife, this inspection did not appear as bad as the shambles they had been subjected to when Generals Joffre and Haig had inspected them in the mud; however, it did entail another long march to be reviewed by a general in a car, which lasted about a minute and then was followed by another long march home. But nothing really got serious for the battalion until the 34th Division came under the command of III Corps.

On 7 February, David moved up to Armentières with A and C companies. He shared a billet with another padre who was attached to the 103rd Brigade in the village of Erquinghem Lys, just south-west of Armentières on the banks of the River Lys. The Revd Edward Francis Duncan was a Protestant rector from the Kilflynn Church, Ballyorgan, Limerick, in Ireland. His church was built in 1812 as a place of worship for the Protestant population of the Castle Oliver Estate. Duncan had joined the 26th (3rd Tyneside Irish) Battalion, The Northumberland Fusiliers, after he had been commissioned as a chaplain in 1915. His men and colleagues alike respected him. His report said, 'He always had a joke or a hearty tale for all.'[30] He and David would become good friends over the short period of time they worked together. Their billet was a deserted cottage within the village, and they shared it with several other officers from brigade HQ.

Even though the division was only in reserve, it was not long before the 18th Northumberland Fusiliers suffered its first loss. On 14 February, while working just forward of the Bois-Grenier (BG) line trench only a few feet from his own dugout, an artillery shell killed Private Wallace Henry Travis. The whole area had been subjected to bombardment directed by ever-watchful German observation posts on Aubers Ridge. What was left of his body was unceremoniously dragged back and laid on the ground just behind the BG line. His fellow soldiers quickly covered him with a few hessian sacks (used normally for trench wall construction); then they left to await the arrival of the padre. There is no doubt that Travis' pals were upset at the way they had to deal with him, but they simply had no choice if they did not want to risk suffering the same fate. German artillery was so accurate that any troops gathering in groups above a section in strength were routinely targeted.

David heard of the death and was summoned the next day. Someone loaned him a bicycle, which he used on the roads leading to the BG line. On his way there, the road came under heavy bombardment. David heard the whistling of incoming shells and had to take cover. The shells fell all around, causing him to be 30 minutes late; but thankfully he arrived unharmed. As the burial party dug Private Travis' grave, David collected 'a few little blue flowers'[31] from the corner of a field. He opened his pack, took out the Union Jack, and placed it on Private Travis' body. The bright colours dazzled in contrast to the dark bleak mud of the trenches. This was David's first burial in France – the first time he had used the flag for this purpose. He would have known from that moment that this was the right thing to do – the look upon the soldiers' faces said it all. Each time he used the flag for a burial after that, he felt that it spoke to all present of 'Dear Old England', and he believed the blood-red cross gave Christians 'sure and certain hope of the resurrection'.[32]

Once the hole was dug and Private Travis' body was laid inside, David was ready to start the service. A major whom David had not met before came along and dismissed all except four of the men. He was concerned that any larger gathering would draw more German artillery fire. For that reason, David cut the service short, simply reading John 11:25 ('I am the resurrection and the life…'), followed by the Committal and the Lord's Prayer. As they stood around the grave together and as the light started to fade, David dropped some of the flowers he had collected onto the body, and the men then filled in the grave. They placed a rough cross with Private Travis' name and the date he died into the ground. David and the four men climbed back into the trench where David visited and spoke with more of Travis' friends before heading back to his billet in the dark.

Later that night, David wrote to Henry and Martha Travis, the parents of Private Travis. It was the first time he had to write to the family of a soldier whom he had buried. As the artillery and machine-gun fire continued from the front-line trenches, he was probably struck by the cold and terrible realisation that this was going to be the first of many letters he would have to write. But he had already seen how by incorporating the Union Jack into the burial service, in some small way he was helping those left behind in the trenches. He hoped his letters to his soldiers' families back in England also would help them, in some small way, to come to terms with their tragic loss.

On 24 February, Major-General Edward Charles Ingouville-Williams (known affectionately to his men as 'Inky Bill'), GOC 34th Division, took over responsibility for the left division in III Corps's front. The winter had been a wet one, and the land around the British front line south of Armentières was constantly under water. The area to the rear of the 34th Division front line ran parallel to a small stream. A and C companies were quickly put to work trying to keep the trenches dry, laying miles of boards and walkways throughout the division's lines.

The villages surrounding Armentières, like Erquinghem-Lys, had suffered some damage from artillery fire. The cottage where David was billeted had lost part of its roof, but they were quite comfortable under the portion that was still intact and undamaged. Luckily, Armentières itself had so far been left mostly unscathed. The town still functioned, with many estaminets and patisseries open. So, life away from the trenches, for those lucky enough, could be quite tolerable at times.

Despite the constant bombardment and noise of the front lines, David did find some time for quiet reflection in the small back garden of the house. On several occasions, he sat for what seemed like an eternity and allowed his mind to wander, thinking of better times and his wonderful family back in Kent. And it was here, as he would later describe in the 1931 article in *Our Empire*, where he first saw the 'rough cross of white wood' and wondered who was buried under the cross; it was here where he said that his idea to return an unknown comrade back to England would first take shape.[33]

Over the next few days, David spent a lot of time going back and forth to the trenches – mostly at night, but on several occasions he had to run the gauntlet of German artillery fire during the day. Being called forward to bury the steady toll of front-line casualties became a regular feature of his daily routine. Two days after he'd buried Private Travis, David went to bury two more soldiers who had been shot by a German sniper who had caught them both with their heads above the parapet.

Private James Reed was with the 26th Northumberland Fusiliers and Private J. N. Walker was with the 18th Northumberland Fusiliers. Both were married, but because Walker was a Catholic, David would bury Reed, while a Catholic priest would come from divisional HQ to attend to Walker. After another shortened service, held against the backdrop of steady gunfire, David went back into the front-line trenches with the men who had helped bury Private Reed. Once they were back into the relative safety of one of the dugouts, he saw that one of the men was in a corner, obviously upset. A young officer pulled David aside and told him that he was Reed's brother. David was struck by the strength and courage he had displayed; he had shown no outward signs of emotion until they arrived back in the platoon's trench.

'Keep up your heart, old lad,' David said as he sat down next to him. Reed looked up, wiping away a few tears that he was unable to hold back.

'Oh, you may be sure of that, sir,' Reed said, forcing a smile onto his face.[34]

A dogged determination quickly returned, fighting off the grief that had temporarily overcome him. David and Private Reed sat quietly for a while longer before the padre bid farewell to Reed and his pals, then headed back to Erquinghem-Lys.

That evening David wrote to Private Reed's wife, Mrs Grace Reed. About a month later, he received a response, which he kept. He sent the letter home to his wife with the note, 'This is an example of the kind of letters we get all the time.'[35] In her letter, Grace wrote, 'I would like to know about my dear one, did he leave no message for me? He was wearing my ring do you know if it was buried with him? I would not like anyone else to have it.'[36]

David and his fellow clergymen offered comfort and spiritual guidance to all who needed it. As well as normal church services in barns and the larger farmhouses for platoons and companies, David held communion services for as few as two or three at a time; whoever wanted it, whenever they wanted it, he made himself available. On several occasions, just a short distance from enemy positions, deep in a small dugout or corner of an old trench, David laid out his flag on a table or a box or even an upturned bucket to be used as a makeshift altar. Through this kind of personal and close interaction, he started to gain the trust and respect of the soldiers he came into contact with.

Over the course of his time at Erquinghem, David became fully immersed in the life of a front-line soldier. He always was quick to state that he had it easy compared with the average infantryman. But David spent as much time as anyone in the trenches, and his first experiences of war obviously affected him greatly. It was the everyday mix of tragedies, stubborn resilience and camaraderie shown by ordinary men that seem to hit home the hardest. Friday, 3 March 1916 was one such day.

David was heading to the front line to visit the battalion that had taken over the night before when he got word that a billet housing soldiers from D Company, the 26th Northumberland Fusiliers (who had relieved his battalion), had taken a direct hit from an artillery shell. He immediately turned around and headed for their battalion HQ. When he arrived he found out that what he had heard was indeed true. Men tried to remain calm as they helped injured soldiers and were busy searching the rubble for buried survivors.

David had been with D Company the night before. They were happy and cheerful, looking forward to a few days in a 'cushy' billet away from the front line. But now Private John Bennett was dead, another called Twining was so badly wounded the doctors didn't think he'd live long, and many others were injured too. In a letter to his wife, David wrote, 'I was talking to the men of D Company in the trenches last night … they all escaped injury for four days in the trenches – I felt the whole thing to be inexpressibly sad … my eyes filled, in spite of all my efforts.'[37]

After he had done all he could, David headed to the trenches where his battalion was positioned. It was calm and peaceful at the front line in contrast to what the men of D Company, 26th Northumberland Fusiliers, were dealing with several miles behind the trenches. Some of the men had seen the artillery shells fly over their heads and wondered, 'Where were they dropping?'[38] Heading back to Erquinghem, David met up with some D Company men. As they walked, several talked about Bennett, their comrade who had lost his life earlier that evening. 'While there is all this fearful sadness, one cannot help being moved with the calm bravery of these new volunteer soldiers', David wrote.[39]

Before he got back to his billet, David decided that after the day's tragic events, he needed to pray. The closest 'House of God' was the Roman Catholic Church. David recounted the experience: 'I knelt at the altar rail. All was still for a while … an English Roman Catholic chaplain came and knelt in the centre of the Altar and began "Benediction". The church was all in darkness. He couldn't see who I was.'[40]

David's religious pluralism had roots in his younger years and grew under the tutelage of Bishop Chavasse. But a willingness to worship alongside Catholics showed he really did practise what he preached. The next day, when it came out that Private Bennett was a Catholic and had been buried by a Protestant chaplain, David made light of it in a letter to his wife: 'I don't suppose the Great Redeemer cares which chaplain buries a man as long as it's done reverently after the manner of Joseph of Arimathea.'[41]

It really didn't matter to David, but he recognised it might matter to men like Edward Duncan and other Irish Protestant chaplains who came from very Catholic areas of southern Ireland. He knew that his friend had to deal with a completely different level of sectarianism in Ireland, even worse than he'd seen during his time as a curate in Liverpool, but it was still something that David never really understood, as he expressed: 'So far I have only learnt that our Englishmen do not care a pin whether a man is High or Low, Broad or Catholic, or a Dissenter, whether he gives allegiance to Canterbury, Rome or General Booth.'[42] In David's eyes, they were all Christians engaged in a struggle against satanic forces trying to destroy their way of life.

David and Edward would part company just a few weeks later when David was sent south to Vimy Ridge where he joined the 47th Division. And although they only knew each other for a short time, they were now good friends and stayed in touch, writing when they could. On 31 March 1916, Edward wrote to David after he left for his new unit. The contents of the letter clearly showed that they had become close friends:

> My Dear Railton,
> What a desperate hurry you went away in. I thought at least I have would have been able to say Goodbye. Now that you are gone I cannot tell you how much I miss you. In the short time that you were permitted to be with us you gained the good liking of officers and men alike in a heartfelt way. Everywhere that I go, they are speaking of you. I believe you have gone to a very fine set of men and I take it that you were selected for that work because your good qualities were known and appreciated… Now goodbye, and may God bless you wherever you go. Forgive me for all my peculiarities, and believe me to be always,
> Your sincere friend,
> EF Duncan CF[43]

David was attending a course at the Padre's School in March 1917, when he heard of Edward Duncan's death. He remained composed, but later, whilst on a train returning to his division, he wrote to his wife about how upset he was by the loss of his friend:

> As soon as I got here I heard that Duncan had been killed at Arras – he was my colleague with the Northumberland Fusiliers. Deep down I agonise but – I suppose there must be some reason for it. You can imagine where my thoughts were. Words fail me, partly for fatigue and noise, and partly the sorrow.[44]

★★★

The sound of hobnail boots on the gravel and the billet door being opened brought David back to reality.

'Padre Railton?' a voice from behind the half-opened door said.

'Yes?' David responded.

'Sorry to bother you, sir,' the soldier said in a thick London accent. 'You're needed up at the cemetery tonight, sir. A couple of lads were hit by artillery fire earlier. The Transport Officer said he can give you a ride most of the way there, but he's leaving in about 10 minutes.'

'Thank you, Corporal, I'll just get my things together and head over that way now.'

David quickly grabbed all his belongings, threw his pack over his shoulder, and rushed out of the billet.

CHAPTER 3

Vimy Ridge

'All men make mistakes, but only wise men learn from their mistakes.'
WINSTON CHURCHILL

Sunday, 13 August 1916, Noyelles-en-Chaussée, the Somme

David usually enjoyed feeling the warm summer sun on his face, but after a long night on his feet marching on dusty French roads, the shade provided by the apple tree he sat under was a pleasant respite. The foliage and branches, heavy with ripening fruit that had not been picked or already fallen to the ground, were perfect cover where he could collect his thoughts and write a letter. It was a strange experience to look up to the sky and see it free from clouds and a perfect blue, yet he could still hear an occasional rumble of thunder in the distance. David and his battalion were many miles from the front line, but everyone was acutely aware that the 'thunder' was the sound of British guns pounding away at German positions further up the Somme valley.

After halting the German offensive at Vimy Ridge, the 47th Division was moved off the line for a rest in the Bruay-Diéval area, the men were left alone to lick their wounds away from the front line for several weeks. With no responsibility outside of the battalion, they spent their mornings carrying out routine administrative and logistical tasks before enjoying the spring afternoons playing sports. It was a much-needed rest far away from Vimy's barren, shell-ravaged landscape. The division then was sent north to a quiet sector of the front line near Angres. In contrast to Vimy, their positions were what one officer described as 'flowery trenches' – so called because grass and plants were able to grow in front of the parapets due to the lack of machine-gun and artillery fire.[1] From this position on the line, the division was tasked with carrying out a series of bluff operations, sending out large raiding parties in an effort to disguise the build-up of troops in the Somme area. One month later, the 63rd (Royal Naval) Division replaced them so they could head south to join those troops in reserve that would eventually be moved forward to join in the Somme offensive.

Because of the concentration of troops behind the main front line of the Somme, there was hardly a building that was not being used as a billet. So David was delighted when he received word the battalion was to stay in place and bivouac in the orchard for another night. The weather was good, so he would make the most of this opportunity on the Sabbath and set up an area where he could offer communion and prayers. Within the hour, he found two bales of hay in the ruins of a neighbouring barn. He would write to his wife, 'We had a little altar in a field under a tree. Your cross was fastened to a tree and the Union Jack and a fair linen cloth covered the Holy Table as usual.'[2]

Some weeks earlier, David had procured a gramophone, which he had carried with the battalion's baggage train. Wherever he could, after the men had halted for the day, he had it rushed up to his location.[3] Soon music gently drifted on the breeze through the trees. For many men it had a soothing effect. Some complained that it reminded them of home too much, making them melancholy, but for most it reinforced love of their homes and families, reminding them why they were there and what they were fighting for.

David soon realised the music had a calming effect upon most of the men. After the war, doctors and medical professionals treating returning soldiers for shellshock and shattered nerves used music extensively in the recovery process. As early as 1920, *The Times* acknowledged its usefulness, with this hyperbolic headline: 'Music Cure for Shellshock'.[4] At this time, David probably did not know the science behind it, but he was well aware that his gramophone, like his flag, brought the men of his battalion some welcome comfort.

That evening he led a communion service attended by about 20 men. Many sat on the periphery listening to the sermon and service. Although they did not attend officially, they were quiet enough to hear his words and the congregation singing hymns such as 'Now O Father'.[5] At the conclusion of the service, as he did most evenings, David walked around the battalion and talked to the men. Sitting under a tree chatting to several soldiers, they discussed their experiences of the war so far, thoughts of what life might be like after the war, and what it would be like going up against the Germans again. Some of the men had been with the battalion since they arrived in 1915 and had seen action at Festubert, Aubers Ridge, and Loos. But for most men, the main talking point was the battle at Vimy Ridge – the experience of being attacked and having to give up hard-won land. It was still a bitter pill to swallow, and now they were eager and glad to get back on the offensive.

★★★

The German attack on Vimy Ridge began on 21 May 1916, but for David, it felt like it had actually started much earlier. Since he had arrived with the 47th Division, he could tell from the officers and men that something was building. In March 1916, the British front was extended south by 20 miles so that the French 10th Division could be moved south to Verdun where they had come under huge pressure from a German attack. The poor condition of the trenches, and the fact that they were hard to defend because German artillery could fire unsighted from behind the ridge, led to a request by the Third Army Commander, Sir Edmund Allenby, that the existing line be withdrawn between 3,000 and 4,000 yards, where they could create a much stronger defensive position. From a military perspective, it made perfect sense. But because the French had lost so many lives taking the ridge the year before, it was politically impossible for General Haig to allow such a withdrawal despite the opinions of his commanders on the ground. In hindsight, this decision might have been correct politically, but it was going to cost in lives lost.

Although this sector had been quiet, both sides adopting a policy of 'live and let live',[6] the Germans had been busy secretly bringing forward specialised mining troops. Despite being able to see each other, both sides worked unmolested on their respective trenches. The Germans were able to mine all the way under the old French trenches undetected. Once the British discovered what the Germans were up to, they countered with Royal Engineer tunnelling companies. Both sides started to detonate camouflet charges to disrupt one another's mining activities. A camouflet charge was used to cause an explosion beneath an enemy tunnel that created a cavern without breaching the surface, and was used primarily as a counter-measure to enemy mining and tunnels. Each time a mine was detonated and resulted in a crater at the surface, infantry would rush forward trying to gain control and hold the far lip of the crater. Over the course of about a month, the British had got the better of these types of engagements, forcing the Germans to launch a major offensive.

★★★

David remembered the first of the German mines exploding on the night of 26 April. He had been called forward to a cemetery where he had conducted burials for two soldiers who had been killed by a German shell hitting a communication trench earlier that day. After both men were buried, David headed towards the billets to join the 20th Londons. With him was a burial party consisting of one NCO and six men who were happy to be leaving the front line before their battalion was replaced. At around 3:30 A.M., as David and his party were passing the destroyed village of Carency, a massive explosion shook the ground several miles away, as he recalled in a letter: 'at once a violent bombardment began, such as I have never heard or seen … the ground on which we stood was fairly high up, and we could see the lines of the trenches illuminated by the flash of the guns'.[7]

Several hours later, after finding his new billet in the corner of an old barn, David awoke to news that it was a planned attack and one where the Germans had actually broken through the British front line of trenches. The explosion they heard and felt from almost two miles away was a massive German mine exploding. Royal Engineers knew what the Germans were up to, so a company of men from the 6th Londons was ready and prepared to seize the near side of the lip of what became known as 'New Cut Crater'. Rifle fire from the 17th and 18th Londons ensured that the advancing German infantry could not exploit any weakness in the front line caused by the explosion.

Two nights later, the Germans exploded another mine but this time David was much closer. At the moment the mine was detonated, he was moving along the communication trench named Coburg Alley and was showered with dirt. Then there was another mad scramble to shore up any breach whilst the defenders came under heavy bombardment. One officer and several men from the 20th Londons were buried alive. David helped with the wounded, as he recalled in a letter: 'I stayed until our wounded came along our trench – far behind the actual fire line, and I helped the men who were not stretcher cases. One poor chap had to be piggybacked down the trench, he was so heavy. We took it in turns.'[8]

★★★

Since he had arrived at the 47th Division, David found himself being moved from unit to unit within the 141st Brigade. On 29 April, David was at the 47th Division HQ; the Senior Chaplain had sent for him. If he was going to be moved to another unit, then David would object to being taken from the men with whom he had developed such a close bond. Throughout the war, even when being promoted, David was not afraid of telling those in authority that he was against being moved and wanted to stay with his men, even to the detriment of his own career. This was a trait that he had obviously picked up from his father. George Scott Railton once wrote: 'There is nothing more painful to The Salvation Army Officer than to have to go away from the people to whom all his life has been for a time devoted, in order to take up a new post.'[9]

Whether it was being recalled from America because he was needed in London or being moved between units in France, they both showed a common concern for those they were trying to serve and help. But in each case, they realised that there was nothing they could do about it, fully immersing themselves in their newly appointed roles despite an initial reluctance to move. Helping those in need with kindness and compassion was the common goal of both father and son, no matter where they were.

The Senior Chaplain of the 47th Division was the Revd Harold Bell, who had served with the volunteers and then the Territorials since 1897. As well as being a parish vicar, Revd Bell had served the British Army loyally. But at the age of 43, he was starting to feel the years. After the 1915 battles at Aubers Ridge, Loos, and Festubert, it became glaringly obvious that being a padre at war, even at the divisional level, was taking its toll. Regardless, Revd Bell was not going to leave his post voluntarily. Like David Railton and many other padres, he felt he was needed in France; it was his duty to both God and Country. Only deteriorating health later in 1916 forced him to be invalided back to England.[10]

The details of the meeting between Bell and Railton are unknown – how strongly David objected to being moved, or how Bell had explained the decision is open to speculation. But what is known is that David became the padre of the 1/19th (County of London) Battalion, London Regiment (St Pancras), later that day, and on the same day, he wrote to his wife complaining about two chaplains leaving the front line to return to England. David's earlier move away from the 18th Northumberland Fusiliers in 1916 had come about because there were not enough padres with infantry battalions. As the Army rapidly expanded, so did the establishment for padres. Yet despite authority being given in Army Council Instruction Number 231 to double the number of chaplains with the Army,[11] it took a while to locate the right men and for them to arrive with front-line units.

Even as numbers of chaplains working in France and Belgium increased, the number of chaplains returning home after just one year was not helping the shortfall. Clearly, David felt very strongly about it, writing to his wife, 'It is simply scandalous that all officers here have to stick it out for the duration of the war ... but a chaplain who has got to know the men well goes off because he has had enough of it – and his year is up.'[12] This testimony lends support to accusations that some Anglican chaplains were ineffective during the war. As David and many other gallant chaplains would go on to prove by their actions, those scrambling to return to their parishes in England were in the minority, and later accusations concerning Anglican chaplains were unfair and mostly unfounded.

★★★

Standing in the orchard, David talked with some of the men. No matter where they were, even in the trenches, he tried to find an opportunity to talk. Unfortunately, it often coincided with the times when he was coming forward to bury one of their comrades, but the men seemed to appreciate him being there in the trenches with them all the same. He had not been with them long before the battalion could see that the dedication was paying off and his presence was clearly starting to benefit the men. Everyone from the officers down through the ranks knew that they could talk to Padre Railton. No matter what the time of day or whatever was troubling them, he could be found. W. J. Bradley wrote of David in 1965, 'His easy manner made him immensely popular.'[13]

★★★

By early May 1916, tunnels dug by the Royal Engineers were ready to be detonated, and on 3 May at 4:45 P.M., several huge detonations went off simultaneously. Men of the 21st Londons rushed forward under cover of artillery and machine-gun fire and seized the forward edges of the craters. Three large craters, named Momber, Love, and Kennedy, were formed from the explosions. This kind of mining and counter-mining went on unchecked for several more weeks.

All the while, David and his fellow chaplains were busy trying to serve the men of the 47th Division the best they could. Whether it was a small communion service in a partially burned barn, a field, or the dugout of a forward position, David prayed next to men who seemed to be continually tested and tried more each day. During that time of uncertainty at Vimy Ridge, everyone seemed to be nervously waiting. Not knowing if or when the next eruption of death and destruction would come from underneath their feet had started to take its toll.

On the morning of Sunday, 21 May 1916, as men were working hard getting their sections of the line in good shape after a period of intense mining, suddenly the whole of the 47th Division's front line came under heavy bombardment. The men stopped working and sheltered where they could. Later in the afternoon, the bombardment intensified with a box barrage – artillery fired on three sides of a given area to prevent escape or reinforcement of the enemy while allowing one's own infantry to advance safely into that area. Those in poorly fortified communication trenches had to shelter as best they could – in shell craters or by digging holes with their bare hands, doing anything to try to get below ground.

***

The role of British Army chaplains in combat during the early stages of the war was not well defined. Some chaplains had been close to front-line troops during the long retreat from Mons in 1914, with several being taken as prisoners of war. Most were restricted to rear area hospitals on the French coast many miles from the fighting troops. Consequently, men complained that they never saw chaplains anywhere near the front. There appears to have been confusion and disagreement amongst general officers, who had differing opinions whether chaplains should be allowed to even visit troops in the front line.[14] In the First Army a formal scheme of 'Battle Posts' specified the position of the Senior Chaplain and three chaplains for the field ambulances of a division. The division's Royal Artillery chaplain was to be in a central position where he could move between the batteries of the division. All remaining chaplains were sent to Advanced Dressing Stations (ADS) or Regimental Aid Posts (RAP). The Battle Posts would vary according to local conditions. In the Fourth Army in June 1916, Army Commander Henry Rawlinson issued an order via his Assistant Chaplain General, clarifying that the appropriate place for chaplains during an engagement was with a medical unit. The only exception was the chaplains attached to the Royal Artillery.[15]

Even by 1916, some padres were never seen near the trenches. Whether they were ordered to stay away or not is unknown, but many, including author and poet Robert Graves, thought that some padres were using 'orders' as an excuse. And even if they were ordered to stay away, Graves wrote, 'Soldiers could hardly respect a chaplain who obeyed these orders.'[16]

David Railton had no doubt whose fault it was: 'It is a mistake on the part of the authorities, which will cost the church dearly. I have told my seniors so, but law is law, in the Army as well as out of it.'[17]

Many chaplains disobeyed any such orders, bravely joining men they were ministering to at the front line, even paying the ultimate sacrifice with their lives. But by late 1916 divisional commanders allowed local arrangements for the battle positions of padres. It became the responsibility of the Senior Chaplains of divisions to decide where chaplains should be positioned, and, providing they did not hamper operations, no restrictions were placed on their movements.[18]

★★★

During the bombardment at Vimy Ridge on 21 May, David and his fellow padres moved back to the rear to help initially at the Main Dressing Station (MDS). Three miles back behind the lines, it was situated near the village of Estrée-Cauchie, known by all as 'Extra-Cushy'. The MDS consisted of a small group of huts used by the French as a hospital during their occupation of the Souchez-Carency sector of the line and were known officially as Quatre Vents. They were perfectly suited as an MDS, and on the afternoon of 21 May, with the bombardment continuing at the front and with the 142nd Brigade being called up from its reserve position, it looked like the 5th (London) Fd Amb soon would become very busy.

With the artillery barrage intensifying and the extent of the German attack becoming apparent, the Senior Chaplain picked padres to make their way to the ADS at Cabaret Rouge – David being amongst them. He grabbed his equipment then headed outside with several other padres and climbed aboard a waiting truck. They headed west towards Villers-au-Bois, where 141st Brigade HQ was based, then on to Carency. They walked the last mile to the ADS, which was located about a mile and a half south-east of Souchez.

Cabaret Rouge was at a collecting post called 'Point G' at the end of the communication trench that bore its name. It was called Cabaret Rouge because there had been a small red-bricked, red-tiled café on the site bearing the same name before it was destroyed in 1915.[19] It was the perfect position for the ADS, as most troops had to come through this natural bottleneck on their way back from the front line. The 19th Londons' HQ dugout was a little further north at the foot of the ridge.[20]

When the padres arrived at the ADS, medical staff personnel were fully stretched, coping with a flood of wounded soldiers coming down off the ridge. Padres worked with the doctors and medics, helping the most severely injured and dying in their last moments. If a soldier passed away while a padre was with him, then the padre noted the soldier's details from their identification tag. David was in the habit of writing this down in his official Correspondence Book (Field Service) – Army Book 152, so he could write to the family at a later date. Many of his Correspondence Books are still held by the Railton Family.[21] The scores of letters he received throughout the war years and afterwards represent just how important a letter from a padre who had spent the last moments with their loved one meant to family members.

Casualty evacuation throughout the First World War was difficult. In the beginning, the scale of the war and mass casualties caught everyone by surprise. It proved to be even harder when the enemy was attacking, while the line was fluid and with the fighting moving back towards the various medical aid stations. But a tried-and-tested system employed by the RAMC throughout the war (still used in a modified form today) saved many lives.

Once a soldier was wounded, regimental stretcher-bearers would bring him for examination by the Regimental Medical Officer (RMO), who would initiate treatment at the RAP. From there the divisional field ambulance would take over responsibility for evacuating and caring for wounded soldiers. Field ambulance stretcher-bearers would take casualties back to the ADS, ideally situated about 400 yards behind the front in tents, a house, or a dugout if any were available. At the ADS, doctors and medical staff would control bleeding, immobilise big fractures, change saturated dressings, administer morphine, and occasionally conduct emergency amputations and minor surgeries to prevent loss of life. With the casualty now stabilised, they would be transported to the MDS by horse-drawn ambulance. There the casualty would be given much more treatment and definite triage. From the MDS they were taken back to a Casualty Clearing Station (CCS) for any required surgery. After recovery, the casualties would be transported by train to the base hospitals near the Channel coast at Étaples, Rouen, Le Havre, and Boulogne.[22]

★★★

At 7:45 P.M. that evening, the artillery barrage lifted briefly; seconds later, it started again. This time the artillery sounded slightly different to David and others at the ADS. The barrage on the front-line trenches was lifted and moved to the rear with increased intensity. Some soldiers around the dressing station might have known that the lifting of the guns to the rear could only mean one thing: German infantry was now advancing somewhere along the line. At Cabaret Rouge, David and his colleagues continued through the night to care and comfort increasing numbers of wounded and dying soldiers arriving from the front.

The Germans had in fact concentrated their attack to the south on the less well-entrenched positions of the Berthonval sector of the 140th Brigade. The 7th and 8th Londons took the full force of the attack. The 142nd Brigade had now moved up into the divisional reserve and communication trenches to stop a major breakthrough. But the German attack and advance into British trenches were brought to a halt by the brave actions of a few officers and men of the 140th Brigade who faced the worst of the enemy bombardment and attack. The 19th Londons may not have been in the direct path of the German infantry's advance, but they still took losses. As well as losing several men killed and wounded, an officer and a soldier attached to the 8th Londons were posted missing, presumed dead.

The next morning David and his fellow padres started the task of burying the dead. Across the road from the ADS lay a cemetery that was first started by the French but soon filled up with more and more dead British soldiers. Most of the men buried there would have died at the ADS or while being carried to it. There was an increasing number of unidentified bodies laid in rows to the side of the cemetery awaiting burial.

Today in the cemetery at Cabaret Rouge are the remains of 7,650 soldiers who died in the First World War, over half of whom remain unidentified.[23] Grizzly remains of a young soldier torn to shreds by an artillery shell with nothing to identify him or his regiment was what padres like David Railton had to deal with every day, and it was the reason why so many families never found out what had happened to their loved ones.

In 1907, British Army Order No. 9 authorised the issue of an aluminium 'Identity Disc' about an inch and a half in diameter to be worn around the neck on a length of cord under the soldier's uniform. Each disc would be stamped with the soldier's name, rank, number, regiment, and religious denomination. With a small professional army, it was not cost prohibitive; but, after war was declared, metal discs were too expensive to be issued to the entire Army.

In 1914, most newly enlisted soldiers were issued a round disc of the same size, but it was made of red/brown vulcanised asbestos fibre. The new discs worked well. However, there was still no way of identifying a body post-mortem. When a soldier died, the disc was removed in accordance with regulations, leaving the body without an identity. Some bodies were so mutilated that without an identification tag being left with the remains, it would have to be buried 'Identity Unknown'. Military planners had not thought ahead about the issue; but, in their defence, like most of those in command, no one could have imagined that there would be casualties on the scale that David and his fellow padres faced at Cabaret Rouge Cemetery and across the Western Front during the war. Some soldiers wore a second, privately purchased bracelet or tag, but most did not.[24]

In September 1916, Army Order No. 287 authorised the issue of a second, green-brown shaded octagonal or lozenge-shaped disc. This identity tag would be attached to the original disc by a 6-inch piece of cord, and if a soldier died, it would be this disc which was removed; the original would stay with the remains of the soldier. Although this would do little to help at Vimy Ridge and the Somme, the second disc became general issue in November 1916, making the gruesome task of identifying remains of dead soldiers a little easier.[25]

All through the day, only stopping briefly to eat, David and his colleagues continued the process. Every soldier who had either died, arrived dead, or was unidentifiable was given a Christian burial beneath his flag. Even under these terrible conditions, David noted the soldier's name, sought an address for his next-of-kin, and wrote a letter as soon as he could. There is no way of knowing how many men he buried or how many letters he had to write to the parents of young soldiers killed, but the fact that there are no letters home to his wife during the battle is perhaps a testimony to how busy he was.

Between his work at the ADS and any sleep he could manage, David tried to visit the men of his battalion who were enduring terrible conditions up on the ridge. He went as much as he could and often on his own. Occasionally, he would visit with the Commanding Officer (CO) and Regimental Sergeant Major (RSM) when they moved forward to consult with company commanders. From what we know of David, it would have been hard to pull him away from his work at Cabaret Rouge; however, we also know that he wanted to get back to the front line, and he would have been looking forward to seeing the men of the 19th Londons again.

As David walked forward up the communication trenches with the CO and RSM, he learned what the situation was like at the front and how the battle had progressed. The battalion lines had held well, but it was obvious that the Germans had been concentrating on a line where the two brigades met further south. That is where the major problems had occurred. If the pressure continued and the Germans pushed further into trenches south of them, then British positions all along Vimy Ridge would be forced back or run the risk of being out-flanked.

David continued walking along the communication trench system that led to Coburg Alley. The communication trenches were full of reserve soldiers from the 142nd Brigade. They were spread out and dispersed as best they could in an effort to keep casualties to a minimum, but they had to be ready to go at a moment's notice. Once they reached the battalion's front-line trenches, David left the CO while he went for a briefing by his company commanders in a dug out.

David liked to move amongst the various companies talking to the men. He was always amazed by the way they kept up their morale. Far from being dejected and worried about the German siege on the line, they were upbeat, even cracking jokes. In turn, David's spirits soared as well. He couldn't help but feel sorry for the Germans. If this was their best shot, and the British Tommy was still standing and laughing in their face, then the Prussians and their army might as well turn tail and head back to Berlin. Continuing the fight was futile because they were most surely going to lose.

On the night of 25 May, while David was still helping at the ADS for the fifth night running, the 6th Brigade took over from the 141st Brigade, allowing his battalion to withdraw. The next morning, David found a truck from divisional transport heading away from the front line and secured a ride. He was exhausted; despite the rutted and cratered roads, he slept for several hours.

That evening, the battalion re-grouped about 10 miles west of the Vimy Ridge front line. The next day they would be moving for a rest period in the area of Bruay and Diéval some 20 miles north-west of Arras. Billets of one sort or another had been found for most of the men. No one complained of their rudimentary nature: a barn, a pile of straw, or even under some old canvas in a field. Anything was better than the constant fear of being sniped, bombed, mined, or hit by an artillery shell.

After David wandered through the various billets talking to the men, he joined the CO and most of the other officers in an abandoned farm building they would use as a temporary mess. Spirits were high because the battalion had not felt the full brunt of the attack, taking relatively light casualties. The 47th Division suffered the loss of 63 officers and 2,044 other ranks killed, wounded and missing.[26]

The CO confirmed there was talk of a new offensive to the south later that year and that after they had received replacements and conducted a period of training, the division would undoubtedly be involved. No one said so directly; most were looking forward to being on the front foot again and pleased to hear about talk of a new offensive. But unspoken opinions about the way the defence of Vimy Ridge had been conducted were commonplace through the ranks and reflected in the divisional history written in 1922: 'The magnificent spirit which refuses to yield to the enemy any ground, however useless, is worth much; but were the Higher Command justified incurring the resulting losses?'[27]

Stubbornly holding on to the ridge because it was not politically acceptable to the French was not a strategically sound decision and had cost many British soldiers their lives. The whole Vimy defensive line, especially in the north opposite Souchez, could have been moved back to the area around Cabaret Rouge where it would have been much easier to defend. Everyone hoped that those in command would not make the same mistakes again as they headed towards a new offensive on the Somme.

CHAPTER 4

The Graveyards

'Believe me. Nothing except a battle lost can be half so melancholy as a battle won.'

ARTHUR WELLESLEY, DUKE OF WELLINGTON

Saturday, 23 September 1916, the Somme, France

Above the columns of soldiers of the 19th Londons, who were marching on the main road from Albert to Amiens, were clear blue skies, but beneath their feet, a road badly rutted with patches of deep, soft mud, still wet from the storm two days earlier. The band from the 3/19th Londons had joined them at Bécourt the day before and now led the battalion as it marched away from the front line to rejoin the remainder of the brigade in former billets at Bresle.[1] The band played most of the way there but had to stop on several occasions when the road, which was the main thoroughfare to the front line, got too narrow and congested with troops and supply wagons heading back towards the front.

During the march, David tried to move amongst the men, chatting and joking as much as he could. For the most part they were quiet but polite. They knew what their padre was trying to do, and they appreciated him for it. But nobody wanted to talk; they all had a glazed look over their eyes, and the skin seemed to want to sag from their faces. These young men were visibly aging before his eyes, getting old long before their time. High Wood had exacted a terrible toll, not just in casualties during the battle – clearing the battlefield of the dead was proving to be worse. During the four days the men had to carry out this grisly and thankless task, David could see what it was doing to them.

Just outside Albert, David marched down the outside of the column and came up alongside Major Fair, who had assumed command of the battalion during the battle at High Wood. He saluted and marched alongside his new CO. David wanted to express his concerns about some of the men. Even though he wasn't sure what they could do to improve the situation, he thought Major Fair should be made aware that some of the men were in a bad way.

The general consensus among the few remaining officers was that they would be heading back into the fray once they had received a new draft of recruits. Although it was the Germans being gradually pushed back – General Haig's belligerent approach of continued attacks despite heavy losses – the British soldiers' lack of food, supplies, and shelter was having a major effect upon the strength of some of the divisions.

'What do you suggest, David?' Major Fair asked quietly. He had listened to the padre's concerns, making sure that no one else could hear their conversation.

'What about a memorial service to commemorate those who were lost?' David asked. He hopped over a hole in the road, then got back into step.

'I think it's a good idea, Padre, but I'm not sure that a regimental church parade will do much for morale after what these lads have been through. I'm sure they've had their fill after all the burial services. But I do think we should commemorate the loss of our friends somehow.' Major Fair paused, seemingly deep in thought. 'Is there a way we could do this with it being a little different from a normal church parade?'

'You are the Commanding Officer, sir. We can do this any way you think that would be in the best interests of the men,' David replied. He didn't want to come across as some pompous parson tied to strict ecclesiastical rules. 'I think a short commemoration service for the whole battalion followed by a celebration of Holy Communion later in the day for those that wish to attend would be appropriate,' he offered. 'You could address the battalion beforehand, and if I could be so bold, I would be most honoured if you'd choose the hymns and read a lesson of your choice.'

Major Fair paused again to think for a moment having heard David's suggestions.

'Yes, I think that would be fine, Padre. Let me have a few hours to mull it over, and I will get back to you later. But I think if we do have it, it should be tomorrow morning, nice and early, before the brigade tasks us with anything else.'

David acknowledged Major Fair with another salute then moved over to the side of the road and rejoined at the back of the battalion. David liked Major Fair; he thought that the regiment couldn't have been in better hands after the loss of such a talismanic leader as their previous CO. He hoped and prayed that the men, who had endured so much over the past few days, would be given sufficient time to heal. He knew that in all likelihood, Major Fair's remarks about having the commemorative service as soon as possible pointed to the fact they would probably be heading back to the front line in the near future. David knew that he had probably not seen the last of High Wood.

★★★

My darling Ruby,
The battle is over for our men for at least a week. The Brigade has lost over nine hundred, but the positions were won… We are now burying the bonny comrades who were with us before – it is dreadful! Many men, who have stood it all, cannot stand this clearing of the battlefield. I don't know what to tell you. I expect it would be censored. I am writing standing. We are in the open and there is not even a seat after this day's downpour.

You will have read full accounts about the fighting at High Wood. It has been a great victory, but the cost was and is too much to bear. We are without so many men who were here on the Twelfth Sunday after Trinity. They all went 'there' bravely and up to the last calmly and cheerfully, and some Brigades suffered even more severe losses. Some battalions are worse off even than the poor 19th.

Yes, we lost our dear Colonel and 10 other officers out of the 14 that went. Several of them had their last Communion with me in the trenches just before the battle… No words can tell you all how I feel, nor can words tell you of the horrors of the clearing of a battlefield. This battalion was left to do that. Several men went off with shell shock, and two were wounded. I am certain the shell shock was caused not just by the explosion of a shell nearby, but by the sights and smell and horror of the battlefield in general. I felt dreadful but had to do my best to keep the men up to the task. We were not badly shelled, but when you stand over the body of a man whom you know, and lift the body on to a stretcher and a shell explodes close by, even the bravest men can crack.[2]

'Come on lads, let's be having you,' the Sergeant Major quietly barked. 'The sooner we get this done, the sooner we can get away from this place.'

The working party clearing the battlefield had stopped to take a break. Like David, some had taken the opportunity to quickly write a few lines to their families; however, many just sat there, staying low, staring into the distance. Most had a look of dread on their faces; what horrors awaited them the next time they lifted a piece of wire or pulled away at some discarded ammunition box stuck in the mud? David put away his letter; he'd finish it later that day once they were back with the rest of the battalion. He got up and started to help the Sergeant Major rouse the men to work.

For many of the 19th Londons, High Wood was the first time that they had been on the offensive. Before the battle, they were eager to get after the Hun. Although the 47th Division had been involved in the 1915 battles at Aubers Ridge, Festubert and Loos, the offensive on the Somme was on a completely different scale compared with any carried out by the British Army thus far. Although they had heard casualties were more severe than expected, they were told the Somme offensive was working and the Germans were being pushed back.

Reinforcements arrived at the battalion during June and July 1916, which brought all units of the 47th Division up to full strength. Fully recovered in numbers after Vimy Ridge, David and the rest of the battalion started marching south on 1 August. The weather may have been set fair, but it was blistering hot and the roads were covered with dust, several inches deep in places. Most of the marching was done in the early morning hours, after a breakfast at first-light, and with a dire warning ringing in their ears: 'Orders were that no one was to fall out unless unconscious. If so he'd be treated as a deserter.'[3]

Columns of soldiers from the 47th Division hit the dusty roads with a halt being taken in the afternoon, allowing the men a respite from the worst of the summer heat. Five days' marching brought the division to St Riquier, a small village just to the east of Abbeville. The divisional history describes these as 'pleasant days',[4] but if you'd asked your average Tommy after a long day's march, he might have told you otherwise.

The division spent the next two weeks training for what everyone knew was coming. Although they all realised it would soon be their turn to be thrown into the attack – which had already been going on for over a month – the morale of the men was high.

Many of the new men arriving in the battalion, originally recruited from the St Pancras area of north London, now came from the length and breadth of the country, their accents not originating in London. To keep his spirits up, David's wife had sent him sprigs of heather, which he shared with several officers and men who had joined from Scotland.[5] Most of these Scottish 'Derby Men' pinned it on their lapels for good luck. Before conscription became law, Lord Derby started a voluntary scheme whereby young unmarried men were taken first. These recruits were known as 'Derby Men'.

On 20 August, the division was on the move again. This time they were heading back towards the front, west through Ailly-le-Haut-Clocher, Villers-Bocage, and Baisieux, with the division finally billeted near Bresle. Upon arrival, they came under the command of III Corps, and on 1 September, two months after the start of the Somme offensive, the battalion, along with the rest of 141st Brigade, started rehearsing for an attack on High Wood on a flagged course.[6]

★★★

The idea of a new major offensive in 1916 originated from a meeting of Allied commanders in December 1915. The initial plan of a campaign on all three fronts soon fell apart when it became apparent that Russia would not be ready in time and that Italy's reliability as an offensive power was becoming doubtful. These problems were highlighted in a 'Paper by the General Staff on the Future Conduct of the War'.[7] Military commanders on the General Staff saw no prospect of a new front being opened because there was 'no chance of any great new army being furnished by France, Russia or us during the next six months'.[8] Casualty figures from operations of 1914 and 1915 were now above half a million, and of those about 205,000 had been killed. But despite mounting political pressure, and with no new ideas from the General Staff of how to promulgate the war differently, the Chief of the Imperial General Staff had no other option than to recommend to the War Cabinet that the main theatre area of operations remain in Flanders and France and that offensive operations should take place in the spring.[9]

General Haig, who had just replaced General Sir John French as commander of the BEF, wanted any spring offensive to take place in Flanders, closer to the coast where his attacking divisions could be more easily supplied and he could involve the Royal Navy. It was General Joffre who first suggested the idea of an offensive on the Somme. In December 1915, Joffre told Haig that a French attack on the Somme would be greatly assisted if a British attack took place north of the river between the Somme and Arras. To Haig, an attack in the Somme over one further north in Flanders was still not preferable, but he liked the idea of a simultaneous and coordinated offensive. Joffre preferred the Somme to Flanders because it had remained largely untouched, and he considered the ground perfect for an offensive on a grand scale.

It is open to debate whether General Joffre chose to deliberately ignore intelligence about the German defences in the Somme clearly laid before him by his own staff, especially after the German attack on Verdun began in February 1916. For whatever reason, he chose to ignore all the warnings. Somme historian, Terry Norman says, 'Despite the fact that, it's being a quiet area, the Germans had taken the opportunity to transform many key positions in that part of their front into underground fortresses.'[10]

Geology also was on the defender's side. Underneath was 'a massive chalk layer beneath the gentle landscape – perfect for the excavation of deep chambers'.[11] Some historians consider the Somme the worst possible place the Allies could have attacked, as Malcolm Brown argues: 'On a front of over 450 miles, from Flanders to the Swiss Frontier, there was no better defensive ground than that provided by the country of the Somme.'[12]

The Germans were unhurried and placed their defensive positions with meticulous care. Their positions on the Somme were sighted and built with one thing in mind – inflicting maximum casualties upon the enemy. If the Allies wanted to win on the Somme, then it was going to come at a heavy cost.

The Somme offensive opened on 1 July 1916, and, by any standards, it was a disaster – the worst day in the long and storied history of the British Army. Exact numbers of casualties sustained that day will never be known for certain, but generally it is thought to be about 57,000, with about 19,000 of them fatalities. In the following weeks, British infantrymen inched across the countryside of the Somme seizing woods, ridgelines, and villages. Names such as Delville Wood, Montauban, Beaumont Hamel, Thiepval, Mametz Wood, Flat Iron Copse, and Contalmaison would be forever etched on the British conscience as places where its youth was slaughtered. In years to come, what Verdun was to the French, the Somme would have the same meaning for the British people.

Throughout July, August and into September, the battle developed into a series of short piecemeal attacks that became attritional in nature. The German first- and second-line defensive positions were bludgeoned and finally overrun, and the British front line crept on to the top of the Bazentin Ridge. Losses were still increasing, but the 'push' continued on. General Joffre was in no hurry to call a halt – the offensive in the Somme was reducing pressure placed upon his besieged troops at Verdun. And although there had been no decisive breakthrough, Haig continued the offensive relentlessly. He knew that if they 'were to win the war, then the German Army had to be defeated in the field'.[13] Victory would come through attrition on the Somme, and Haig believed that because of his actions there, by the end of 1916 Germany would be a spent force.

★★★

Lying between the Bazentin Ridge and the Germans' third line of defences in front of the villages of Flers and Eaucourt L'Abbaye, High Wood was clearly visible from the newly captured British positions. Sitting in low-lying ground, it dominated the surrounding area and was a perfect position for the enemy to strengthen and hold. A trench system called the Switch Line, which ran through the northern side of the wood, meant German troops could be moved up to strengthen the positions there at short notice.

By the time David and the 19th Londons arrived at High Wood, it was a wood no more. Its dense trees had been reduced to stumps, and the Germans were now deeply entrenched in what remained of it. High Wood was nothing but 'Dead trees, dead earth, dead water – nothing lived here except rats, flies and men'.[14] First attacked by the 7th Division in mid-July, briefly penetrated by a cavalry charge and then having repulsed a further nine attempts to take it, High Wood rightly deserved its fearsome reputation.

★★★

During their long march to join the battle, David and his men were made aware of what two years of intense shelling and attacks had done to some of the French towns. Sat astride the main axis of attack in the British sector of the Somme, the town of Albert had been reduced to rubble and its population evacuated. Less than a mile and a half from the front line at the start of the battle, it became a huge British base camp and the main route through which all troops and supplies had to pass on their way to the front.

Albert, a place of pilgrimage for Christians since the Middle Ages, with its late 19th-century church and the imposing red-bricked basilica of Notre Dame de Brebières, was left battered by continuous artillery bombardment. On 15 January 1915, a shell hit the gilded statue of the Virgin Mary, depicted holding her infant up to God, at the top of the spire. It did not fall to the ground but was left hanging horizontal, as if Mary were holding her baby to the people on the ground. After that a superstition grew up around the statue: when the Virgin statue finally fell, the war would end. A variation was that the side that finally brought it crashing down to the ground would lose the war. The tower was destroyed by British artillery during the German spring offensive of 1918, and the statue fell to the ground that April.[15]

David baulked at the wrecked French towns he witnessed. His loathing of Germans and of the acts of wanton destruction perpetrated by their army is evident in many letters home to his wife: 'The German spirit is of the Devil, and it is hell poison.'[16] And because of it, attitudes of even mild-mannered clergymen (considered the most forgiving of those on the battlefield) were hardening. If there were to be peace, then Germany would be made to pay for what they had done and only after it had been defeated. Even as early as 1916, David was calling for the kind of punitive terms that the victorious Allied war leaders would later exact from the vanquished Germans at Versailles in 1919:

1. Germany forfeit all land outside of Germany.
2. Germany pays war indemnity.
3. Germany forbidden to have an army or a navy.[17]

★★★

On 10 and 11 September, the 47th Division relieved the 1st Division in the front line and waited for its turn to try to capture High Wood. Together with the 20th Londons, their objective was to attack in the second wave, clear the wood to the north, and then take the trenches known as the Starfish Line just north of that. Before the attack, because of the close proximity of opposing trenches, there would be no artillery barrage at High Wood despite the rest of the front receiving a three-day bombardment. Also for the first time, a great new weapon – 'the tank' – would be employed on the battlefield. Eager to give the infantry a huge boost and the element of surprise, General Haig rushed the new, and as of yet untried and untested, tanks into service. Four of the new vehicles would support the attack directly through the wood.

Unbeknown to the men as they cleaned their weapons and prepared themselves for the battle ahead, some of their senior officers were deeply concerned. The division's commander, Major-General Charles Barter, saw major flaws in the plan, especially as High Wood, the position his division was tasked to take, had successfully repulsed attacks for the past two months. Along with the commander of the 141st Brigade, Brigadier-General McDouall, Barter went as far forward to the wood as he could to look upon the ground on which he was being ordered to attack. Tank officers expressed doubt whether their machines could negotiate the tree stumps in places like High Wood.[18] Barter recommended to the III Corps staff that he temporarily evacuate the trenches to give the artillery a chance to be effective so the wood could be cleared prior to the attack. He also asked for the tanks to proceed along the sides of the wood, picking off enemy targets within the tree stumps as they went. Lieutenant-General Sir William Pulteney, III Corps Commander, and his staff rejected this recommendation. He insisted there would be no artillery bombardment before the attack; the tanks would proceed through the wood on the morning of 15 September, as the infantry attack was taking place.

Despite the fact that the 47th Division had to advance through High Wood (the worst terrain on the entire line of the 4th Army advance), and having never been close to the wood himself, Pulteney showed no flexibility and overruled his commanders on the ground. He did not heed the warnings even when he was quizzed by General Sir Henry Rawlinson, the 4th Army commander who had heard from tank 'experts' that they would not be able to get through stump-riddled terrain like High Wood.[19] Historian Terry Norman suggests Pulteney wanted 'High Wood as a vast lane for the passage of four precious tanks and without a hint of a barrage.'[20]

Throughout the First World War, the British Army was an institution in which most officers kept their opinions to themselves even when they saw something going terribly wrong. Acquiescence of a bygone era – that a senior officer's orders should not be questioned under any circumstances – was still prevalent. Whether it was Pulteney, his commander Rawlinson, or even General Haig – none of them appreciated being told that there were flaws in their plans. This unwillingness to listen to subordinates brave enough to speak up, even though they would be tragically proven right, meant that many young men were needlessly and unnecessarily slaughtered at High Wood.

★★★

A week before the battalion moved through Albert on its way to the front, a second Anglican chaplain was sent to the battalion. Only commissioned a month earlier on 8 August 1916, Padre Robert Edward Monro would soon face a baptism of fire. Both he and David would laugh and joke about their Scottish heritage, but Monro was more of a Londoner than a Scott despite his surname. The son of a clergyman preaching in the poorer parishes of the East End of London, Monro graduated from Oxford, then became the vicar of St Matthias' Church in Bethnal Green.[21] As with most padres who worked with David during the war, they would become good friends. They stayed in contact after David's departure and promotion in 1917. Monro was badly wounded during a gas attack at Bourlon Wood in 1917, and this would have a huge effect on him for the rest of his life. Despite this, he was still listed on the Territorial Army Reserve of Officers (TARO) as a chaplain until 14 December 1939, when he reached the age of 60. On his record is noted, 'Shellshock – not to go to the front'.[22]

The night before the attack at High Wood, David and Robert Monro conducted services in the front-line trenches. In a break between communion services, David found a quiet corner of a dugout, huddled around a candle, and wrote to his wife: 'We have got "there", our men are waiting their turn. God help us all… We had some splendid services yesterday – I hope they did some good. The men are in great form. A good few are inwardly anxious but they put a cheery face on it all.'[23] David also described the services they had conducted before the battle: '50 or 60 men in a dark building lighted by only a few candles and one acetylene lamp is wonderful! Your cross is on the wall, and two candles and the oak cross on the altar, the Union Jack underneath.'[24]

The men spent the night packed into the trenches contemplating the fact that they would be attacking this dreadful place in just a few hours. Despite the noise of artillery fire landing either side of High Wood, there was a strange silence throughout the battalion's lines. Most men lay quietly awake while a few slept. David moved through the trenches where he could. Few men wanted to talk. Some prayed with him, and others looked scared, but most were in good heart and looked forward to the light of dawn and the issue of the rum ration.

Orders were given and confirmed – for an infantryman, the plan was very simple and had been practised over and over. The 47th Division was well prepared, as historian Terry Norman notes: 'No one could accuse the division's battalions of not being well-rehearsed for the coming battle.'[25] Two battalions, the 18th on the left and the 17th on the right, would attack through the wood supported by four tanks along the whole length of the 141st Brigade front. These two battalions would secure the far end of the wood. The 19th Londons would then move through the wood and take the Starfish line of trenches beyond it. Finally, the 20th Londons would push through to the final objective. Everything was set except the tanks.

Of the 36 tanks that started out the evening of 14 September at a snail-like pace, only 30 actually made it to the front. At zero hour, those that did make the start line moved so slowly they were soon left behind as the first wave of infantry attacked. The four tanks that were allocated 'lanes' in High Wood were abandoned in a ditch, broke down, caught fire, or bellied on a tree stump. As predicted, the tanks found moving through High Wood quite impossible. They were of no tactical use at all.

At 6:20 A.M., the first two battalions advanced straight into withering enemy machine-gun fire that came from undamaged German trenches. Deeply dug bunkers within the woods sprayed bullets along the front, while platoons of German infantry directed accurate rifle fire on the advancing Londoners. Casualties were very heavy.[26]

At the same time, David and the rest of the battalion started to move into the assembly trenches, but they were full of HQ staff of the battalions already attacking the wood. Despite this, the men of the 19th Londons quickly took their places along the parapets of the trenches. At 7:00 A.M., whistles blew; the battalion climbed up the ladders and went over the top.

Good luck boys. God bless, David said to himself. He closed his eyes, put his hands together, and recited the Lord's Prayer as bullets whistled above his head. *Our Father, who art in heaven, hallowed be thy name…*

As soon as the battalion charged forward through the tree stumps and shell craters, they were cut down by 'heavy enfilade fire'[27] coming from their left. Battalion Commander Lieutenant-Colonel A. P. Hamilton saw right away that the attack had stalled badly. Wounded soldiers from the leading battalions headed back to the sanctuary of the trenches. Men from both waves of the attack were mixed together, all trying to stay alive. The battalion's wartime diary describes what happened next: 'Lt-Col Hamilton clambered out of the communication trench calling upon men to follow and was killed almost immediately by a machine gun bullet.'[28]

By mid-morning, it was obvious that High Wood was a problem. Everywhere else the line had moved forward as planned. The New Zealand Division on the right and the 50th Division on the left achieved their first objectives and took the Starfish line in front of their positions. Their leading troops were now in danger of taking fire in their flanks from unmoved German infantry and machine-gun posts on the north end of the wood.

Seeing the attack was being held up and that the four tanks had failed to have any positive effect, the 141st Brigade commander, Brigadier-General R. McDouall, asked divisional HQ for a barrage to be aimed directly at the wood's western and north-western corners. General Barter trusted his brigade commander's judgement and immediately ordered that all divisional artillery assets bombard these positions. Coupled with trench mortars being fired on the eastern side and bombing attacks along the edges of the wood led by 19th Londons' platoon commanders, Second Lieutenants Crump and Chandler,[29] German resistance began to crack, with many defenders laying down their weapons and surrendering.

It took several hours, with many of the attacking infantrymen still having to take shelter and fire from shell scrapes and craters, but by 1:00 P.M., High Wood was cleared of Germans. The 47th Division accomplished what several other divisions had been unable to do – take the most heavily defended position on the Somme battlefield. But as the hours went by, euphoria and relief were soon replaced by misery and despair when the casualty figures started coming in.

News that the battalion had lost its charismatic commanding officer soon spread. But there was little time for grieving – there was still a battle to be won. At noon, Major Charles Fair, the battalion's second-in-command, was sent forward from brigade HQ to take command of the battalion. All battalion second-in-command officers had been kept away from the front in case their commanding officers became casualties. When he arrived and saw that all the lead battalions were mixed together, with many officers missing, the decision was made to form a composite battalion under Lieutenant-Colonel Norman of the 17th Londons.[30] After the war, in a letter to the official war historian, Major Fair described what he did when he arrived at the wood:

> The situation was still obscure. I took some Lewis guns through the wood and posted them on the NE side in old German trenches as a precaution against immediate counter attack. Units were hopelessly mixed in the wood and just outside it. We gradually got them disentangled during the next 24 hours.[31]

After David saw his men over the top and had said a prayer for their safety, he moved back through the support trenches to the RAP. The trenches were already littered with bloodied and dying men who had managed to crawl back into them. He helped carry wounded men before he found stretcher-bearers to get them to an aid post. One young lad had taken a bullet to the chest and appeared to be bleeding badly. One look from the doctor told David all he needed to know. David knelt by the soldier's stretcher and held his hand, praying with him as the light in his eyes went out.

The doctor, Captain Wesley Bennett, RAMC,[32] now worked as fast as he could trying to save wounded men, stabilising them enough to be moved back to the ADS, located about a mile to the rear at Flat Iron Copse. Most of the time he patched them up or just made them as comfortable as he could before they died. Bodies of those who did not make it were taken outside the tent and laid in a row. A canvas sheet covered their heads. As the hours went by, the number of bodies increased.

***

That evening there was a consolidation along the entire front – an attempt to hold on to the ground that had been won at such a high cost. Because of the heavy losses at High Wood, every available man was needed. Even those in support roles within the battalions and brigade were allocated a position to defend. Orderlies, store men, transport drivers – anyone that could fire a rifle was sent to augment quickly re-shuffled platoons within the newly consolidated battalion. Although that night and the next day were generally quiet, there was now a considerable shortage of rations due to the confusion of units.[33] Many men who would normally have been making sure that supplies got through were now on the front line.

For a second night, 16–17 September, the tired and hungry men, still holding on to the captured positions of High Wood, surrounded by the ghastly sights and smells of the untouched battlefield, faced the real prospect of having to fight off possible counter-attacks from the direction of Flers. Fortunately, they did not materialise, and the next morning, the 24th Londons, who took over responsibility for the entire wood, relieved the composite battalion.

The men of the 19th Londons who had survived marched away from the battlefield. If they felt any sense of relief at leaving, hoping they had seen the last of that horrible place, then they were mistaken. Everyone knew that casualties were high; the few officers and NCOs left to organise the men as they headed towards Mametz Wood spoke volumes. But it was only after the roll was called and a further estimate of casualties was made that the full horror of what had happened at High Wood became known. Eleven officers and 294 other ranks were killed, wounded or posted missing.[34]

Whether David stayed with the doctor at the RAP throughout the battle or moved back to the ADS at Flat Iron Copse is unknown. Either way, he was back with the men as the battalion rested in the open at Mametz Wood on the afternoon of 17 September. At 6:00 P.M., they were ordered to move up to the Bazentin 'Circus', a trench system taken from the Germans that connected the woods of Bazentin-le-Petit and Bazentin-le-Grand. When they arrived, they were duly turned around and sent back because there was no room in the trenches. In the open again and with the weather deteriorating, they were ordered to move at 1:00 A.M. The battalion's wartime diary briefly describes what the men were going through: 'Order received to move to trench between the Bazentin-Le-Grand and Bazentin-Le-Petit. Heavy rain and roads in very bad condition. Lewis Gun carts proved utterly useless. Accommodation bad and men now suffering from exhaustion and cold. Cookers finally arrived at 6am.'[35]

That morning, to make matters worse, the cold, wet and hungry men now faced the distinct prospect of either being sent back into battle or being tasked to bury dead comrades who were still lying where they fell. The war diary account continues: '30 bombers were supplied to 140th Brigade for operations in neighbourhood of Flers', and a 'burial party of one officer and 15 ORs supplied for High Wood'.[36]

David marched with the burial party back to High Wood. Once they arrived, the scale of the task at hand became apparent. His small burial party was simply not big enough; those in command had grossly underestimated how many men would be needed. For the next three days, the battalion would supply 'large burial parties',[37] meaning anyone fit and able from the battalion would be used. Their task was to locate and recover the bodies of their fallen comrades. The men slowly moved across sections of the wood where the battalion had advanced, looking for bodies then removing them to a central area where they would be buried. It was a thankless task, and David noticed that the morale of the men started to fade the longer they stayed at High Wood.

On the south-west side of the wood, a makeshift cemetery of sorts had formed. A large shell hole was being used, which would eventually be the burial site of 47 men from the 47th Division. Subsequent burials would take place around it.[38] Each time a burial took place, David would cover the body of their fallen comrade with the Union Jack and conduct a short service before they lowered the deceased into the ground. There simply was no time for anything more.

During that first day at High Wood between burials, while he was searching a patch of ground just ahead of the trenches, David recognised the twisted, contorted body of their CO, Lieutenant-Colonel Hamilton. He was lying alone at the bottom of a shallow crater. His body was forward of the trenches he had scrambled out of after he realised that the attack was not going to plan. David called over two men who had a stretcher with them. They placed the Colonel onto it and lifted him out of the shell hole. David took out the Union Jack from his haversack and laid it over the body. Then, as carefully and respectfully as they could, despite the treacherous ground over which they had to travel, they moved the flag-draped body to the cemetery where many of the battalion's officers and men were being interred.

David removed all the Colonel's personal belongings he could find and then cut off his rank insignia and his buttons; he left his Military Cross ribbon, which he had won at Loos the previous year. He was not sure whether Mrs Hamilton would want this, but he had to make a judgement call. David thought about his own wife and what she would have wanted to keep if it were him lying dead on the battlefield. In a letter to David a few weeks later, Mrs Hamilton confirmed that he had made the right decision.[39] There is no exact record of the burial of Lieutenant-Colonel Hamilton. But, piecing together the few sources that are available – a description of Major Fair's 1920 battlefield tour, information from the Commonwealth War Graves Commission, and David Railton's own words – we can put together a fairly accurate description of what probably happened.

While visiting the Somme with friends just two years after the Armistice, Major Fair wrote, 'The machine-gun dugout at the "circus", which served as H.Q. after High Wood has gone but a curious shaped tree which I remembered was there. I could not find Colonel Hamilton's grave, presumably it has been moved.'[40]

After the war had ended, many small cemeteries around the Bazentin Ridge were closed, with bodies reburied at the Flat Iron Copse Cemetery where Colonel Hamilton lies today.[41] David Railton, writing after the war (in the voice of the Flag) noted, 'I remember being taken to the rest service for Colonel Arthur Hamilton, Major Trinder and Captain Peter McGinn. It was very close behind the ground on which they had fought and fallen.'[42]

Piecing together all this evidence suggests that it is very likely that David decided to have the burial party transport the Colonel back to the area of the 'Circus' where the regiment was still situated. He would be buried there, with the whole regiment in attendance, on 19 September 1916, with Major Trinder and Captain McGinn, before the battalion moved to the old German line between Fricourt and Bécourt later that day.[43] David described the difficulty under which the service was conducted: 'Just as the service began, two or three guns which were close to us opened fire and yet when the padre said they would sing "Abide with Me" every officer and man lifted his voice in defiance.'[44]

The most likely burial site was the Cross Roads Cemetery just a short distance (200 yards) from the 'Circus' dugout (mentioned by Major Fair) at the crossroads close to the northern end of the Bazentin-le-Grand wood, a half-mile from High Wood. This small cemetery of only 19 graves was closed after the war, and the graves were moved to Flatiron Copse Cemetery. Major Trinder, 18th Londons, lies there too, but no record of Captain Peter McGinn has been found.[45]

It's hard to understand what the loss of Lieutenant-Colonel Hamilton would have meant to the battalion. Many officers had died, and Hamilton was not the first CO to have lost his life leading a regiment into battle. However, it is very clear that Hamilton was deeply admired, even loved, by those who served under him. Major Fair described the loss of his CO 'as if I had lost a brother, we have been so constantly side by side in every sort of corner for nearly eleven months'.[46] David described Hamilton as 'our dear colonel',[47] and he also wrote, 'I admire our colonel', while describing an occasion when he gave up his tent for his men during a storm.[48]

Lieutenant-Colonel Hamilton was not a cap-badged officer of the London Regiment. According to Major Fair, he 'was a regular soldier who had been commissioned into The Queen's Royal West Surrey Regiment in 1905. Prior to taking command of the 1/19th he had been Adjutant of the 18th Londons.'[49] He won the Military Cross at the Battle of Loos and was presented the medal by King George V in London.[50]

A few weeks before the battalion went over the top at High Wood, Hamilton was told that he was to return to his regiment. After 11 months with the 19th Londons he did not 'seem to want to go in the least'.[51] It seemed that Major Fair and the men who considered his departure 'another blow'[52] didn't want him to leave either. In the build-up to the Somme, while the battalion was at Bresle, Sergeant-Drummer Spanner came up with a 'brilliant idea'[53] to show how much the battalion appreciated their CO. He worked diligently to collect all the signatures of the officers and NCOs of the battalion on the 'drumhead' of a damaged regimental drum.[54] He persuaded his corporal to draw the London Regiment's badge on the drumhead, which he intended to present to Colonel Hamilton when he left. The drumhead, now a precious 'Roll of Honour', was framed and presented to Mrs Hamilton.[55] It gives an accurate and somewhat sombre snapshot of the battalion before High Wood.

David Railton wrote to Mrs Hamilton on several occasions.[56] Colonel Hamilton's sister became a friend of David's mother after the war while she was living in Thanet. In a 1972 letter to Andrew Scott Railton, she explained how the drumhead came to be in the possession of the Railton family: 'We were present at Westminster Abbey when your father presented the flag. It was my mother's wish that the drumhead signed by all the officers of the regiment should be given to your father.'[57]

★★★

When the battalion arrived back at their billets in Bresle, the brigade was waiting for them. 'We had a great reception when we rejoined the rest of the brigade yesterday and we marched in with our band playing',[58] Major Fair recalled. It was as if the rest of the brigade understood what a terrible undertaking the 19th Londons had been tasked with. They were slapping backs and shouting their support. The band played, and although their spirits were low, the men of the 19th Londons marched back with their heads held high. The battalion had not been hit the hardest (11 officers and 78 men killed), so it made sense to those in command that the task of battlefield clearance should be done by the 19th Londons. But if the battle at High Wood had not taken a heavy enough toll, then the torture of cleaning up the aftermath of the battle had.

***

That evening, despite being tired from the march, David headed to divisional HQ to report in person to the Senior Chaplain. He wanted him to know that he thought there might be several cases of shellshock caused by their battlefield clearance duties and wanted to ask his advice. When he arrived, there seemed to be a strange atmosphere; he could sense that something was not right. Although there had been huge losses over the past few days, this did not seem like a headquarters that had just won a great victory. The new Senior Chaplain, Revd C. T. T. Wood, who had only just taken over from Revd Bell, did not know much except that he had heard of possible command changes in the coming days. David was intrigued but thought nothing more of it.

A few days later, Major Fair broke the news that divisional commander, Major-General Charles Barter, was leaving the division. Nothing else was said and no other explanation was offered except that it was a routine change in command. Unbeknown to the rank and file of the 47th Division, Barter was sent back to England in disgrace; dismissed and charged with 'wanton waste of men'.[59]

If officers and men had known the reason why Barter was leaving, then some may have felt conflicted. Despite the fact that he was well regarded by most, the division had lost 4,500 officers and men at High Wood. If there ever was a charge of 'wanton waste of men' to be levelled at a commander, then surely it should land squarely at the feet of General Barter. Many would have felt little sympathy for the general; David's battalion alone had suffered enough, and there were battalions that had nearly been wiped out.

Gradually over the next weeks, months, and years, a much different story emerged. The 47th Division was officially criticised for its 'lack of push'.[60] No one associated with the division could understand: a 'lack of push' from a division whose commander was charged with 'wanton waste of men'? After the war, veterans of the 47th Division would form their own opinions. They heard about General Barter's request to III Corps before the battle, asking for artillery to be used before the attack and the tanks to move along the edge of the wood rather than through it. Barter fought for the remainder of his life to clear his name. He was haunted by what happened, continuously lobbying for an official enquiry. Despite being cleared by an unofficial investigation and subsequently knighted by the King, Barter would never forgive or forget.

In 1919, at a dinner in London to honor the 47th Division, General Barter rose to his feet to make a speech and used the public occasion to set the record straight:

> I was charged with wanton waste of men entrusted to my command at the battle of the Somme. I repudiate that charge with indignation. The measures taken which led to this loss were either in opposition to my representations, or I was not responsible for them. I was dismissed at an hour's notice with disgrace from my division. I was dismissed at an hour of the most brilliant achievement of the division – the capture of High Wood, which several other divisions had made futile attempts to take. I think it is unexampled in military history that a military commander should be disgraced in the hour of the success of the troops under his command without any attempt at investigation.[61]

Most people now agree that the decision to remove General Barter from his post was totally unjustified and came from the III Corps commander. General Pulteney needed a scapegoat for the losses and the fact that one of his divisions was held up so badly at High Wood. It was his decision to overrule Barter that directly caused the high casualty rate at High Wood. He was covering up his own incompetence. General Haig did not see through this blatant miscarriage of justice – in fact, it appeared that he too believed it:

> The 47th Divn failed at High Wood on 15th September and the GOC was sent home! Barter by name. Now Gorringe has taken over command. He arrived on Sunday, so he has not had time to make his personality felt. I told him to teach the Divn Discipline and Digging.[62]

Pulteney continued as III Corps Commander. In 1917, his corps suffered high casualties and lost considerable ground during the German counter-attack at Cambrai. But it was not until 1918 that General Pulteney finally lost his command, when his incompetency could no longer be covered up by firing subordinate generals instead of himself. Richard Holmes wondered why he had been so well protected: 'It is hard to see how he managed to survive for so long, though his old Army connections probably helped: he was a Scots Guards officer.'[63]

★★★

The next day, companies were free to conduct what the 19th Londons' War Diary describes as 'refitting and specialist training' in the afternoon.[64] But in the morning, the battalion formed up in a three-sided square for a ceremonial parade. At the open end was 'the new band of the 19th'[65] and in front of them a table covered with the Padre's Flag. On top of that were a simple altar cloth, two candlesticks and a wooden cross in the middle. Once the Senior Company Sergeant Major (in the absence of RSM Ridout, who died at High Wood) handed over the parade to the Adjutant, Captain R. C. G. Dartford, and those few officers left alive had fallen in, Major Fair came into the square, stood the parade 'at ease' and addressed the battalion.

Writing about their grandfather, Reginald and Charles Fair note: 'There is no record of the speech Charles made or what lesson he chose, but the hymns were particularly apt. The first three were subdued but providing solace, no doubt reflecting the mood and needs of his men. A display of jingoistic patriotism would not have suited the occasion.'[66]

It would not have been the time for a sabre-rattling call to arms, and if the speech did in fact mirror the hymns, it surely would have been focused on quiet reflection, allowing everyone the chance to grieve for friends and comrades in arms. The first three matched the mood perfectly and the rousing 'For All the Saints Who from Their Labours Rest' lifted everyone's spirits.[67] He would have reminded them that although they had won a great victory, there would be other battles ahead that would require equal effort and sacrifice.

Later that evening, David continued the task of writing to the families of those 89 men who had fallen at High Wood. Before the battle a

'Nominal Roll & Next of Kin' (one for officers and one for the men) was compiled. The lists included the name and address of each man's next of kin – the person whom they wanted to be informed should they be killed. David's copy of the 'Officer's Roll & Next of Kin' is amongst the many items kept for over a century by the Railton family. Looking at it today makes one wonder how men like David Railton coped with this task. Next to 11 names David wrote, 'Killed'.[68]

Also in the Railton Collection is a scrap of paper with faded writing in pencil: 'To be opened if I get killed. Captain LJ Davis, 1/19th London Regiment. Mr & Mrs Arthur Davis, 11 Cleve Road, Hampstead, London NW'.[69] On David's 'list' next to Captain L. J. Davis, he wrote, 'Killed' and 'Sent letter for parents'.[70]

★★★

A century later the Somme still haunts the British psyche. Nothing has been written or said since the slaughter of the summer of 1916 that has convinced the British people that the Battle of the Somme in 1916 was anything more than one long tragedy. The tragedy of it was not lost on men like David Railton and Charles Fair, who carried around with them for the rest of their lives the horrors they experienced during battle. And yet, even after such terrible losses, it seems their spirits and conviction to the cause never wavered. They were still 'enormously proud'[71] of what the battalion had achieved and expressed what most men of the battalion felt: 'It is an honour to be here.'[72]

Of all the tragedies and losses at the Somme, one would prove to be the bitterest of ironies. It involved David and the 19th Londons and showed that tragedy could strike all classes and all families from every walk of life. From the homes of the working classes amongst the backstreets of north London, to those of a minister of the government, the tragedy of the Somme spared no one.

Of the many well-documented blunders that took place in the planning of the Somme, the lack of operational security around the date and time of the attack would be one of the harshest lessons learnt. German commanders were well aware of the obvious build-up of troops in the area of the Somme, so they knew roughly from where the attack was coming.

Their spies were hard at work gathering information concerning the date. A few German agents had heard rumours of a British attack around Whitsuntide planned for 11 June. Another agent's report said the attack would come a week later, which left the German High Command worried about the Whitsun holiday date. But they needn't have worried. The Germans were able to garner some very important information for themselves by reading the London newspapers on 2 June.

British minister Arthur Henderson MP gave a speech at a meeting of munitions factory owners and workers in Leeds. During this meeting, he was asked why the Whitsun Bank Holiday was to be a normal working day. Henderson knew he had to be careful because of the need for secrecy. He tried to be clever with his answer but did not do a very good job: 'How inquisitive we all are! It should suffice that we ask for a postponement of the holidays and to the end of July. This fact should speak volumes.'[73]

This gaff would not have had such importance had the censors done their job – it's safe to say that German agents were probably not at this meeting in Leeds. Instead, this very pertinent information was published. In all fairness to the Labour MP, his was not the only slip; it was just one of a list of security failures from which the British would need to learn if they wanted to defeat the German Army.

The bitter irony lies in a grave of Plot 1A at the London Cemetery and extension at High Wood.[74] There lies Captain David Henderson, son of Labour MP and Cabinet Minister Arthur Henderson, killed during the attack of 15 September 1916, and buried by David Railton during the battlefield clearance.[75]

CHAPTER 5

The Military Cross

'The bravest are surely those who have the clearest vision of what is before them, glory and danger alike, and yet notwithstanding, go out to meet it.'

THUCYDIDES

Saturday, 19 December 1916, Devonshire Camp, Busseboom, Belgium

The paraffin lamp in his hut not only provided the light he needed to write, but also a touch of warmth to help David thaw out after his long walk back to camp, even if its effect was minimal. Although winter had not officially begun, it felt like the middle of February, having been unseasonably cold since mid-November. David was already feeling the effects. In the letter he was writing, he told his wife, 'My right foot is a mass of chilblains.'[1] Everyone hoped that the early blast of freezing weather they were experiencing was not a sign of things to come. Unfortunately, they would be very disappointed – the bitter winter of 1916–17 in northern France and Belgium would end up being labelled the coldest in living memory.[2]

★★★

After the 47th Division was finally withdrawn from the Somme on 14 October 1916, what was left of the division marched to Albert and entrained for the long journey north. Because of the congestion of troops being moved on a single railway track, with trains desperately trying to get supplies to the front given priority over trains moving away from the front, the division spent many hours in railway sidings. David vented to his wife when he wrote, 'We have come about fifteen miles in twenty-four hours! Vive la France!'[3] But that didn't matter to the men. Even though they were crammed into railway cars meant for cattle, most seemed happy just to be away from the front and appeared to be in no hurry to go back. In the same letter, David wrote, 'At about 8am, the men hacked a footer about for a while. It is easy to give warning of a move on. The train creeps out so slowly, and the men run from the field and get in at their leisure.'[4]

It was apparent that food was going to be in short supply throughout the journey because 'permission was given for the iron ration to be consumed'.[5] The iron ration was comprised of preserved meat, cheese, sugar, tea, biscuits, and salt, carried by all men only to be used in the event of being cut off from regular supplies. As the train moved away from Albert and passed through undamaged villages, some of the men were quick enough to slip away and purchase local produce such as eggs and bread.[6]

For the next two days, their train headed south-west to Amiens, then north-west along beautifully unspoiled parts of the Somme valley to Abbeville before heading north to the coast and the hospital area at Étaples. Although frustrated by the snail-like pace of their journey, blaming 'some staff ass or asses'[7] for messing it all up, David enjoyed travelling through the beautiful countryside when they were actually moving: 'The river with trees flanking, and all the leaves in the beauty of their autumn tints … all the rushes and reeds seem to have gathered the golden sun and every colour into their graceful selves.'[8]

After another night on the train, they headed east, back towards the sound of the guns and the front-line trenches of Flanders, arriving east of the Ypres Salient. Divisional headquarters was set up at Hooggraaf close to the town of Poperinghe. In 1922, Alan Maude, whilst writing the war history of the 47th Division, described the landscape east of Ypres as 'a dull and depressing slice of country'[9] – flat and featureless, crisscrossed by irrigation ditches, with several 'squalid clusters of houses' banded together in villages.[10]

This barren farmland was covered with an ever-increasing number of hutted camps; this was where the men of the 19th Battalion would be billeted when they were not in the divisional front line. The good thing about there being so many camps was that each unit, upon leaving the trenches of the Ypres Salient, would return to the same one. This way they 'came to regard it as theirs taking more pride in its upkeep and amenities generally than if they had only been casual occupants'.[11]

***

David looked up at the paraffin lamp again. He still hadn't warmed up properly since arriving back at the camp several hours ago. It was good to be out of the wind, but the cold seemed to seep in from every direction, up through the floorboards or between gaps in the wooden boarded walls. No matter how many layers of clothing he put on, there was no escaping it. Even though he wanted to stay warm, he kept a watchful eye on the lamp, making sure that it was not getting too hot next to the wooden beam from which it hung. Back on the Somme he'd seen for himself what could happen to paraffin in a confined space.

After finishing a letter to his wife, he started one to Mrs Elsie Clark, wife of the late Captain Sydney Clark, RAMC, who had been killed on the Somme on 2 October 1916, age 47. This was the second time he had written to Mrs Clark. In response to his initial letter, Mrs Clark had written back to David seeking more information about her husband's death. Most of the time when a family wrote to him requesting more details, David passed the letters on to someone in their company or platoon. He generally didn't have the time, but occasionally he responded more than once in exceptional circumstances. On this occasion David considered the circumstances surrounding the death of Captain Clark truly exceptional. He explained that he was with Captain Clark when he died, and that the captain had died instantly and was buried with the dignity befitting such a fine man. But he would not tell her what else had happened that day – nor would he tell anyone all the circumstances surrounding her husband's death, not even the circumstances that led to David being awarded the Military Cross.

***

After a few days in Bresle recovering from the Battle of High Wood and with the platoons bolstered by the arrival of 250 new recruits replacing those men lost, the 19th Battalion headed back into the fray. On Sunday, 1 October, at 3:15 P.M., as the right-hand battalion of a brigade attack, the men of the 19th Londons advanced on the village of Eaucourt L'Abbaye. The village, which consisted of a group of houses clustered around old abbey buildings, and was reputed to have extensive cellars, looked like it was going to be another hard nut to crack. Initially, constant machine-gun fire from the west corner of the abbey held up progress, but tanks supporting the infantry took care of them. By the evening the battalion had taken its objective, rushing through the village, then hastily digging defensive positions on the far side. On the second day of the attack, despite there being gaps in the line caused by confusion and bad weather around Eaucourt L'Abbaye the prior evening, the 23rd Londons were able to move forward and consolidate the line.[12]

Between the destroyed villages of Martinpuch and Flers and about a mile behind the newly established front line, there stood a huge bunker that had been converted into the division's ADS after it was captured from the Germans. Appropriately named 'Cough Drop', the bunker was dug deep into a bank and had three entrances. It was a haven on an otherwise war-ravaged landscape and the perfect location for a dressing station with 'accommodation for some seventy stretcher cases'.[13]

As the battle got under way on 1 October, David held a church service for the troops of the divisional transport company some miles behind the front line. Afterwards, in a very emotional letter, he conveyed his fear for the men who had already been through so much. 'I shall go up to the dressing station shortly, it is all terrible. A fearful fight is proceeding.'[14] After the heavy losses of High Wood, he obviously expected more of the same. 'Last night in divisional orders, the Military Cross was awarded to one of our Lieutenants. Today he is killed.'[15] After he arrived at the ADS, David spent the night helping doctors and medical personnel. The ADS was under temporary command of Captain S. Clark, RAMC, of the 5th (London) Fd Amb.

On the morning of 2 October, British positions around Eaucourt L'Abbaye were being consolidated. At the same time, unbeknown to anyone, someone inside Cough Drop had not been paying enough attention to a primus stove while making themselves breakfast. The stove caught fire and burned the table it was standing on. A medic who saw it happen went to get what he thought was a plastic container full of water and threw it on the fire. But the jug was full of paraffin, not water; so what once was a small fire and should have been easily contained, now engulfed into a raging inferno that quickly spread throughout 'the well-timbered dugout'.[16]

Despite a valiant effort from everyone at the ADS who helped put out the fire, the dugout was destroyed. No one was injured, but a lot of stores and valuable medical supplies went up in smoke. According to the divisional history, 'Far worse was that this precious haven, where in an emergency, so many wounded could be housed out of harm's way, had "gone west" for good.'[17]

Over the next two or three hours, as much as could be salvaged was recovered and dragged outside. Doctors and medics of the ADS worked hard to make sure it would still function as a dressing station for at least a day or two, until a replacement could be found. Canvas sheets were raised on the sides of the dugout so injured soldiers could still be cared for under some kind of shelter. David does not mention the fire in letters home, but he was there and presumably helped in the recovery. Later events of that day might have pushed the fire at the ADS into distant memory.

There is very little factual evidence to allow us to say for certain what happened that afternoon – David never spoke of why he was awarded the Military Cross. All we have is what he wrote in letters to his wife regarding the death of Captain Clark and the official transcript that appeared in *The London Gazette* on 25 November 1916:

> Rev. David Railton, Temp Chapln to the Forces, 4th Class, A, Chapl dept. For conspicuous gallantry in action. He rescued an officer and two men under heavy fire, displaying great courage and determination. He has on many occasions done very fine work.[18]

Although we probably will never know with absolute certainty what happened, using what evidence we have, such as newly uncovered letters, handwritten statements, and newspaper reports, we can put together a plausible account.

After the fire, it was business as usual for the medical personnel of the 5th (London) Fd Amb. Stretcher-bearers brought in more and more injured men from various battalion aid posts. Doctors were able to continue working, but they were limited in what injuries they could treat. There were to be no surgical procedures of any kind because all morphine had been destroyed along with most forms of anaesthetic; and as soon as they heard artillery shells, they all had to dive for cover. A canvas sheet did not afford them the same protection that the dugout had.

Sometime in the afternoon Captain Clark heard there was 'a wounded man reported to be lying somewhere in the forward area'.[19] Whether he asked David to go with him or David volunteered to join Captain Clark and the stretcher-bearers is unknown. David never mentioned going forward on this kind of search before, but as was his habit, he would not have made a fuss in any of his letters home if he had. It is possible that if this rescue had passed off without incident, then we may have never heard of it.

Tanks were used in the support during the attack on 1 October. A short account of the attack appeared in *The Times* of 12 October 1916. Of the four tanks that supported the infantry during the advance on Eaucourt L'Abbaye, 'One was unable to proceed, and operated as a stationary fort. Subsequently it was abandoned. While escaping an officer was wounded. Two of the men refused to leave him, and stayed for two days in a shell hole between the lines.'[20]

Captain B. H. Liddell Hart describes it somewhat differently in his book, *The Tanks*:

> When the battalions of the 141st Brigade were held up short of the German trenches, these two tanks drove from the flank and along the trench-line, so shaking the defenders that the 141st Brigade was able to capture the trenches and push on beyond the village of Eaucourt L'Abbaye. But the tanks became ditched, and had to be abandoned when the enemy counter-attacked.[21]

Which account is correct, whether it was one or two tanks that were abandoned, is unclear. But what is certain is that the enemy had the opportunity to get behind the 141st Brigade when there were gaps in the line or during the counter-attack. At least one German sniper was able to use 'the gap on the right of the 50th Division in the Flers line'[22] to move forward and take up a deadly firing position in an abandoned tank.

That afternoon, 2 October, Captain Clark, David, and the men detailed as stretcher-bearers tasked with locating the wounded man were searching in an area forward of the ADS. To their knowledge, the ground had been cleared of the enemy as the front line had moved well forward. Suddenly, and without any warning, a shot rang out. Instinctively, everyone hit the ground. From this point it is very difficult to know exactly what happened. Two days later, David wrote to his wife mentioning the incident: 'Captain Clark was killed by my side, or strictly speaking, a few paces behind me, and four others were wounded. God alone knows how I was missed.'[23] However, there is no mention of David's actions or any explanation of why he was put forward for the Military Cross.

Whether the 'four others' were wounded trying to get Captain Clark back to the ADS after he was killed is difficult to determine. All we can be sure of is that the sniper was hiding in a discarded tank in front of Eaucourt L'Abbaye, and David was either alone or surrounded by wounded men from the stretcher party. The men David rescued were probably the tank crew mentioned in *The Times* who had stayed with their officer and then were trapped in a shell hole for two days, pinned down by the sniper.

In a letter to his mother two months later, David wrote, 'The credit of my M.C. belongs more to an officer and two other men than to me.'[24] Just a few days after the incident he found out some details about the sniper: 'I hear that the vile villain who killed Captain Clark, the doctor, and wounded four others of our "wounded party" was in a tank. This tank had been discarded and burnt by our men after the advance.'[25]

Whatever heroic deed David performed that day, he truly believed that he did not deserve the medal he was subsequently awarded. 'Of course this kind of thing happens constantly among officers and men of the Army, but as a rule our padre paths are freer of it.'[26] Always putting the fighting soldiers first, he was quite clear who he thought should have received the medal. 'God alone knows how little I deserve it compared to many of our combatant officers and men.'[27]

Sometime after the incident, David filed a report concerning one of the men who was with the 'wounded party' that day. Whether it was typed up and filed is not known – this testimony was handwritten in pencil, undated, and remains with the Railton Family Archive.

Statement as to the character of Private S Filmer

I have known Pte S Filmer for a considerable time. I believe he has always been of a character creditable to the battalion. I witnessed an action of his in the Eaucourt L'Abbaye sector, last October, which proved his worth as a soldier.

An officer who was searching for wounded was hit by a sniper. Two other officers who were with him called for assistance. Pte S Filmer, together with 2 other men immediately left the trench with a stretcher and carried him back to the trench under constant fire from the sniper. Four members of the party were wounded. I feel sure that any combatant officer who had watched the steady way in which Pte Filmer acted on that occasion would say that his conduct was such as to bring credit to the battalion.

Signed: D Railton[28]

It is not known who filed the report stating that David had shown 'great courage and determination',[29] or what the details were. But at some stage after Captain Clark had been shot and placed on the stretcher by Private Filmer and two others, David must have crawled forward and dragged back the officer and two men from the crater they had been hiding in. Whether other men helped or not is also unknown, but either way it would have taken great resolve to have put himself in harm's way three times against a sniper who had just killed Captain Clark.

The citation published in *The London Gazette* concludes by saying, 'He has on many previous occasions done very fine work.'[30] David always said that he thought the officers and men deserved all bravery awards because they were constantly in harm's way. But he was not only being recognised for what happened on the afternoon of 2 October 1916; he also was being recognised for all his efforts since joining the 47th Division: the many hours he spent helping the wounded at Cabaret Rouge, visiting his men in the trenches at Vimy Ridge, and what he did in the aftermath of the battle at High Wood when the battalion had been tasked to clear the battlefield. David Railton was constantly risking his own life for his men, although he never would have agreed with such a statement. David did not consider himself brave, nor would he have called himself a coward. But neither was he the kind of man who needlessly sought danger, risking becoming a casualty himself. He would have been no use to the men if he were dead or severely wounded.

★★★

A little over a month before the 'Clark incident' and before the battalion had arrived at High Wood, David had a chance encounter with an old friend. He was standing in a field when he saw a column of soldiers marching. At first he thought it was the Northumberland Fusiliers. After running half a mile across a field, he realised it was the Liverpool Scottish. They were wearing rain-proof sheets and so he could not recognise them in their kilts from a distance. David recalled, 'I walked for miles with Chavasse… How they filled me with joy. I yarned with Chavasse for a long while … the Bishop of Liverpool had not been so well. He had just come back from leave having seen him.'[31] Having served as a private soldier in the Liverpool Scottish, David obviously felt a great affinity for the regiment. And knowing the son of his great mentor, the Bishop of Liverpool, obviously made the time he marched with them even more enjoyable.

Captain Noel Godfrey Chavasse, RAMC, the battalion's doctor, had already made a bit of a name for himself in the Liverpool Scottish. In 1915, at Hooge, he had been awarded the Military Cross[32] for spending the good part of three days searching areas the battalion had advanced over, helping rescue the wounded, and making sure everyone had been accounted for. He also had been 'Mentioned in Dispatches' for 'gallant and distinguished service in the field' at Sanctuary Wood.[33] As well as for his bravery, he had a reputation for looking after the welfare of his men, and they respected him because of it. On at least one occasion, he paid for 1,000 pairs of socks to be sent from England for all the men of his battalion.[34] He also set up canteens, hot urns of cocoa, and other facilities wherever he was able, with the aim of keeping the men healthy and well – both physically and mentally.[35] He courted the wrath of those in command for being sympathetic towards soldiers who were obviously suffering from shellshock.[36]

On 7 August 1916, just three weeks before Noel Chavasse and David marched together, the Liverpool Scottish had been involved in the attack at Guillemont on the Somme. Despite being wounded, Captain Chavasse spent two days and nights rescuing men from the ground between the front-line trenches, 'although fired on by bombs and machine guns. Altogether he saved the lives of some twenty badly wounded, besides the ordinary cases which passed through his hands.'[37]

Noel Chavasse went on leave after the battle to recover from the injuries he had sustained. When he met David on the Somme, nothing had been announced concerning his acts of 'courage and self-sacrifice'[38] at Guillemont. What they talked about is unknown, as neither of them mentioned any details in their letters home. Noel Chavasse made one quick reference in a letter to his parents: 'On the way up we met Railton who is a chaplain out here and who looks very well. He asked to be remembered to you.'[39]

David's reaction to unwanted publicity after the award of his Military Cross clearly shows he was not seeking awards of any kind. But it does seem plausible that his conversation with such an inspiring and brave man as Noel Chavasse might have influenced David's actions on 2 October.

Whatever the motivation, he made the conscious decision to put the lives of an officer and two men above that of his own. Even after David found himself pinned down by a German sniper, he went back out to rescue the other two men, when the safest option would have been to lay low and wait for someone else to come and deal with the situation.

On 26 October, 1916 (while David was at home in Folkestone on leave) *The London Gazette* announced that Noel Godfrey Chavasse, MC, RAMC, had been awarded the Victoria Cross.[40] Whether David knew anything about Noel Chavasse's actions at Guillemont is unknown. But what is certain is that he would have been delighted for his friend and mentor, the Bishop of Liverpool.

★★★

David returned to his battalion on the morning of 5 October, after the battle for Eaucourt L'Abbaye was over and the battalion had been relieved. They were withdrawn back to the area of the Quadrangle trench system near Contalmaison.[41] The battalion stayed busy for the next week re-organising companies, training, and getting ready to leave the Somme with the remnants of the 47th Division to head north. There were very few men from the battalion at the ADS with David during the incident surrounding the death of Captain Clark and the rescue of the officer and the other two men, so there would have been no mention of it when he returned to the battalion. Based on what we now know of David, he would not have brought it up in conversation unless he was asked.

After the train journey to the Ypres Salient, David was granted leave and travelled back home to Folkestone.[42] He arrived back at the battalion on Monday, 13 November 1916. As he was climbing onto battalion transport to head back up the line, having dropped off a bag at Devonshire Camp, the Transport Officer, Captain MacLagan, called over to him.

'Many congratulations, Padre.'

'What for? Dodging mines and those wretched Boche U–Boats in the Channel?' David answered as the transport convoy was pulling away.

'No – MC,' MacLagan shouted back.

'Well, I knew you would have some jokes old Mac, but they won't work tonight.' David laughed, leaning out of the window.

'It's no joke; it came out on orders last night,' he shouted again as the transport moved away.[43]

Nice try, Mac, David said to himself.

Several hours later, David arrived back with the battalion who were situated in the 'right sub–section of the Bluff Sector of the front-line'.[44] As he entered the battalion HQ dugout, he was greeted by several officers, each eager to shake his hand. The last person to greet him was Major Fair, who had a broad smile on his face. He came down the steps into the dugout and pinned the purple and white medal ribbon on his tunic. David was surprised, visibly embarrassed, and did not know what to say.

'If this is true, then I really shouldn't wear it until it's gazetted.' He babbled his words slightly and started to take it off.

'No, you mustn't.' Major Fair raised his voice. 'Put it on at once; it was sent for you from headquarters.'[45] 'Congratulations, David,' his voice much lower now. He shook his hand and smiled.

That evening David did his rounds through the companies who were on the battalion's section of the line. Everyone greeted and congratulated him. Word had gotten out; their padre had been awarded the third highest honour for gallantry that their country could bestow upon an officer – he had done something extraordinary that day. Later he held several short services within the confines of the trench's cramped dugouts. Each time, they were crammed full of soldiers wanting to pray with him. He wrote, 'They seem to be really pleased that I have got it.'[46]

Although he wore the medal ribbon, he would have to wait another 12 days before the medal was presented and the news publicly announced. On 25 November, the official announcement was made in *The London Gazette*,[47] and the next morning after a church service, David received his Military Cross from the new Commanding Officer, Major Friend. Two other members of the battalion received bravery awards as well – a Distinguished Conduct Medal (DCM) and a Military Medal (MM).[48]

A week after the announcement was made, several local Folkestone and Kent newspapers praising their 'Brave Chaplain'[49] quickly picked up the news. His vicar, the Revd Canon Tindall, led the chorus of praise, saying, 'Mr Railton is one of those men who never thinks of himself. Anyone who knows him will feel that he is just the man to do an unselfish act.'[50]

The East Kent Times led their article with 'Heroic Chaplain – Rescue Under Fire – Military Cross for member of Thanet Family'.[51] *The Folkestone Express* and the December issue of the *Folkestone Parish News*[52] also covered the news.

All this publicity made David feel very uneasy. At first his modesty seems like something most honourable men of his generation typically would say. But underneath, there was a genuine fear that being awarded the Military Cross would jeopardise the close relationship he had with his men. In a rare 'uncut' letter to his mother, written in December 1916, which has survived intact, he shared this fear:

> What has however distressed me dreadfully is the long-winded account of me in the local paper, which has reached me from Folkestone. Oh how these officers and men hate it. How they scorn the man who somehow gets all his life put into the papers because he has been awarded the M.C.
>
> I want you to do a great thing for me. If any of the local paper people ask for information, give them the official Gazette account and nothing more. Only a little while ago an officer got the M.C. Several people got him boomed in the local paper. A copy was sent out here. That officer's name has since been a by word for swank in the battalion.
>
> When a padre is boomed it is worse still as we are supposed to be so humble. I mention all this because the Folkestone paper, and even the Parish magazine, has boomed me so much that – well – if it gets known in the brigade it will do me and my work much harm.[53]

But his dislike of any publicity did not dampen the warmth with which he was congratulated. One such letter from the Deputy Chaplain-General

(Major-General) reflects what many thought of David in light of his bravery, despite his fear of being 'boomed'. Bishop Llewellyn Gwynne wrote to David on 5 December 1916, 'I am sure you deserve the coveted distinction. You have set a splendid example and I am proud of you.'[54]

★★★

After all the fanfare died away, David never again mentioned the award of his Military Cross, nor does he ever again mention his friend Noel Chavasse. In September 1917, while David was just a few miles away at the HQ of the 19th Division, Noel Chavasse's name once again appeared in *The London Gazette* for actions that would make him the most famous hero of the entire war:

> For most conspicuous bravery and devotion to duty when in action. Though severely wounded early in the action whilst carrying a wounded soldier to the Dressing Station, Capt. Chavasse refused to leave his post, and for two days not only continued to perform his duties, but in addition went out repeatedly under heavy fire to search for and attend to the wounded who were lying out. During these searches, although practically without food during this period, worn with fatigue and faint with his wound, he assisted to carry in a number of badly wounded men, over heavy and difficult ground. By his extraordinary energy and inspiring example, he was instrumental in rescuing many wounded who would have otherwise undoubtedly succumbed under the bad weather conditions. This devoted and gallant officer subsequently died of his wounds.[55]

Captain Noel Godfrey Chavasse, VC, MC, was awarded posthumously a Bar to his Victoria Cross. He was the only man to win two Victoria Crosses in the First World War and still is only one of just three men to have ever been honoured this way.[56] He died peacefully at one o'clock in the afternoon on 4 August 1917, at the 32nd Casualty Clearing Station at Brandhoek[57] and is buried at the Brandhoek New Military Cemetery.[58] Just before he died, someone asked him why he had kept on working even though he was so badly injured. He replied, 'Duty called and duty must be obeyed.'[59]

CHAPTER 6

The Winter of Death

'Sometimes even to live is an act of courage.'

LUCIUS SENECA

Sunday, 29 April 1917, Headquarters, 19th (Western) Division, Westoutre, Belgium

David had only been with the 19th Division for less than two weeks but already he felt like he was 'becoming a clerk'.[1] He hated being tied to a desk with a seemingly endless stream of paperwork to attend to. Despite his promotion, he was not happy that he had moved to another division. The distance he had travelled was short. Westoutre was just a few miles south of where he had been billeted in Busseboom, and he was close enough that he frequently saw officers and men of the 47th Division, who made a point of calling him 'Major Railton'.[2] This playful teasing showed their deep admiration for David, but it did nothing to lessen his despair at having to leave them.

He described the news of his promotion and move to the 19th Division as finding a 'bomb on my table',[3] vowing to try to get the appointment overturned. However, he knew it would be impossible to get the decision reversed: 'I know it will be difficult as an order is an order in the Army. Of course I feel it would be a big mistake for me to leave here just now. I do not know these men and officers.'[4] Despite an appeal to the Senior Chaplain of the 47th Division, David was appointed Senior Chaplain to the 19th (Western) Division on 16 April 1917, and promoted to the rank of Chaplain to the Forces Class 3 (Major).

After what David had endured during the bleak winter months of 1916–17, being in the relative comfort of a divisional HQ must have felt good even though he would have never admitted it. And although he clearly felt guilty being away from his men, his 33-year-old body would have been grateful for the break. From letters written to his wife, we get a clear impression of what the winter of 1916–17 was like. They tell of the coldest winter of the war and in one of the worst places: the trenches of the Ypres Salient.

★★★

After the excitement (and unwanted attention) of being awarded the Military Cross, David was happy to get back into the routine of carrying out his duties with the 19th Londons and with the 141st Brigade. At 8:00 A.M. on 19 October 1916, the new commander of the 47th Division, Major-General G. F. Gorringe, took command of the Bluff and Hill 60 sectors of the line to the south-east of Ypres.[5]

Ypres sits at the bottom of an eight-mile arc of ridgeline that surrounds it like a massive geographical amphitheatre. The height of the ridge is no more than 150 feet tall, but because of the flat terrain to the east, it allows an unobstructed view of Ypres and the surrounding countryside. Because of the topography, this part of the Ypres Salient was of vital importance to the overall strategic position of the British defences. The Germans viewed it the same way and that was the reason they had expended a great deal of men and resources trying to take it the previous June. That winter, even though the weather would produce conditions where men struggled to just survive in the trenches, the strategic importance of their piece of the line meant there would be no let-up in hostilities for the men of the 47th Division.

Travelling to the front line from Devonshire Camp, David would go by road either on horseback, horse-drawn carriage, or in a motorised truck if one happened to be heading that way. As he travelled east through the flat farmlands south of Ypres, he would have been able to see clearly the damaged church spires and buildings of Ypres across the open fields. As he continued to the east, houses and villages were much more picturesque, with 'what had been beautiful gardens and well-wooded approaches'.[6] Like most of the Belgian countryside behind the front lines, the buildings showed signs of damage from artillery fire, although many were still habitable.

As he came closer to the front line, the ground rose up gently to a ridgeline. The importance of this ground and the difficulty in defending it was reflected in the narrowness of the sector occupied by the entire division. At just 2,300 yards wide, starting from the Ypres–Comines Canal on the right (Bluff sector) to the Zwartelen Spur, north of the Ypres–Comines railway, on the left (Hill 60 sector), it was going to take a substantial force to defend it. Two of the three 47th Division brigades would be permanently in the line, with four battalions for the front and support lines in the Bluff, Ravine, Verbrandenmolen and Hill 60 sub-sectors; two battalions in local reserve at the Railways Dugouts and Woodcote House; and two further back at Swan Chateau and Halifax Camp. The third brigade would be out of the line spending its time in one of their camps west of Ypres. So, from October 1916 throughout the brutal winter into early 1917, men of the front-line battalions would spend two-thirds of their time rotating through the trenches.[7]

After the 47th Division took over responsibility, the 141st Brigade were the first brigade in reserve out of the line. The 19th Londons carried out company and battalion training,[8] with new officers and men being brought up to speed before the 141st Brigade went into the Bluff Section of the line. They took over from the 6th Londons on 30 October 1916.[9] The same day, just to 'remind the enemy there was still a war on', an organised bombardment of the enemy's front and support lines opposite the Bluff occurred, 'with considerable damage being done'.[10] Three companies were in the trenches, with a fourth carrying out 'working and carrying parties' at night while in reserve.[11]

On 15 November, David wrote to his wife from the Bluff sector. In the letter, he describes the daily tragedies that befell the battalion: 'Yesterday morning I chatted in the front line with one of the jolliest young officers we have. At night he went out and was hit. I hear he has since died. How jovial he was and oh! It is all too miserable.'[12] The officer was 2nd Lieutenant W. B. Bovey, son of Alfred and Jennie Bovey of 165 St John's Hill, Battersea, London. He was buried at the Lijssenthoek Military Cemetery.[13]

In the same letter, David describes a problem faced by members of the clergy in the trenches. They struggled with how to connect with their men, while at the same time remembering that they are men of God when the men act or say something that is not appropriate: 'Our clerical ways have upset so many of these men … it does not matter what they say, but it does matter whether they withdraw and get politely aloof, and never heed a word you say or come for advice.'[14] Later in the letter, David shows that despite trying to keep up his cheery manner around the men, the war was really starting to wear him down: 'I am in a mood at present wherein I am tired of the war. Tired of seeing wounds and death and mud and filth… Oh, what a grouse! And probably in ten minutes I shall be laughing with the others.'[15]

On 17 November, whilst resting at the RAP, David's mood seems to have improved. He was pleased hearing the news that the authorities were going to build 'an oratory for soldiers at the rest camp in Folkestone'.[16] Through his words, David shows a deep understanding of soldiers and illustrates how careless use of the English language by some members of the clergy, who were out of touch with the men, could trigger preconceived notions of class that dissuaded soldiers from embracing the church: 'Only don't let them call it an Oratory, if they value the soul of the soldier… Call it Rest Room, or Quiet Room, or even, Soldier's Chapel, or almost any plain English phrase.'[17]

The Rest Camp at Folkestone was set up to help soldiers during their wait going to and from the Western Front. Some stayed as little as two hours, some as long as two days. Between 1917 and 1918, as many as 8,000 soldiers passed through the Rest Camp each day.

The battalion remained in the Bluff sector of the line until it was relieved on 18 November, when they returned to being the 'out of line brigade' back at Devonshire Camp.[18] For the next 10 days they recouped in the relative comfort of the hutted camp, carrying out training at both the company and battalion level. It was during this time that David was awarded his Military Cross.

David did enjoy church services with the battalion, where every man was on parade. Reading his letters, however, we get the distinct impression that he was happiest conducting services when soldiers were not 'ordered to attend' but came voluntarily and partook in Holy Communion because they wanted to. He conducted one such small service on 28 November, just before the battalion was heading back to the front:

> How inspiring! A little hut, kit all-round the walls. A drum belonging to one of the drummers in one corner. A little table and on it the Union Jack and 'fair white linen cloth'. Two candles at each side on the table. Another candle on a box at the left-hand side and another one on a beam behind. A Sergeant and four men formed the congregation … I read the Gospel – the Sergeant quite naturally took the candle off the box and held it near me. All so natural and reverent; and so on to the Consecration and to the end… After the Blessing there was a pause and a hearty handshake all round. The Sergeant asked me to find out what had happened to a wounded pal of his. I promised to do so, and did my best to comfort him.[19]

It was not long until the 19th Londons were sent forward again, this time to the dreaded Hill 60 sector. From 28 November to 2 December, the battalion was in support with companies spread out behind the front line around the Railway Dugouts, Swan Chateau, and Battersea Farm.[20] David moved forward with the battalion, writing to his wife on 2 December from the Railway Dugouts: 'All goes well. I am just off to give some of the men a turn of the gramophone – they love it. Alas! One of our men (17th) a man of 19-years' service was killed accidently last night in one of the tunnel billets.'[21]

Hill 60 was always active, as it was the highest and most prominent feature on the Ypres Salient. It was first occupied by the Germans in November 1914 and 'gave observers an excellent view of the ground around Zillebeke and Ypres'.[22] It is not really a hill at all – rather a large mound of dirt, 200 feet high, created many years earlier from the spoilage of digging out the cut for the Ypres–Comines railway. Nonetheless, both sides coveted Hill 60. It was fought over, captured, and re-captured in 1915 before eventually coming into British hands on the first day of the Battle of Messines Ridge in 1917. Like High Wood's reputation on the Somme, Hill 60 had the reputation of the place to be avoided on the Ypres Salient. The whole area was heavily shelled and mined; the smell of exposed, decaying corpses and lingering gas from earlier attacks hung heavy in the air. All the while, soldiers had to carefully move about the trenches with their heads stooped low due to fear of falling victim to snipers looking down from their relatively lofty perch.

While he was in the support trenches of the 20th Londons on 2 December, David wrote to his wife about the loss of another soldier to a German sniper on Hill 60. He describes the despair felt for him by his comrades: 'The most popular man in the 20th was sniped today. This caused a great sorrow... He was always willing and merry. As he went along the trench today, officers and men greeted him... He was due for leave shortly ... God help his people.'[23]

The 19th and 20th Londons rotated through the Hill 60 Sector trenches twice before finally being relieved on 20 December when they headed back to the brigade reserve area and David rejoined the 19th Londons at Devonshire Camp.[24] But the final days on the salient before they could head back to Devonshire Camp and start to celebrate Christmas would be far from quiet. On 18 December, the 1st Australian Mining Company were expected to detonate a camouflet charge under a German tunnel. Most front-line troops were expecting it. Earlier that afternoon, David wrote, 'Certain things are expected tonight. This battalion (20th) have to "stand to" at 1.30am.'[25]

For some time, mining companies all along the Messines Ridge had been tunnelling under German lines, placing huge amounts of explosives under their positions. So the risk was obvious, and all troops around Hill 60 were warned as such. The charge exploded, destroying the German tunnel without detonating 'the large mine'[26] in place under German positions. Two days prior, German artillery heavily bombarded the whole divisional front line. A direct hit on a 19th Londons dugout killed an officer and three men.[27]

On 21 December, just a day after leaving the front line, the Commander-in-Chief, General Sir Douglas Haig, inspected the 19th Londons and other troops of the 141st Brigade. The previous night, David wrote of some speculation surrounding his visit: 'I suppose this means we are to advance or to be withdrawn for a bit ... for about two months, we have heard numerous rumours. We were to go to Ireland, India, Egypt – all at once or in turn!'[28]

Waking to horrible weather the next day, the men probably feared the same ordeal that David and the Northumberland Fusiliers had experienced a year earlier when being inspected by Generals Joffre and Haig. But this time, due to the weather, the inspection was conducted inside their camp with the men staying in their huts. That evening David wrote to his wife describing Haig as a 'sympathetic soldier' for not subjecting the men to the rigours of a pointless inspection in the rain, sleet and cold after a gruelling stint on the front line: 'He sent a message ... he would see the men in their camps... It was very splendid of him ... Haig is getting on in years, he could not stand tramping around so well. Well, he did ... he is a characteristic English soldier and gentleman.'[29]

The official history of the division agrees that it was a rather low-key visit, saying that General Haig spent time 'chatting informally with many officers and men, and expressing himself as much gratified with the appearance and steadiness of the units under unfavourable conditions'.[30]

Throughout the war and the years that followed, despite all that he had been through, David always spoke highly of Sir Douglas Haig. Even as public opinion started to form a harsher opinion of the Commander-in-Chief, David didn't have a bad word to say about him. He seemed to understand the burden leaders like Sir Douglas Haig had to carry, admiring the top generals the same way he admired average private soldiers in an infantry battalion: 'How nice all "top-men" and "bottom-men" are! The "in-betweens" vary so.'[31]

Despite the hardships they faced, the losses they suffered, and the terrible weather they endured, the infantry battalions of 141st Brigade were lucky, getting out of the line just in time for Christmas. Although David would say that he never had it as rough as the men, he had been there with them and suffered through it too. He limped because of the chilblains in his feet, and he had felt down at times, but his Christmas spirit helped him through, as he described in a letter: 'How beautifully Dickens speaks of Christmas. I have just re-read *A Christmas Carol*. "I will honour Christmas in my heart and try to keep it all year ... as Tiny Tim observes, God Bless us everyone." Glory to God in the highest.'[32]

The first Christmas of the war, December 1914, was marked by unofficial truces being observed at many locations along the line. Stories of the 'Christmas Truce' were well known and would become folklore, going down as possibly 'one of the most remarkable episodes in the history of warfare',[33] with as many as 100,000 soldiers from both sides involved.[34] Most positions just saw a temporary cessation of hostilities for a day or two, with both sides observing a policy of 'live and let live'. However, in many areas, German and British soldiers agreed to a truce by shouting across no-man's land, 'We are not going to fire tomorrow. We will have a holiday and a game of football.'[35]

The same Scots Guardsman said several of his comrades' bodies were recovered during the truce. 'The Germans helped us bury them on Christmas Day.'[36]

After news of the truce and fraternisation reached the ears of the Army's commanders, strict orders were put in place for future Christmases of the war. Both British and German commanders were encouraged to harass the enemy throughout Christmas to prevent a repeat of 1914. The 47th Division sent out 'a series of patrols along the X Corps front',[37] and the Germans responded on Christmas Day by shelling the front lines, 'causing considerable alarms, damage and casualties'.[38]

For David and the 141st Brigade, thoughts were not of a Christmas truce fraternising with the Germans. Too much blood had been spilt, and too many good men would not be returning to families for them to consider sharing the celebration of the birth of Christ with the enemy. They were all just thankful to have 'the good fortune to be in divisional reserve',[39] far away from the hell of Hill 60 or any other sector of the Ypres Salient. But they did seem determined to make 'the most of their opportunity of celebrating Christmas'.[40]

Many platoon and company parties took advantage of their being in reserve by trying to get their hands on a turkey or two. David also describes several examples of charity from men who had been through the rigours of the front line only to think of – and help – those less fortunate, rather than themselves: 'I met an officer yesterday... He was in a hurry. He said, "We are giving 200 Belgian children a Christmas tree." How delightful! Some how these officers have collected for 200 children, and the love of our Lord.'[41]

One evening just before Christmas, the RSM and sergeants of the battalion asked David to read an extract from Dickens' *A Christmas Carol*. He read the first chapter, summed up the remainder of the book, and read the last chapter in its entirety. As he was coming to the end he noticed a hat being passed around: 'I was rather embarrassed, as I wondered what it meant. Presently the RSM stood up… He handed the contents of the hat (it was 14 francs, 40 centimes) to me. He begged me to accept it for any fund that I would like.'[42] The RSM insisted that if David could not use the money for a local cause he wanted him to send it to Mrs Railton to be used for a fund in England. Fourteen francs (12 shillings) is equal to roughly £35–40 today – a tidy sum collected for charity from working class men.

Even though they were in the relative comfort of the reserve brigade area, 10–12 miles behind the front lines, everyone knew they could be in danger at any time, and on Christmas Eve, David was reminded of this: 'The guns have just begun afresh. We were so lucky today. A dud Archie fell plump near the hut where we had a service 5 yards away – the place packed! Praise God for that escape!'[43] An 'Archie' is the shell from a 13-pound anti-aircraft gun usually mounted on the back of a truck.

On Christmas morning David arose at 5:00 A.M. to help with a tradition dating back to the 1890s when officers serve 'Gunfire' to soldiers in their beds at reveille when a regiment is serving overseas. After helping the men start the day with hot black tea and a shot of rum, he spent the day conducting services and visiting men in their huts with the CO, and finished by helping 'a drunken sergeant quietly to his bed'.[44]

Christmas really lifted David's spirits; the contents of his letters to his wife describe the joy he felt, despite suffering from the cold. The life of Jesus Christ was at the centre of David's belief, and he held the celebration of Christ's birth as the most sacred time in his life every year. Whether he was in the trenches or back home in England, David held the true spirit of Christmas close to his heart. In 1921, on the 'Twelfth Night' preaching at St John's in Margate, David gave a practical demonstration to his congregation of the true 'meaning of Gold, Frankincense and Myrrh'. After the 6:30 P.M. service, an offering was taken – 10 pounds, 19 shillings and five pence. In his notes, David explained:

> Gold (2 sovereigns and 2 half sovereigns) was offered together with frankincense and myrrh at the altar. The gold was given to a poor man – in church before the congregation for the benefit of the child that was born in his household this Christmastide. The myrrh was received and taken to the hospital by a nurse in uniform. The frankincense, having been lit, remained burning at the altar.[45]

It must have been just the break from the trenches that he needed. Unfortunately, the realities of war and the hardships of winter would return all too soon. On 28 December, the 19th Londons left Devonshire Camp and headed back to the Ypres Salient. This time they 'relieved the 8th Battalion in support to the Canal Sub Sector'.[46] The companies were positioned some distance apart along the entire length of the sector at 'Woodcote Farm, Strong point 7, and the Bluff Tunnels'.[47] Although these positions were in reserve behind the front line, David had a lot of distance to cover if he wanted to visit the men.

That same day he left the lines at 6:00 A.M. and walked for many miles, returning later in the pouring rain. In the evening he wrote to his wife explaining that he now loathed the winter – the seasons were no longer equally all 'God's joy' to him: 'The phrase, "the winter of life" used to sound such a pessimistic sentence … at last I am now able to understand it. At least it teaches me to sympathise with the aged … it just means the horrid, vile, hell portion of life.'[48]

On 30 December, David and his men moved forward into the line once again. That night he wrote, describing the appalling conditions, explaining how his spirits were at an all-time low and praising the resilience of the men: 'Now I received at this time a special visit from the "Devil"… For a long while I could not shake it off… I was guilty of Envy… At last I dismissed the Devil … "God help the poor lads," I thought. This is the only way.'[49]

David finished the year with his men in 'wet trenches', described in the battalion's war diaries as being in 'extremely bad condition'.[50] For him 1916 was a year he would never forget. Although he would remain on the Western Front for almost two more years, it is obvious that 1916 is the year he would find most troubling. It had started with him leaving for France and it had ended with him in Belgium. One year must have felt like a lifetime – Armentières, Vimy Ridge, the Somme, and the Ypres Salient. And, unfortunately for David and his men, the war was far from over.

The tone of his letters to his wife in the early days of 1917 indicates he was suffering. Despite it all, he pushed on, seemingly regaining strength each time he visited the men. It's obvious that they benefitted from their contact with him, but it went both ways. Through all the darkness and gloom of a cold and wet January in 1917 shone a bright and unwavering determination to help support his men, no matter what difficulties they found themselves in. When adversity was thrown his way and his faith was tested, he fought temptation to succumb – and won. His faith grounded him, and time and time again he turned to it for strength.

> If Our Lord had not suffered on this earth on the Cross, I would blaspheme God all day if I believed in God at all. I only believe in God in this war because I believe in Jesus Christ the Crucified.[51]

Between 8 and 11 January, the battalion was in reserve at Swan Chateau and described in the war diary as 'working and carrying parties supplied at night'.[52] On 8 January, David had to 'track through mud and slime'[53] to bury a young lad from the 18th Londons. His name was Private F. Topham, and he was buried just behind the front line at Woods Cemetery.[54] David writes: 'He had been with us since the beginning. Five of his brothers have been killed. Fancy six brothers killed in one family! Who would not loathe Prussianism. God help our men.'[55]

We cannot confirm for certain that Private F. Topham was one of six brothers killed during the war; however, his mother, Mrs Mary Anne Topham of 88 Bedford Road, Walthamstow, London,[56] is linked to the loss of four more Topham boys – three of whom could have been her sons and a fourth that was probably a nephew. Whether it was four or six matters not. The effect of losing so many members of one family would have been devastating beyond belief. David felt the suffering and wrote to his wife of the pain that the Topham family must have been enduring: 'Pray for all relatives. The faithful departed are in Peace ... no need to pray for them, even if it were reverent. But pray for the relatives, they are in ceaseless agony. Six sons gone! God give us, not just victory, but annihilating victory.'[57]

The next day, David wrote to his wife with news that he had received another accolade. But in his modest and unassuming way, he didn't understand why he'd been chosen: 'I was "Mentioned in Dispatches", I cannot think why. If the army has acted with such grace towards chaplains, may our children love dear old England and all our fearless soldiers and be forever ready to do all they can for them.'[58]

The word 'Emblems' is listed on David's Medal Roll Index card[59] under his medals, meaning he is entitled to wear the Oak Leaf upon his Victory Medal. There is no known record of why he was awarded this honour, and, like the award of his Military Cross, he would never mention it again. He was "Mentioned in Dispatches" for a second time in 1918 whilst Senior Chaplain of the 19th Division. His divisional commander wrote of him, 'For his excellent work on all occasions since joining the 19th Division. Has always displayed the greatest possible energy and his devotion to duty has produced the best results.'[60]

Despite David's reluctance for any acclaim, it is obvious from the Military Cross and twice being 'Mentioned in Dispatches' that his work was appreciated by those in authority. But more importantly for David was that the men he was dedicated to benefitted from his work. In 1965, Mr W. J. Bradley wrote to David Railton's son, Andrew Scott Railton, describing memories of his father during the winter of 1916–17. He describes the conditions faced by the men and how a service conducted by David Railton in early 1917 had a huge effect upon him and the men:

> After turns in the line we were brought back into reserve at this dreary place and housed in extremely leaky huts. Our days there were spent on roadwork, trying to drain off the water into already waterlogged fields covered in sleet and snow. We were never dry and seldom warm, and many of the men suffered from trench foot and dysentery. Most of them were very depressed. He [David Railton] used to come along to the huts each evening and natter to us on all subjects, take a hand at cards and finally prayers. His easy manner made him immensely popular with us all.
>
> One Sunday night there was to be a service at the Church Army Hut in the village and as he was to preach everyone turned out early to get in to hear him. We had to wait outside in the sleet and snow for half an hour before the doors opened and within minutes the place was packed to overflowing. He was late arriving but it made no difference, everyone sat waiting, reading or writing letters. Half an hour went by before he arrived straight from the line plastered in mud from head to foot. He apologised for keeping us waiting, washed some of the mud from his face and hands, put on his surplice and the service started.
>
> When it came to the sermon he said that he would not take a passage from the bible as his text, and he put it down. He started off with, 'When I came in to this hut tonight, I was fed up, bloody fed up, and I will take those words for the

subject of my talk.' He then spoke of our lives in the line, our leaking huts and the exhausting work on the roads, all in appalling conditions, and then switched to the life of Christ and how He at times he must have been 'fed up' too. You could have heard a pin drop as he carried the men with him. At the end of the address he said that owing to the late start, if anyone wished to leave there was just time for them to get to their billets before roll call, but those that wished to remain to the end of the service, he would be responsible to our COs. The entire congregation stayed to the end. The final hymn was 'Onward Christian Soldiers' and I have never heard it sung with so much enthusiasm in my life. When I left the hut my tin hat felt like a Halo and that service boosted the morale of everyone there, and for me it lasted right through the years on active service and I think has influenced my whole life.[61]

Over the next two months, David and his men rotated through the front lines. They occupied both Hill 60 and Canal sub-sectors, with spells behind the front in reserve at the Railway Dugouts, Halifax Camp and Swan Chateau. When the brigade was relieved, about every four weeks, they would return to Devonshire Camp.[62] The importance to both sides of the area of Hill 60 and the line south to the Ypres–Commines Canal meant that there was never an easy spell in the front line or even behind the line in reserve. All through the early months of 1917, the sectors were active with enemy artillery fire, snipers picking men off individually or raids by both sides. All the while the harsh winter continued unabated.

During this time, David's letters home continued to describe the cold and wet conditions. He also described the tragic events that unfolded daily, including examples of his being there to help the fighting men, as well as how he drew strength from them:

A most unusual tragedy happened yesterday. I went up to 'Strongpoint 8' to take the Rest Service for three machine gunners … but here is the tragedy … the shell came from one of our guns… It entered the back of the dugout … short of the Boche line.[63]

As I write in the dugout, drops of water fall from the roof. Snow has fallen and there are no warm dry places in the line. I do so love these men. Yet more and more the strain increases.[64]

Oh, this bitter, bitter winter! I never knew the terrors of winter before. Even when I used to appeal for the poor I did not know how fearful it was for them. I thought I did. I did not. Never properly dry, never really warm.[65]

An officer said to me at breakfast, 'I don't believe the cold affects you, Padre. I believe you're an Eskimo.' Thank God I can still keep up an appearance – but I am so freezing that my whole frame shakes as I write.[66]

One of the things that seemed to get David through this terrible time was the spirit and humour that was constantly on display. A soldier's ability to laugh and joke in the face of adversity is well known, and it was in abundance in the trenches:

> The humour of the English soldier supplies fresh life to us all. How I laughed yesterday! On a frozen pond were three soldiers. There is nothing strange in that, but I thought I had seen every possible winter-sport in Switzerland... Not so! These three were playing football on ice! One had a sandbag over each boot. Up and down went the ball. Bump went the men, but ice or no ice – the national British winter game shall be continued.[67]
>
> During the 11am church parade, the Commanding Officer received a message. He came to me and said he was sorry but he was being called away. When I returned to camp – what a sight one little corner of it was. A fire had broken out in one of the huts... This was why the Commanding Officer had left Church Parade. Later, he smiled when I met him. 'Padre,' he said, 'Do you realise that when I left the church we were singing, Lead, Kindly Light?'[68]

As the weeks went by, David and his men wished for any signs of spring. But just as they thought, 'spring must be coming',[69] they were plunged right back into winter. On 23 March, David wrote to his wife of waking up to find even more snow had fallen in the night: 'I suppose the filthy weather is more upsetting than anything ... after this fearful winter ... it is terrible for everybody, but for the dear lads in the trenches it is an untold Hell. Shall we ever get the summer?'[70]

As spring eventually took hold, everyone started to become aware that in addition to the warmer weather, there definitely was something else 'in the air',[71] and they would soon be 'called upon to carry out some form of offensive operations'.[72] But just as plans were being drawn up, rumours started to circulate that something else was happening much further to the south.

All along the front line from Arras to as far south as St Quentin, it was rumoured that the Germans were up to something. British troops near Arras reported seeing German lines opposite them being shelled by German artillery. Accounts by patrols started to filter through, describing enemy trenches that had been fiercely defended just a few days before as now abandoned. Over a period of several weeks it became evident that the Germans were withdrawing.

To the British and French it became known as the 'German retreat to the Hindenburg Line'.[73] In his dispatches, Haig describes the events as 'The Enemy's Retreat – The Great Withdrawal'.[74] But it was no retreat. It was a well-organised, high-risk tactical withdrawal called Operation *Alberich* that would shorten the German Line by 25 miles and drastically reduce the manpower needed to defend it. The shorter length of line freed up 13 divisions of infantry and 50 batteries of heavy artillery. For the Germans, there really was no alternative. As the Somme offensive of 1916 came to an end, two massive bulges in the line at Noyon and on the Somme created untenable defensive positions. Their reserves were at an all-time low, and they knew an early spring Allied offensive was inevitable.

For the British and French it meant they would have to move forward and establish new lines in ground that had been devastated by the withdrawing defenders. As German troops retreated they blocked roads with felled trees, cut down orchards, and set fire to villages and towns – they were determined to leave nothing for the British and French. The withdrawal, masterminded by Ludendorff, may have been yet another public relations disaster because of their 'scorched earth policy', but it was considered by many as a shrewd move.[75] Because the Allies failed to spot the construction of a new line, the *Siegfried Stellung* (Hindenburg Line) – built by German reserves and civilians, and Russian prisoners of war – they missed a perfect opportunity to attack when the Germans were most vulnerable. A lack of initiative and the devastation of the ground meant the Allies failed to exploit the German withdrawal. The Germans now were set in much stronger positions that required less manpower to defend.

The withdrawal to the Hindenburg Line did not directly affect David and his men – the trenches and defensive positions opposing them did not move. But some of the 13 newly deployed divisions were moved north, placing more pressure on already hard-pressed sectors of the Ypres Salient. More importantly, Allied plans decided upon at Joffre's chateau in Chantilly the previous November were now thrown into chaos. Joffre's fall and replacement by Robert Nivelle, as well as Lloyd George's ascension to Prime Minister, negated most of what was discussed at the Chantilly meeting. Following disagreements between Haig, Nivelle, and

Lloyd George, a compromise regarding Nivelle's proposed offensive and diversionary attacks was reached in February 1917. The delay meant that there would be no major attack before 1 April. German intelligence learned of the Allies' plans; Ludendorff was told just two weeks after Haig, Nivelle, and Lloyd George had met.[76] The risks involved with the withdrawal were now drastically reduced; Ludendorff knew that his troops could retire to his new defensive line unmolested.

Operation *Alberich* had reduced Nivelle's area of attack by a third. Undaunted, even on the advice of Haig who had always preferred a British attack in Flanders, Nivelle was determined to push ahead. His 50 divisions and 5,000 guns would attack at the River Aisne on 16 April 1917, the result of which would have disastrous and far-reaching consequences for the French Army. Seven days earlier a British diversionary attack at Arras was the prelude to his much-vaunted offensive. Like most attacks before it, Arras would end as an attritional slog. But it did produce several notable victories. Over the same ground David and the 47th Division had fought back German attacks 11 months earlier, four Canadian divisions produced a remarkable victory and took most of Vimy Ridge in just a few hours.

While all this was taking place to their south, soldiers of the 47th Division continued their seemingly endless routine of rotating through the front-line trenches on the Ypres Salient. They continued to put up with terrible weather, being constantly sniped, bombed, shelled, and on the lookout for enemy trench raids and attacks. On 8 April (Easter Sunday) 1917, David and the battalion were in the 'Hill 60, Right sub-sector'[77] of the front line. They had been there since 27 March and were due to be relieved that night. It had been an extremely busy period. The war diary of the battalion describes what took place:

> German bombardment on our frontage – rather severe causing some damage to our trenches and also a few casualties – all our men working hard during the night to repair damaged places – enemy snipers very active on our front during most of the night – Casualties 1 OR killed – 9 OR wounded. Weather very cold – frost at night – misty early in the morning.[78]

That night, before they headed back to Devonshire Camp, David wrote to his wife, describing an incident that showed while morale and belief in the cause was as high as ever, not every man was comfortable to be celebrating Easter:

> Yesterday I heard some of the men talking loudly together next door… One man said, 'It was Good Friday yesterday. On Good Friday Jesus Christ died to save us. Tonight the 18th Battalion are going over to see how many Boche they can kill.' I am going to look him up. I recognised the voice. It was said bitterly. I fear he thinks the last part disproves the first. God help him and all of us.[79]

Back at Devonshire Camp, after a long spell at the front line, the men needed a rest and to try to stay warm. The entries in the war diary for Easter Monday and the next three days read:

> 9th – Battalion occupied in bathing and cleaning up – very cold with frequent snow storms during day. 10th – Companies at disposal of OC's for refitting and all interior economy – very cold with strong wind and slight snow. 11th – Very cold with strong wind – heavy snow during afternoon – battalion marched to Steenvorde for a short period in the Corps Reserve.[80]

On Easter Monday, while the battalion were recovering in Devonshire Camp from their time at Hill 60, David travelled the short distance to Talbot House in Poperinghe where he attended an Easter service. It is not known whether he helped or officiated, but he did keep the Order of Service.[81]

★★★

Seven miles west of Ypres, the small Belgian town of Poperinghe – known by British soldiers as 'Pop'[82] – was at the centre of a massive troop concentration defending the Ypres Salient. Although it was still within range of the larger German guns, it provided a safe haven most of the time and became a centre for troops in reserve to enjoy a little rest and relaxation. For many centuries since the earliest days of warfare, where there were soldiers in large numbers, there would be alcohol and seedy places where the world's oldest profession was offered to lonely men many miles from home. For those trying avoid such places, there was the St Joseph's Church Army soldiers' club, which was at 54 Rue de Musse, and the Church Army Recreation Hut by 70 Rue de Ypres. Both were open free to those in khaki between the hours of

10:30 A.M. and 8:00 P.M. daily.[83] But for most troops out of the line, apart from cafés, estaminets and brothels, there really was no place in 'Pop' for soldiers to go.

The British Army mirrored its class-conscious society at home, so there were several officers' clubs which soldiers were prohibited from entering. 'Skindles – a nickname given to a café after the original Skindles in Maidenhead'[84] – was located on the same street as Talbot House. In the main square was another café, 'known as A La Poupee, open only to officers'.[85] David did frequent officers' clubs from time to time where he wrote to his wife and enjoyed a hot meal: 'I addressed my last letter from an Officers' Club at the base… Curiously, padres run both clubs. At both you find splendid rooms, meals etc. It is crowded sometimes, even the Prince of Wales comes here.'[86]

Whether David was talking about Talbot House is not known. It was run by a padre but was by no means exclusive to officers. Upon entering there was never any doubt that it was a club that accepted anyone. Above the door hung a sign that read, 'Every-man's Club', and inside above the entrance of another room was a sign that proclaimed, 'Abandon all rank, ye who enter here', a re-working of Dante's famous idiom.[87]

The Revd Phillip 'Tubby' Clayton was the driving force behind the idea of a club for all ranks. The rented family home (whose occupants had fled the war) came to be called Talbot House. It was named after Lt Gilbert Talbot, who died at Hooge in 1915, and was the brother of Clayton's fellow padre, Neville Talbot. Talbot House soon became known to soldiers as 'Toc H'. The letters TOC were the British Army signallers' code for 'T', and H was H.[88]

The name would stick and the success of Talbot House would grow into a movement. By the 1920s, this movement would expand to about 70 Talbot Houses in cities all around Britain. By the start of the Second World War, there were Talbot Houses throughout the world. Today, despite going through a financial crisis in 2008, Toc H continues to thrive. Many soldiers (author included) have enjoyed the comforts of a Toc H while serving abroad in the Army.

David and Tubby Clayton not only were acquaintances, but also would work together in the years to come on several occasions.

Reading correspondence between them gives a sense that this was more of a working relationship than the kind of friendship David had with many other members of the clergy. But there is no doubt that the two men respected each other. In a 1933 letter, Clayton said this of David after he had agreed to take up a new position: 'I have seldom had a finer letter, and bits of it stand out as a sheer truth about the church and the strange times ahead… I believe it is your kind of outlook that is needed. Meanwhile we must collaborate more closely.'[89] And they did collaborate more when David became a Toc H padre in Liverpool and also after he moved to Scotland.

***

For David and his men, the winter of 1916–17 was a terrible ordeal. Most First World War historians now agree that it was the worst winter of the war, and it took its toll on both sides. The combatants on the Western Front were not the only ones to endure the hardships of a brutal winter. In Germany, a failed harvest came just before the same brutal cold endured by David in Flanders and became known as the 'Turnip Winter'. Food was so scarce that all that many Germans had to eat was the turnip.[90]

In Britain, times were hard for the civilian population too. German submarines were sinking dozens of British merchant ships, which meant that both food and fuel were in short supply.[91] Back in Folkestone, it affected the Railton family: 'How relieved I was to hear that you got some more coal! If Folkestone people find it hard to get fuel – they should pull down some of the ugly things that disfigure the town … advertisement boards, and the wooden and iron pier!'[92]

On 14 April 1917, the day he received the 'bombshell' news of his promotion and move to the 19th Division, David was still with the battalion at Steenvoorde, 6 miles south-east of Poperinghe.[93] Although he was obviously down at the prospect of leaving the battalion he had been with through such trying times, something he heard that night must have raised his spirits, too: 'I overheard an officer telling one of the farm girls that I was their Cure. That I was a true Comrade to them – had won a medal and was *Toujours gai* [always cheerful].'[94]

The next day, David presided over his last 'church parade in a barn'[95] with the 19th Londons. It must have been an emotional time for him. There is no record of what he said, and he does not mention it in any of his letters. But in a 1965 letter to the Railton family, Mr W. G. Bradley describes a very similar church service in a barn. He also sums up perfectly the bond that existed between David Railton and his men, especially during the winter of 1916–17 on the Ypres Salient:

> It was our Company's turn to supply the duties and we were told to report to the Q.M. stores to draw picks, spades, and brooms and report to the padre who wished to use a half demolished barn for services. This we did and proceeded towards the place where his Union Flag was flying, the sign he used for whenever he was available. We were met by a great crowd of fellows coming down the road with the padre and about a dozen others with arms linked leading ... all willing volunteers from other companies. There were so many troops wanting to help, that the work was done in no time at all and the barn made ready for the next day. Every man who could do so took Communion that morning in relays... He was without doubt an outstanding man and did much to help and guide us in those difficult times. When he was transferred from us to another unit, his loss was felt by us all, but the memory of him and what he achieved amongst us, remained. The Revd David Railton was an inspired man.[96]

CHAPTER 7

Private Denis Blakemore

'I am of the opinion that it is necessary to make an example to prevent cowardice in the face of the enemy as far as possible.'

FIELD MARSHAL DOUGLAS HAIG

Friday, 31 August 1917, Headquarters, 19th (Western) Division, Saint-Jans-Cappel, France

The small room in the farmhouse building David used for his office had a leaky roof. Despite still being in one piece, the corrugated tin had seen better days. Expanding rusty holes around the nails banged into the rafters now let in the summer rain. His staff, which usually consisted of a corporal clerk and an orderly, had done their best, finding a few buckets and pails that caught the drips. But the room was filled with a metronomic dripping sound every time it rained.

The major offensive in Flanders had got underway on 31 July 1917. It would become known as the Third Battle of Ypres, the long-awaited breakout from the bulging line of trenches forming the Ypres Salient, which the British had stubbornly held since late 1914. Initially, according to author Everard Wyrall, 'the first of the 1917 Battles of Ypres, had been a distinct success for the 19th Division'.[1] But August successes would soon turn into a muddy stalemate at Passchendaele that autumn. David had heard from divisional staff officers and had seen with his own eyes during visits to the front line that forward progress had drastically slowed.

He looked up again at the roof as the incessant dripping continued, and he remembered looking down from the newly liberated ridgeline across the barren, flat battlefield north-west of Ypres. Like the many miles of the battlefields on the Somme he had seen in 1916, the flat plain from where he stood showed the results of three years of constant shelling – there was not a trace of vegetation. But unlike the Somme, the shelling in Flanders had destroyed the field drainage system, which for hundreds of years had kept the water at a manageable level so it could be used as arable farmland. As soon as the predicted annual rains began, the flooded fields turned into a swamp.

★★★

Before any offensive could take place at Ypres, a major strategic piece of ground – the Messines Ridge – had to be taken. Situated between Armentières and Ypres, two lines of German defences sat at the foot and on top of the ridge running between Messines and Wytschaete. These positions allowed the Germans to completely dominate the town of Ypres and the British positions of the Ypres Salient. Of course the Germans also realised the importance of the ridge, as one historian points out: 'For more than two years the enemy had devoted the greatest skill and energy to developing the natural advantages of his position.'[2] Farmhouses and buildings along the ridge were turned into strongpoints augmented with hundreds of purpose-built bunkers, constructed with reinforced pre-cast concrete blocks.[3] After the German withdrawal to the Hindenburg Line in the spring, the shortened distance of their new line meant that more troops could be sent north to bolster positions of strategic importance. The Germans had every intention to hold Messines Ridge's strategic advantage and not give it up without a fight.

Planning for the assault had started 18 months before. It didn't take a military genius to realise that if an attack was to be launched from the Ypres Salient, then the Messines Ridge had to be in British hands first. Knowing that an attack in Flanders was high on General Haig's list of priorities, in January 1916, 2nd Army Commander, General Herbert Plumer, tasked Royal Engineer mining units (British, Canadian and Australian) to dig under enemy positions. Over a million pounds of explosives were placed into 19 mineshafts which ended directly under German front-line trenches and strongpoints.[4] The scale of the preparations was enormous. 'Six mining companies, all with personnel drawn from mining and related industries'[5] were put on the task. Even a giant mechanical tunnelling machine, used during the construction of the London Underground, was transported over.

When David arrived at the 19th Division in late April 1917, he was already aware that something big was about to happen. The 47th Division had also been preparing for the impending action at Messines Ridge, which David described as 'the Great Events'.[6] He'd seen the on-going tunnelling operations for himself during his time at Hill 60.

The 19th Division's front of attack, according to Wyrall, 'was bounded on the south by the Vierstraat–Wytschaete road, and on the north by the Dipendaal Beek'.[7] The infantry battalions of the 56th and 58th brigades were instructed to stick to strict timings, taking marked lines on the map at a precise time. They were tasked to 'capture the first three objective lines, Red, Blue, and Green lines; the 57th Bde was then to pass through and capture the fourth objective, the Black Line'.[8]

All along the 10-mile front between St Yves and Mount Sorrel, troops sat and waited, hoping that those in command had learnt the lessons from previous battles. But they need not have worried; the extra time allowed to put in place General Plumer's brilliant plan meant the enemy would be totally overwhelmed. Peter Oldham describes the forces deployed and how Messines Ridge was to be taken. 'Nine infantry divisions, assisted by 72 of the latest model tanks, the Mark IV ... and a massed machine gun barrage, were allocated objectives to be taken in waves.'[9] The Second Army's Barrage Map,[10] complete with conversion table, told every platoon commander, down to the minute, exactly where the creeping curtain of artillery and machine-gun fire would be falling as they advanced. Timing was everything.

Despite their well-organised trench systems and concrete bunkers, the German defenders at Messines Ridge were about to experience an early version of 'Shock and Awe'. Shock and Awe is a military doctrine 'that uses overwhelming power to paralyze the enemy's perception of the battlefield and cripple its will to fight'. The doctrine was written by Harlan K. Ullman and James P. Wade in 1996, a product of the National Defense University of the United States, and gained popular usage during the 2003 invasion of Iraq.[11]

David and many other staff officers were about to see this awesome and frightening show of overwhelming firepower for themselves. They went to the top of the wooded Kemmel Hill (also now known as Mont Kemmel or the Kemmelberg). Despite having detailed knowledge of the preparations that had taken place, no one could have imagined what was going to happen. At 3:10 A.M. on the morning of 7 June 1917, stood on top of the concrete observation post at the top of Kemmel Hill, it must have felt like a scene from *Dante's Inferno*. Just a mile and a half away and in direct sight of the front line, those watching would have been aghast at what they saw. Wyrall recreates the scene:

> Immediately the ground trembled and shook as if a violent earthquake was in progress. There was an ear-splitting roar, which numbed the senses for the first few seconds, leaving the body incapable of movement and the brain inactive from the violent concussion. The sudden sheets of fire, which shot up into the air resembled flaming waterspouts. Clouds of smoke and dust hung over the enemy's trenches while the mangled bodies of Germans were flung about in all the ghastly contortions of a violent death.[12]

All along the front, artillery and machine-gun batteries opened up and the infantry rapidly advanced. Wyrall continues: 'The enemy left alive in the front-line and support trenches surrendered immediately; their power of resistance had gone, the awful holocaust which had passed over them had left them incapable of further resistance.'[13]

That evening, British troops were back in control of the Messines Ridge having suffered only very light casualties. For the British Army, the attack at Messines Ridge was a resounding success.

★★★

David looked at the pile of mail and files his clerk had just placed on the table. 'Thank you, corporal,' he said.

He immediately opened the first of several letters that were on top of the files. His clerk knew that his boss liked to read letters from his family before anything else. Then, underneath, he would put all mail personally addressed to him. The letters sat on top of the pile of other administrative work that required David's attention.

After reading the letter from his wife a second time, David folded it back in the envelope, then put it into his pack that was on the floor. Next he went back to the other letters sitting on top of the file mountain. The first one he opened looked like it had been posted in France, and he recognised the handwriting.

> Dear Mr Railton,
> Now that the course here is about over I thought I should like to write and tell you how very much I have appreciated it. Thank you so much for making it possible for me to come... I have very much enjoyed being here.
> I am now looking forward to returning to my work tomorrow. I do want you to know that I look upon it as a very great privilege to be with the battalion I am with and also to work under you. I only hope I shall not make as many mistakes in the future as in the past.
> With kindest regards, yours sincerely,
> John J. Wallace.[14]

★★★

David's 19th Division padres had been involved at Messines Ridge and the early battles of Ypres at Pilckem and Menin Road Ridge. David tried his best to direct, guide, and support all padres within his division, ensuring the men were ministered to by competent chaplains. Sometimes a battalion would have to go without having a padre of their own for a while, using a padre from their brigade for routine services and burials, and sometimes David would stand in to cover as well. Some clergymen who applied to be a Chaplain to the Forces (CF) were not up to it. Some were simply not robust enough. They were too much the 'country parson' or did not have a common touch and couldn't relate to the men. They all needed the ability to minister to men from different backgrounds, especially those from poor and working class families.

The Revd John James Wallace first applied to be a CF in November 1915.[15] According to David Blake of the Museum of Army Chaplaincy, 'Wallace failed his first interview in 1915. The Chaplain-General thought him unsuitable.'[16] Notes from his interview describe him as, 'Unkempt, cheery, boyish looking, like a thin boy'.[17] He then re-applied on 18 January

1917 and was accepted. The Chaplain-General's notes were just as ambiguous and uncomplimentary, saying, 'Small, cheery faced, hair not smooth'.[18] But this time, the British Army's establishment for chaplains had been increased and there was still a shortage of padres on the Western Front. Wallace might well have still been unsuitable, but the need for more chaplains in the field might have been the deciding factor the second time around.

On David's arrival with the 19th Division, Wallace was attached to the 8th Battalion, North Staffordshire Regiment (The Prince of Wales's).[19] For reasons unknown, but maybe best described in Wallace's own words – 'I only hope I shall not make as many mistakes in the future as in the past'[20] – he appears to have not been the padre of the 8th Bn N. Staffs in July 1917.

In February 1917, at the headquarters of Bishop Gwynne in the Place de Victor Hugo, St Omer, a retreat house for chaplains serving on the Western Front was opened.[21] Generally referred to as the 'Chaplain's Bombing School',[22] it became a place where chaplains of all ranks and denominations came for 'spiritual renewal of their faith'.[23] Normally sent there by Senior Chaplains or Commanding Officers, some padres arrived 'resentful, war-weary, and irritable but were quickly put at ease and returned to their tasks'.[24] After Wallace returned to the 19th Division, David put him back with his battalion. But while he was away and during the weeks after Messines Ridge, the 8th Bn N. Staffs appeared to have been without a padre.

★★★

David opened the second letter addressed to him marked 'private'. It was from Mr G. L. Blakemore.

> Rev'd and Dear Sir,
> I felt it my bounden duty to write again to you this evening, and inform you that it is only this morning that I received official word from the War Office, notifying me of the sad death of my son Denis.
> It is, as you will readily understand, a terrible shock to us, and the very last thing in the world which we expected to happen to him.
> There is one great consolation in it nevertheless which we shall always be grateful for, that through your sympathetic feelings, and holy administrations, he died, at all events, a good Christian soldier in the faith wherein he was always brought up.[25]

David finished the letter then sat back in his chair. He was silent and still for a few moments as he thought about the letter and the pain the Blakemore family must have been feeling after finding out the fate of their son. As he looked out of the window, watching the rain, he started to recall one of the darkest events of his life; one he knew he would never forget.

***

On the morning of 7 June 1917, at Messines Ridge, soldiers of the 8th Bn N. Staffs were in their positions ready to move at 'zero hour plus two hours and thirty minutes'.[26] They then advanced across no-man's land, passed through the carnage of the German front-line trenches, and moved through the troops of the 56th and 58th brigades who were now busy consolidating their positions on the Green, Red and Blue lines. The battalion was supposed to be in support but ended up leading on the right of the division's front in the attack on the Black line, 'capturing part of the objective'. And, like the rest of the advancing infantry battalions, they suffered 'very few casualties and little resistance was offered'.[27]

While the battalion was forming up, Private Denis Blakemore, a 28-year-old conscript from Bicton, Shrewsbury, was found hiding in a shell hole in the rear of the assembly trenches. His platoon sergeant brought him forward and placed him back with his section as they readied to advance; he was later reported missing by his section commander. After 18 days, Blakemore was arrested in Boulogne while trying to pass off as a member of the Army Service Corps. He was brought back to the 19th Division, where he remained under arrest while he awaited court-martial.

Conscripted into the Army under the Military Service Act of 1916, he was obviously not suited to active service. He came from a large family of four boys and four girls whose father was a retired elementary school headmaster.[28] He did everything he could to get away from the front despite knowing the likely outcome of his actions. He had already been court-martialled earlier that year, charged in November 1916, 'while on active service deserting His Majesty's Service'.[29] He was sentenced to death, but the sentence was commuted to 15 years' penal servitude, which was then suspended by General Haig.[30] So, when he ran away from his platoon before they advanced at Messines Ridge, had he the ability to think clearly and rationally, he would have known that when he was caught he would be charged with desertion and would most certainly face a firing squad.

Mr and Mrs Blakemore both wrote to David before they were fully aware of the truth of what happened to their son, conceding that they were worried about his state of mind: 'It has been one continual and daily fear of his mother for the past month, that something would happen to him out there, in one way or another.'[31] And they acknowledged his previous absence, writing, 'He certainly went away at the beginning through terrible fright in the battle lines, and afterwards was too frightened to return to his regiment, and gave himself up for fear of the consequences.'[32]

Since the early days of the war, the British Army had enforced the death sentence for desertion and cowardice. Just a month after the outbreak of hostilities, on 2 September 1914, Private Thomas Highgate of the Royal West Kent Regiment was tried for desertion and two days later executed by firing squad.[33] A second soldier, Private George Ward of the Royal Berkshire Regiment, had walked away from his position after an artillery shell had killed two men standing next to him. He was arrested six days later, and two days after that, on 26 September 1914, he was executed.[34] From then and up until Blakemore was tried, another 196 men were executed for desertion[35] – clearly not the 'example' General Haig had hoped for, and certainly not enough deterrent to keep traumatised men like Denis Blakemore from deserting.

During the entire period of the war, 3,080 men were court-martialled and sentenced to death, with 314 being executed.[36] Although the vast majority of death sentences were commuted, most of the men who did face a firing squad were put through a trial where the verdict was a foregone conclusion and the trial merely a formality to placate politicians. In 1983, Anthony Babington was the first to fully uncover the truth. He writes, 'It was the first time the true details of these grim and sometimes horrific trials had been revealed.'[37] Several men were not even defended, and, worst of all, most men 'executed for cowardice might these days be judged to have been suffering from battle exhaustion or battle shock, and therefore not fully responsible for their actions'.[38]

Private Denis Blakemore was court-martialled on 27 June 1917 at the headquarters of 57th Infantry Brigade at Mont Noir. Because his battalion and most of the division were engaged in 'considerable activity' on the Oosttaverne Line,[39] there appeared to be no officers available to act on the defendant's behalf. The Field General Court Martial (FGCM) documents list the president and its members as well as all witnesses called. The president is listed as a major of the 8th Bn N. Staffs, and although he was available, it is evident that no other officer was available from the battalion to represent Private Blakemore and speak on his behalf. During the war, there were several occasions when defendants were tried without an officer representing them, with the defendant waiving his right rather than waiting for one to become available.[40] It looks like Private Blakemore was one of these cases.

The proceedings started with the charge being read:

> The accused, No. 40435 Private D Blakemore, 8th Bn N. Staffs Regt, a soldier of the regular forces, is charged with, 'When on active service, Deserting His Majesty's Service' in that he on June 7th 1917, when his company was formed up in the assembly trenches and about to advance to attack the enemy, absented himself from his company and remained absent until apprehended in Boulogne on 19th June 1917.

After the charge was read, Private Blakemore was asked how he pled. 'Not guilty,' was the reply.[41]

Blakemore was now told to sit. In front of him, sitting behind a long table with the president, were the three additional members of the court-martial: a captain and lieutenant of the 10th Battalion, the Royal Warwickshire Regiment, and a captain of the 13th Battalion, the Rifle Brigade. Four witnesses were called during Blakemore's court-martial, each of them sworn in using the Holy Bible.

The first witness was Blakemore's platoon sergeant:

> At 5.40am, 7th June, I called the roll of the platoon to which the accused belongs. This was in the assembly trenches before the advance. After searching I found the accused in a shell-hole to the rear of the assembly trenches. I ordered him to rejoin the platoon, which he did so and prepared to advance. We advanced to our own original front line and I formed up the platoon and counted. I found there was one absent and found out it was the accused. I dispatched a runner to

go and see if he had got mixed in with any of the other three platoons of the company. He came back and told me he could not find him. When we got to the 'Black Line' I found that he was still absent. I again went to look for him but without success. I next saw him under arrest some days later.[42]

The second witness was Private Blakemore's section commander, a lance corporal:

On 7th June I saw the accused about 30 minutes before we went forward. When we were about 150 yards in front of our old front line, I looked around and saw the accused. I did not see him again until the day he was brought back to the battalion.[43]

The third witness was a lance corporal of the Military Police:

On 19th June about 5pm I was on MP duty at Gare Maritime, Boulogne. I saw the accused, and heard him admit to a Lieutenant of the 8th Bn N. Staffs that he was absent from his battalion. I took him to the guardroom where he was detained.

At this time, testimony was added 'By court':

He was in uniform, with an Army Service Corps cap badge in his cap. He was not shaved.[44]

The fourth and final witness was a sergeant of the 8th Bn N. Staffs:

On the 21st June 1917, I was sent to Boulogne. I received the accused from the APM and brought him back to the battalion on the 22nd June 1917.

Once again, another piece of testimony was added 'By Court':

Accused had no badges on at all.[45]

As if the evidence was not damning enough, and despite the 'Not Guilty' plea, without any officer representing or advising him to do so otherwise, Blakemore then took the stand under oath and admitted that he had deserted:

At our original front line I stayed a while and then I went away. I went farther and farther and as far as I could tell went the way that we came from. Then I got on the road and got into a motor lorry and went in it and then I got to Bailleul. Then I got on a train and went to Boulogne. I was there three or four days before I was arrested.

From the court-martial documents, it looks like he was cross-examined and asked why he had deserted. His response was,

> I was too upset to go on with my section. I knew the attack was coming on that morning.

A guilty verdict was pronounced immediately after Private Blakemore had testified.[46]

Before a sentence was passed, the court then heard from the adjutant of the 8th Bn N. Staffs, a second lieutenant. Under oath, he produced a certified copy of Private Blakemore's Army Form B122 (Company Conduct Sheet). This document showed that Blakemore had been previously found guilty of desertion on active service by court-martial in November 1916. The sentence of death was commuted to 15 years' penal servitude, which had been suspended by the Commander-in-Chief on 4 June 1917.[47]

There was only one sentence available to the court. The Commander-in-Chief, who appears to have been aware that Blakemore had not been defended at his trial, confirmed the death penalty, signing the 'Schedule' page of the documents, 'Confirmed, D. Haig FM, 6th July 17'.[48] The sentence of death by shooting was scheduled to be carried out on the morning of 9 July 1917.

It is a long-established tradition and right of every condemned soldier that a chaplain will attend him before his execution. After a soldier was convicted and sentenced to death, each division issued a set of confidential instructions entitled, 'Execution of sentence of death by shooting'.[49] These instructions covered all aspects of the grim ordeal, including listing the responsibilities of all those involved – the Medical Officer, the Assistant Provost Marshal, the Military Police, and the soldier's unit who provided the firing party. An entire paragraph was dedicated to the division's Senior Chaplain who was responsible for providing a padre.[50]

This was not the first time that David had been faced with the prospect of ministering to a condemned man. He was fully aware of the effects of battlefield stress and shellshock. He had seen it at Vimy Ridge and especially at High Wood during battlefield clearance duties undertaken by his battalion. He knew that it made men desperate. Men who were normally fine soldiers started to change, acting without regard to the consequences of deserting while on active service. On the Ypres

Salient in November 1916, some men of the 47th Division who had been through Vimy and the Somme were beginning to crack, as David described in a letter:

> A tragedy today. A man called Blackwell who had deserted shot himself in the guardroom. I went to him when the doctor gave me leave. I fear he will die. He said pathetically, 'write to my wife and tell her it was an accident or something.' Ah! What a place this world is when a man is lonely and without God. He gets fed up – despairs – and does not care for God or man.[51]

The next day he wrote to his wife of another man who had deserted:

> Tonight I have said goodbye to a man who was up on a charge of desertion, he has been ordered to be shot. This sentence has been commuted to penal servitude. He is lucky to get off, I told him never to think he was 'done', always pray to our Lord, look up and after this sentence start afresh in civil life. I gave him a New Testament. He is lucky to get off while another man was shot a short while ago.[52]

David Blake, curator of the Museum of Army Chaplaincy says, 'It appears that it was normally the job of the Senior Chaplain of a division to select the chaplain to attend the execution. They seem to have selected chaplains with experience and whom they could trust to carry out the duty.'[53] In most cases, this chaplain was normally the same one who was attached to that soldier's battalion. If there was no padre with that battalion, then David could have sent someone suitable from the same brigade. In this case, for some unknown reason, it looks like he did not think that Revd John Wallace, who was attached to Blakemore's battalion, was suitable or capable of carrying out this responsibility.

Although he had been around men convicted and sentenced to death, as far as we can tell, up to this point in the war, David had not been called upon to carry out this unpleasant task. It is possible that he considered it a kind of 'rite of passage', a duty that he felt he had to carry out in order to feel solidarity with the padres under his command and with the soldiers that he had come to respect and admire. If he was able to help a man spiritually when he was most vulnerable, preparing him to meet his fate with dignity and strength, then he knew he had to be the one. David also seems to have been the kind of man who would not send someone to do something that he was not willing to do himself.

Witnessing the death of a fellow soldier must have had a huge effect on all those present. Soldiers who were tasked with shooting the condemned man (often from the condemned man's own company or platoon) were told that shooting straight was the humane thing to do, but they often shot wide anyway. The officer in charge may have been called upon to administer the *coup de grace* with his service revolver if his men had not aimed straight and hit the 'small paper disc'[54] pinned above the heart. The doctor, whose sworn purpose in life is to save men's lives, had to confirm the condemned man was dead. Even the military policemen and provost marshal guards charged with escorting the handcuffed soldier and tying him to the post, tree, or wall would have been affected by it. Each one had difficult duties to perform.

But it was the padre who was expected to be able to put away his emotions and feelings. He was the one person that looked into a man's eyes during their final hours and minutes on earth. It was the padre who saw the worst and best in men before they drew their last. And it was often the padre who was most affected in the aftermath of a military execution. There are many first-hand accounts written by padres who spent the final few hours with condemned men. The number and the vivid descriptions of their accounts show the experience had profound effects on them.

The Revd Edward Montmorency Guilford, known as 'Monty', would have his faith tested after he returned from the war. Combined with dissatisfaction of the war, the carnage and loss of life, 'Monty found himself supervising the judicial killing of a bewildered young man'.[55] He spent the last night with Private Joseph Bateman and witnessed his death. His grandson, Peter Fiennes, went on to say, 'The execution of Joseph Bateman had a profound effect on my grandfather.'[56]

The manner in which the condemned men faced their firing squads differed. Some met their fate with anger, some with fear, doing everything they could to try to escape, while others had comrades give them alcohol to numb the pain of their death. Private James Crozier had to be carried to his place of execution he was so drunk.[57] Others were just 'sullen and silent'. War correspondent Phillip Gibbs describes one condemned man being ministered to by a chaplain 'who suffered, torn with pity for that sullen man whose life was almost at an end'. When offered prayers, the condemned man replied, 'I don't believe in them.'[58]

The Revd Richard Griffiths describes one young man who tried to escape as he was led to the firing post:

> From behind, came the prisoner, scarcely able to walk, along a side path, pleading and groaning. Then as he turned the corner on to the grass, he suddenly dashed from his guard and ran wildly across the broken ground, stumbling, panting, straining, able in his despair to reach an astonishing speed, and for the time, able to out distance the men, laden with their equipment. He was eventually caught, and as he came back facing us, he presented a pathetic figure of exhaustion and helpless appeal. He was tied to the stake. His eyes were bandaged.[59]

Private Harry Farr was hospitalised on numerous occasions with an uncontrollable shake, reporting sick four times with his nerves. 'He said he could no longer stand the explosions of artillery and was reported as trembling and not in a fit state.' Nonetheless, he was tried on 17 October 1916, charged with 'misbehaving before the enemy in such a manner as to show cowardice'. Harry Farr went to his death acting nothing like the coward he was accused of being. He 'refused a blindfold, preferring to look the firing squad in the eye'. A chaplain who had witnessed Farr's execution wrote a letter to his mother saying, 'A finer soldier never lived.'[60]

As far as we can tell, like most of his war experiences, David never spoke of the execution of Private Blakemore. His letters to the Blakemore family were probably destroyed many years ago. The three letters (and a note in his own handwriting on the envelope) written to David from the Blakemore family and a couple of names and addresses he wrote down in his notebook, are all that remain with the Railton family today. But without mentioning his name, David wrote a very revealing and moving account of the last hours of Private Denis Blakemore.

Sometime after his flag was used to cover the coffin of the Unknown Warrior on Armistice Day 1920, David wrote a detailed history of the flag itself. He did so in the voice of the Flag, rather than his own. The account was never published – the original manuscript is held by the Railton Family.

> Indeed as long as I rest in the abbey I shall always remember how in the dead of a certain night the Padre got up and took me in his pack into the wood. I wondered where ever was he going for a service at such an hour. In the wood was a little tent and inside the tent three men. Two of them got up and, after speaking with

the padre for a few moments, went outside. Then the tent was closed up. The padre laid me down on the grass and talked with the third man. Then he wrote down in a book something that was being told him. I do not know what this was, but I remember hearing the padre say, 'Would you like your communion, laddie? Because if so, you can have it now.'

Then he came to me and spread me over the grass and laid upon me the chalice and paten that he always used in the central part of that wonderful communion service. Soon after the service the light of the day seemed to be coming and I heard voices of other men. A doctor came into the tent and soon after that the padre left me and took the arm of his friend and went into the wood. The next thing that I can remember is that there was a startling report of rifles and presently I heard footsteps rushing through the wood and all the twigs crackling and the padre snatched me off the ground in a way he had never done before. He did not fold me up. He just crushed me into his pack and ran through the wood and up a hill to a little dug out. He flung me on the floor and stamped up and down. I do not know all he said but the words, 'devilment' and 'blood' and 'misery' kept on coming in and he vowed that he would never use me again and he was done with the Army and would go home. Then he folded me up and went out.

But the next day I remember he said what was the use of being turned out of the Army and possibly depriving the chaplains of the freedom that they were having in intercourse with the men and in correspondence with their relatives and friends. The fact that he and others went home could not cure war, so he decided to stay and he kept me for many more hundred communions.[61]

In one of David's notebooks, an Army Book 152 – Correspondence Book (Field Service), he wrote, 'Monday – Private Denis Blakemore. Spent all night with him until 4.30am – when sentence of death was carried out – God help his people.'[62] Also with the notebook, written on two pieces of a 'Message and Signal' pad, are the following names and addresses he wrote down whilst with Private Blakemore:

Mother & Father – 3 St George's Street, Mountfields, Shrewsbury. Miss GR Perry, Brook House, Stratford.

On the second sheet is written:

G Blakemore, 99 Victoria Road, New Brighton, Cheshire (Brother-jeweller) and wife Mrs Wall 2a Church Lane, Stafford (Landlady)[63]

From his moving, unpublished account, kept safely hidden away by the Railton family since the 1920s, we can see that the death of Private

Denis Blakemore had a deep effect upon David Railton. His admission of wanting to leave the Army after what he had witnessed is quite understandable to us a century later. But a reader of that time might have been shocked at the honesty and the way he had thrown down the Union Jack. It could have been the reason this version of the story, in the voice of the Flag, was never published.

From the court-martial documents and unit wartime diaries held in the National Archive, and the description of the location in David's 'Story of the Flag', there is no doubt that the execution of Private Blakemore took place on Kemmel Hill. David would have known that at the top of the hill was an observation dugout because he and other staff officers of the 19th Division witnessed the mines being detonated and the subsequent artillery barrage at the start of the Battle of Messines Ridge, the same time Private Blakemore had deserted his platoon a few miles away. He would have known that he could go there and vent his frustration out of earshot of anyone else.

At that time, Kemmel Hill was still completely wooded and had been left largely unscathed by the war. However, just a year later, it would look totally different. Of vital strategic importance to both sides, during the German advance of April 1918, there would be two battles fought there, with the 19th Division fighting in the first, 17–19 April 1918.[64] The second battle, 25–26 April, would cost the lives of thousands of French and British soldiers and leave Kemmel Hill completely defoliated, covered in craters and shell holes. The Germans held it until they were pushed off in the final advance by British and French troops in Flanders, which started on 28 September 1918.

After an execution had taken place, it was normal procedure for the body of the executed soldier to be buried in a 'recognised burial ground'.[65] If that were not possible, then the grave would have been dug close to the site of the execution but 'concealed from view of the prisoner as he approaches the chosen spot'.[66] In the case of Denis Blakemore, his body was taken down from the post or tree he was tied to and placed on a stretcher.

After David had composed himself on the top of Kemmel Hill, he walked down through the trees to where the body of Denis Blakemore was being loaded into the ambulance. The body was transported the short distance along the Kemmelbergweg to a cemetery next to a field ambulance unit in the village of Locre (now Loker). Beginning June 1917, it became known as the Locre Hospice Cemetery and contains the graves of 244 men who died in the First World War.[67]

David wrote to the Blakemore family telling them that he had conducted the funeral for their son.[68] The question arises whether he used his flag or not. There is no mention of whether it was used to cover the body. It is reasonable to believe that he would have used it for the burial service the same way he had used it for many hundreds of previous burial services of men who had been killed in combat. Some officers and soldiers may have objected to this, but that would not have worried him. In David's opinion, man had convicted Denis Blakemore, not God. He had paid the ultimate price for his crime here on earth, and he had willingly taken Holy Communion before facing his death bravely.

The task of informing an executed soldier's family invariably fell to the chaplain. Unlike other soldiers' families who often heard from an officer or a friend as well as his chaplain, relatives of an executed soldier normally heard nothing until they received a letter from the chaplain. In the first part of the war, the Army made no attempt to hide the fact that a soldier had been executed. This meant families had the public stigma hanging over their heads; and financially, it left them in dire straits. Any pension granted after the death of a relative was not a right, and along with allowances for children, it could be stopped if someone was labelled as 'not worthy'; and before 1918, families of deserters were considered as such. Blakemore's name is listed in the 'Register of Soldiers' Effects'. Under 'War Gratuity', the words 'Not authorised' are written in red ink.[69]

After 1918, and against Army wishes, the government changed the policy. Families of executed soldiers were informed in the same way as they would for a man who had died in battle, and their widows received a pension, too. The rationale was that it was not the wife or children who had deserted, so they should not be made to suffer. The Army, on the other hand, argued that if these men were treated the same with regards to notification and pensions, then the government would be guilty of undermining military discipline that was considered essential to winning the war.

In the case of Denis Blakemore, David appeared to have spared the family the news that he had died in front of a firing squad. On 25 July, Mr Blakemore wrote, 'I should be further thankful if you could kindly inform me in what action he was in, and when and how he was wounded before coming into your charge.'[70] It was not until 10 August that the family received official word from the authorities that with 'very great regret' their son, Denis Jetson Blakemore, 'was sentenced after trial by Court-Martial to be shot for Desertion … and the sentence was duly executed'[71] on 9 July 1917.

For generals faced with the task of trying to win a war, the need to keep men fighting warranted making examples of cowards. This reasoning has been used over the years to justify British Army First World War executions. Commanders needed to maintain discipline amongst their ranks, and without the threat of the death sentence, desertion would be widespread.

During the Second World War, the death sentence was not available as punishment for men who had deserted. And if the figures provided by Brigadier A. B. McPherson are to be believed – 'that very nearly 100,000 soldiers deserted'[72] – then a case could be argued in favour of the death sentence. In 1942, General Auchinleck, 'one of the most humane as well as one of the finest generals of that war, recommended the re-introduction of the death penalty to deter it'.[73] But if we break down the desertion rates further, as a number per 1,000, as claimed by William More, then those rates were higher in the First World War rather than the Second World War,[74] even with the deterrent factor of the death penalty. In the British military during the Second World War, discipline was not compromised. The fighting capability of British forces was not diminished, even if 100,000 men did desert. Many millions of men, volunteers and conscripts alike, fought bravely and with pride for their country and were ultimately victorious without the threat of a firing squad.

During the First World War, Australian soldiers did not have the death sentence hanging over their heads because of Section 98 of the

Commonwealth Defence Act 1903.[75] It stated that a death sentence could not be carried out unless the Governor-General confirmed it. There are those who would argue that Australians had a discipline problem, and figures show that desertion rates for Australians were at times higher than those of other units.[76] But Australians served bravely in campaigns at Gallipoli and the Western Front and there were no significant breakdowns of military discipline even though Australians were 'free from the shadow of the firing squad'.[77]

In the years after the war, when memorials commemorating those who had died were being erected in towns and villages up and down Britain, whether those men who were executed should have their names included became a passionate issue. Most war memorial committee members and parents of those who fell in the war did not want the names of executed men on memorials. But soldiers who served with – and in some cases had grown up with – men who had been executed, thought about it differently. Some parents refused to allow their son's name to go on a memorial if an executed deserter was also included.

In the Lincolnshire village of Fulstow, families were so divided on the issue of an executed soldier that no memorial was built for the village's 10 soldiers who died in the war. It was not until 87 years later that a plaque with all the names on it was placed on a wall of the village hall.[78] In 1922, at Newport-on-Tay, Scotland, emotions ran so high that two ex-soldiers stole gelignite from a local quarry and threatened to destroy any memorial that did not bear the name of Private Peter Black, a comrade and school friend who had been executed for desertion in 1916 whilst serving with the Black Watch. After a contentious town hall discussion, the committee tasked with the construction of the memorial was forced to resign. In September that year, the memorial was unveiled with all 84 names, including that of Private Peter Black.[79]

It is not known whether the Blakemore family faced the kind of vilification other families of executed men had been subjected to. Denis Blakemore's name appears on two memorials in Shrewsbury churches. The first memorial is at the Holy Trinity Church in the village of Bicton just on the outskirts of the town of Shrewsbury. The list of 11 men is just inside the church and 'significantly his name appears last, as if added as an afterthought'.[80] It is possible that this placement was because his family no longer lived in Bicton. His father was a schoolmaster there but had since retired and moved. His name also appears on the war memorial at St George's Church in the Frankwell area of Shrewsbury close to the family home in St George's Street. According to Peter Francis, 'The interesting thing about the memorial in St George's is that Blakemore's name shows all the signs of having been in the list from the outset.'[81] Whether his family kept his execution a secret or that the people of the parish were more forgiving is unknown.

The fact that many of the men executed in the First World War were, by modern definition, unfit for duty, makes this one of the saddest and most tragic miscarriages of justice in the history of the British Army. And when we look at the composition of the men who were shot, it lends support to 'claims that the executions of soldiers were a class issue'.[82] Of the 306 men shot for cowardice or desertion during the war, only two were officers. Fifteen officers were convicted of desertion and sentenced to death, only to be given a royal pardon. And while shellshock or battle fatigue was not accepted at a trial for most soldiers, an officer who showed signs of shellshock or battle fatigue was more often than not diagnosed as suffering from neurasthenia and sent home. Neurasthenia is the technical name for a condition characterised by lassitude, fatigue, headache and irritability, and is associated chiefly with emotional disturbance.

There are many cases of officers receiving medical care for shellshock when other soldiers were not. Before the Battle of the Ancre, the sad last act of the Somme, Denis Blakemore's own commanding officer, Lt-Col Parish, had been 'shellshocked' and evacuated.[83] Blakemore, who had been through the ghastly first days of the Battle of the Somme with his battalion, deserted on 18 November 1916, the very last day of the battle, about the same time that his CO was being sent home.

For many years, the call to pardon those men 'Shot at Dawn' got louder and louder. Finally, in 2006, 306 men executed for desertion and cowardice were exonerated when Queen Elizabeth II signed the Pardon for Soldiers of the Great War Bill[84] and it became law. In the House of Commons, on behalf of the British Government, Defence Secretary Des Brown finally admitted what many had known since the end of the First World War: 'I believe it is better to acknowledge that injustices were clearly done in some cases – even if we cannot say which – and to acknowledge that all these men were victims of war. I hope that pardoning these men will finally remove the stigma with which their families have lived for years.'[85] Number 40435 Private Denis Jetson Blakemore 8/N Staffs, charged with desertion and executed 9 July, appears in Schedule 1 to the bill.[86]

Added to the court-martial documents of Private Denis Blakemore held by the National Archive is a document signed by the Secretary of State for Defence. It reads:

> This document records that Pte D Blakemore of the 8th Battalion, North Staffordshire Regiment who was executed for desertion on July 9th, 1917 is pardoned under Section 359 of the Armed Forces Act 2006. The pardon stands as recognition that he was one of many victims of the First World War and that execution was not a fate he deserved.[87]

When surviving members of his family visit Westminster Abbey and stand at the grave of the Unknown Warrior, they can look across into the Chapel of St George and know that the old and tattered union flag, 'The Padre's Flag', hangs there for them as well as the many hundreds of other families of men it has covered.

CHAPTER 8

Kaiserschlacht

'One more victory like this, and we are lost.'

PLUTARCH

Sunday, 26 May 1918, Headquarters, 19th (Western) Division, Saint-Germain-la-Ville, France

For soldiers of the 19th Division who had been battered by German attacks just a few weeks earlier and survived, waking up in the sun-bathed Champagne region, now teeming with new life brought on by the spring warmth, must have been a pleasant feeling. The rustic tranquillity of the River Marne south of Reims, with its neat and tidy, picture-perfect postcard villages, was such a change from the more war-ravaged British trenches of the Western Front. Despite being the scene of Nivelle's disastrous offensive a year earlier, the Champagne region was recovering quickly with nature reasserting itself everywhere.

The 19th Division was now part of the hastily rearranged IX Corps under the command of Lieutenant-General Sir Alexander Hamilton-Gordon. Earlier in May, four other equally depleted divisions (8th, 21st, 25th and 50th) had also entrained south to the Champagne region. In an agreement between Haig and the French commander, IX Corps would take over from fresher French troops who would be transferred to the north. By the time David and his division arrived on 19 May, IX Corps had already taken over a 15-mile sector north-west of Rheims between Bermicourt and Bouconville.[1]

IX Corps came under the command of the French who obviously did not believe in the military theory of strength in depth. As soon as they arrived at the front, General Hamilton-Gordon complained to his French superior officer, General Duchene, regarding the positioning of his divisions. Captain Sidney Rogerson writes, 'Far from being in a state of congenial relaxation, they found themselves crammed between the front-line trenches and the Aisne, against all the normal rules of military disposition.'[2]

If the Germans happened to attack there (although considered unlikely), then most of IX Corps would be trapped with nowhere to go. Concentrated German artillery could inflict large casualties in a relatively small area if it chose to do so. But Duchene refused to change the deployment of any troops under his command. 'By his stubbornness and rigidity, for whatever cause, Duchene was condemning the British forces suddenly put under his command to the possibility of annihilation.'[3]

But this did not concern the men of the 19th Division who were many miles behind the front line. With new recruits filling the ranks of battalions, the plan was for the 19th Division to stay in reserve for a lengthy period of rest, training and re-building of its constituent units in the area of Saint-Germain Châlons on the banks of the Marne. When they were deemed ready, the division was going to take over a sector of the line somewhere between Rheims and Verdun.[4]

It's safe to say that when the men of the 19th Division arrived in the Champagne countryside, most would have been very happy with the conditions there. Their lives would have felt markedly better compared with what they had previously been through. Food and provisions were abundant, and they did not have the prospect of having to face an imminent German offensive. But when David Railton arrived on the banks of the River Marne, he received some unwelcome news.

During the move south, David's bag and a sack full of personal belongings and letters from relatives of men he had buried went missing. David was beside himself. Apart from the letters and personal items, his bag and most of its contents could have been replaced easily enough.

But the one thing he treasured the most – his flag – was gone. Many years later on the back of a postcard, he briefly explained what happened:

> For a good few months it (the flag) was lost having been thrown off a train when we were sent to help the French. Together with a sack full of letters, the flag was in the pack. Two men got into the cart. As we travelled they felt a sack or two under them which stopped them sleeping. So they just lugged out the pack and threw it, as they supposed, on to the open truck. But it went unseen in the darkness, into some fields.[5]

David told a longer version of the story in his short history, *The Story of a Padre's Flag*, in the voice of the Flag:

> On that occasion there was rather a lot of 'hustling' whilst entraining and in the darkness and general confusion it was difficult to keep anything in a particular place. There had been some fierce fighting and the padre had collected personal effects of several of the slain and had received many letters from their relatives and friends at home. These were put in several sandbags. The one containing the letters was tied to me, to be kept at all costs.
>
> The padre's man thought the safest place for them would be the Mess Cart, so he put us both there and reported that he had done so to the padre, who was very satisfied that such a good place had been found. As the train moved on its eternally slow way and as the night grew colder two or three men climbed into the cart for warmth. The next thing I remember was a tremendous bump. It took a long time before I found out what had really happened.
>
> Apparently these comrades of mine said to one another, 'This is not a very comfortable bed' and as they felt that the removal of an odd sack or two would ease the situation they naturally thought 'men first, pack second.' Hence I was flung overboard with the letters. Mind you they did not know it was me. But you should have seen the Padre's face and likewise that of his man when they realised that I had disappeared.[6]

David kept the news to himself, hoping that someone was just playing a prank. But after the first service without it and many comments from the men asking where it was, David started to accept the reality that it had probably 'Gone West' for good.[7] 'Meanwhile Dubby [his mother-in-law], of boundless generosity, had purchased and sent me another Union Jack, which I still possess.'[8]

The men who had caused the loss of his bag and the flag were honest and full of remorse. One of the sergeant majors within the division's headquarters had wanted to bring them both up on a charge. But David refused – he didn't want anyone being 'straffed'[9] for what was clearly nothing more than an unfortunate accident. It is not known when the new flag arrived. But his mother-in-law had sent it right away, so it probably arrived before the division moved back north to the British sector. When he had it in his possession, he used it just like the original flag – only a few people knew the difference.

Despite the loss of his original flag, along with the sack of letters and personal effects, David seemed to be happy in the Champagne region. After what he had been through over the past two years, no one would begrudge him this. But most of all, he was really happy for the men. Knowing what his division had been subjected to since he had arrived a year before, he believed strongly that they deserved this rest.

★★★

During the first five months that David had been with the 19th Division, command of the division had changed three times. When he arrived in April 1917, the GOC was Major-General A. R. Montagu-Stuart-Wortley. One of two brothers who were generals, the other, Major-General E. J. Montagu-Stuart-Wortley, who commanded the 46th Division, was controversially sacked after a failed diversionary attack at Gommecourt on the opening day of the Battle of the Somme. Major-General A. R. Montagu-Stuart-Wortley was soon moved to take command of the 32nd Division, and he later rose to the rank of Lieutenant-General. Major-General C. D. Shute was the GOC for just a few months until the return of the 19th Division's previous commander, Major-General G. T. M. Bridges. Shute was in command of the division during the Battle of Messines Ridge and was later promoted to command V Corps.

General Bridges had left the division in April 1917, before David arrived. He was selected to join the British Mission to the United States of America after they had entered the war. The British Mission, of which General Bridges had been a part, tried and failed to get the Americans to send soldiers immediately to fill the ranks of depleted British and French divisions. He returned to the division on 19 June, but on 20 September, he was badly injured whilst visiting the commanders of 57th and 58th brigades at their HQ bunker underneath Hill 60. That afternoon, as he came out of the entrance, a shell exploded close by. A large piece of shrapnel almost severed his leg, which had to be amputated a short time later.[10] General Bridges wrote to David later that year. The letter obviously refers to a discussion they had before his injury concerning mandatory church parades and whether padres in the Army should hold any rank.

> Dear Railton,
> I was sorry not to see you before I left.
> I have thought long and hard over the two conundrums you put to me and have come to the conclusion that your solution is the best on both counts – (ie) that services should be voluntary and padres should give up all rank.
> I can see difficulties in the second matter but they can only be overcome by yourselves.
> Excuse a scrap – don't feel much like writing.
> Best of luck, yours,
> Tom Bridges[11]

Undeterred by the loss of a leg, General Bridges returned to the United States to help speed up the arrival of American troops. He was later knighted and became the Governor of South Australia.

On 22 September 1917, the 19th Division got its fourth GOC in as many months. Major-General G. D. Jeffreys was a Grenadier Guard who had seen action at the Battle of Omdurman during the Sudan Campaign in 1898 and had also served during the Second Boer War. He left the Army in 1911 after having been the commander of the Guards Depot at Caterham, Surrey. On the outbreak of war in 1914, he re-enlisted and saw service at the Battle of Mons with the 2nd Battalion Grenadier Guards, which he was promoted to command a short while later. He went on to command the 1st Guards Brigade and the 57th Brigade within the 19th Division – he was a natural choice to take over as GOC when General Bridges lost his leg. General Jeffreys went on to command the division for the rest of the war. He eventually became the General Commanding the Brigade of Guards and GOC London District.

General Jeffreys was already well known throughout the division. The product of a professional army, he was regarded as a fine soldier. Being a Guardsman, he also had a reputation as a disciplinarian, demanding high standards from the men who served under him. 19th Division historian, Everard Whyall said of Jeffreys, 'Woe betide the slipshod man! Woe betide the slovenly man! Whether in habit, speech, or thought. These received no mercy.'[12] He became a highly respected commander because he would work tirelessly to make sure his men went into battle fully trained and prepared, confident in their own abilities. Wyrall writes, 'No man had a sterner sense of duty, and it was this outstanding characteristic which made him so deeply respected and esteemed.'[13]

After the Battle of the Menin Road Ridge, the 19th Division were not involved in any further offensive operations in Flanders. It was now the division's responsibility to secure its sector of the front line, while the continuing attacks of the Third Battle of Ypres were focused further north. There were tough times ahead for the division – it would continue to lose men while it consolidated and built up its defences, all the while being constantly sniped and shelled. But it was nothing compared with what some divisions were facing a few miles away at a small village called Passchendaele – a name that would forever be linked with misery, suffering and the loss of thousands of British soldiers.

The division came out of the line on 11 November and moved away from the front to the Blaringhem area, just a few miles southeast of St Omer. General Jeffreys told his commanders he anticipated that the division might be out of the line for a period of six to eight weeks. However, he warned them this might be cut short with a return to the trenches in as little as a month.[14] This is where General Jeffreys' experience of years of training men up to extremely high standards came to the fore. He built the training up gradually but systematically, starting at platoon, company, and battalion levels, before building to brigade-sized exercises that covered every situation his soldiers might face in the months ahead. In the preface and foreword of his newly written *Standing Orders for Trenches,* the General laid out in plain language what he expected of his men: 'No good system can, however, exist without discipline. Discipline is the bedrock of military efficiency, and without it a regiment is at once futile in attack and powerless in defence... A battalion should guard its trenches as closely as it guards its honour and name. The word "retire" is never to be heard.'[15]

It seems certain that David respected General Jeffreys; however, David's pathos for his men may have sometimes clashed with his General's strict policies on discipline. The only recorded reference David made to his General is amongst some notes he wrote for Westminster Abbey in 1954. When explaining events regarding the use of his flag during the burial of the Unknown Warrior, he describes General Jeffreys as a 'stickler for detail'.[16] For a Grenadier Guard, this is a compliment, only to be expected in a regiment of such high standards. But David also writes, 'Don't be surprised if he "flares up" over this! He will calm down!'[17]

Of all the letters that were offered by David's wife when she had them typed and consolidated, not one is written during his time serving with the 19th Division under General Jeffreys. Could it be that he wrote to her venting his frustrations and she felt that some of his comments should not be made public? Or was it that he simply did not have the time to write in as much detail as he had done while he was with the 47th Division? Or maybe his wife felt that the letters written by a padre in the trenches would be more interesting to the public than those written by a padre or staff officer at divisional headquarters miles from the front line? We will never know.

There can be no doubt that General Jeffreys was an effective wartime divisional commander and that he ran his division in the finest traditions and standards of his regiment – the facts speak for themselves. But there is at least one occasion when David would have been horrified and probably would have objected officially to the extremes his General was willing to go to in order to maintain discipline, even if it was during the chaos caused by the German spring offensive of 1918. According to Richard Holmes, 'In May 1918, the commander of the 19th Division was refused GHQ's permission to "confirm and have carried out" summary death sentences on stragglers.'[18] If David had known about this, which we have to assume he did, then he must have forcefully argued against his GOC for wanting to have men summarily executed for not keeping up with their platoons and companies.

The only extant letter between the two men shows no signs of tension. It was written on 4 November 1920, whilst arrangements were being made for the burial of the Unknown Warrior in Westminster Abbey.

General Jeffreys was now Commander, The Brigade of Guards and GOC of London District.

> My Dear Railton,
> I was very sorry to miss you yesterday. The Dean had told me that a chaplain had offered him a flag which had been in France, but I did not realise that you were the chaplain and the flag was the one I had so often seen with the dear old 19th Division until I met him yesterday afternoon at a committee meeting.
> The history of the flag which you left for me, is very interesting, and I understand that after the 11th it is to remain in the keeping of the Dean.
> I am very glad to hear that you are settled in a living and hope that you are fit and well. Come and look me up again if you are in London.
> Yours sincerely,
> G. D. Jeffreys[19]

Training had been taking place for less than a month when, on 4 December, the division was told to prepare to proceed south by rail within 48 hours. They would join General Julian Byng's Third Army on the Somme.[20] For the many men who had fought there in 1916, thoughts of a return would have brought back some terrible memories. One can only imagine what David was thinking. The horrors he had faced with the 47th Division at High Wood would have all come flooding back as he and his men entrained for the long journey south.

★★★

Since July 1916, the Allies had been on the offensive. But as 1917 drew to a close and thoughts turned to 1918, it was obvious that the Allies were exhausted and over-stretched. They faced huge problems – problems that would not only be felt in the Cabinet Room of 10 Downing Street or at Haig's General Headquarters, the Château de Beaurepaire, in Montreuil. These problems developed into a palpable fear, as the winter of 1917–18 started to cast its cold shadow across the Western Front.

The Somme offensive of 1916 had exhausted manpower and resources from both sides. But after its withdrawal to a shorter line of defences on the Hindenburg Line, Germany was able to re-distribute its divisions in preparation for renewed Allied attacks that they correctly anticipated in the spring of 1917. Two of these British attacks along the ridges of

Messines and Vimy were startling successes, but the failure of the Nivelle offensive to secure a breakthrough at the Chemin des Dames was to have far-reaching consequences for the French Army, effectively taking away its offensive capability for over a year. Haig's attack in Flanders yielded results at first, but in the autumn rain, his army floundered and became bogged down in the mud at Passchendaele. Finally, the use of over 400 Mark IV tanks failed to achieve any decisive breakthrough, and to compound matters, the British were put on the back-foot after a well-organised German counter-attack regained most of the territory it had lost earlier at Cambrai.

In April 1917, the United States of America declared war on Germany. They had resisted involvement in a foreign war for three years, despite the sinking of the *Lusitania* and many of its merchant ships in the Atlantic. President Woodrow Wilson's hand was finally forced to sign Congress's declaration of war after it had transpired that Germany was encouraging Mexico to invade the United States' southern border. After war was declared it was made clear to their allies that Americans would only fight under the command of American generals. Sending reinforcements to fill their depleted divisions seemed a reasonable request to Britain and France. But for the United States, it was politically unacceptable, and they rejected the proposal entirely.

A crisis of manpower with no immediate prospect of fresh American soldiers forced Haig to make drastic cuts. Losses of 1917 had so stretched many divisions' manpower that some were now not combat ready. In January 1918, he was forced to reduce the strength of infantry divisions from 13 to 10 battalions. Although it was clear that America was committed to the fight, many thought that by the time they had assembled enough divisions, it might be too late – the war could already be over.

For France, the humiliating defeat at the Chemin des Dames in the spring of 1917 would start a chain of events that could have knocked them out of the war entirely. Discontent within the ranks at the way the war was being conducted had been simmering quietly for some months, but the defeat in the Champagne region turned the heat up so violently that it boiled over into open mutiny. The French Army was in disarray. The mutineers were not killing their officers or rampaging through villages and towns; they simply refused to go back to the trenches. Had the Germans realised what had happened, they could have just walked through large portions of the French front line unmolested on their way to Paris. Nivelle's dismissal and the appointment of Philippe Pétain, combined with the selective use of firing squads for the mutiny's ring-leaders, slowly brought order back to the ranks. But it would be some time before the Allies could again rely on the French Army to conduct offensive operations.

In Russia, the army had been in a state of near revolt since its humil-iation at Tannenberg in 1914. Discontent with a monarchy out of touch with its people led to the ousting of Czar Nicholas II in March 1917. The Kerensky-led government now had the reins of power, but its fatal flaw was that it did not end the war. The Lenin-inspired October Revolution, which seized power from Kerensky, knew it had to bring war with Germany to an immediate end. As well as seizing all property and land in the name of 'socialisation', it unilaterally appealed for peace and agreed to a three-month armistice. Although forced to cede huge tracts of land to Germany at the signing of the Brest-Litovsk treaty, Lenin's regime was now able to consolidate its power. Gone were the burdens of fighting a 'capitalists' war'; Lenin was now free to turn Russia into a socialist state.

Germany finally got what it had wished for all along. Since 1914, it had wanted the chance to fight a war on just one front. But the Germans knew time was not on their side. They could not dream of matching the industrial might of the United States or beat the sheer numbers of fresh young men it could bring to the battlefield. But if it could strike a knockout blow against Britain and France on the Western Front before hundreds of thousands of American troops arrived, then the Kaiser would be able to dictate peace terms to the Allies.

War with Russia did not officially end until the Brest-Litovsk treaty was signed on 3 March 1918. However, Russia had effectively been out of the war since the declaration of the armistice after the October Revolution – its soldiers had already decided not to fight, with thou-sands of them returning home. Germany immediately started sending thousands of soldiers to the west. In December 1917, after it took up its position on the front line, the 19th Division experienced the German build-up for itself. Wyrall writes, 'A German stretcher-bearer wandered into the divisional lines and was captured. He belonged to a division lately transferred from the Russian Front.'[21]

By the middle of March 1918, after most of the German troops had moved west, the German Army now had 192 divisions in the field – the Allies, only 156. The German High Command and its army were now ready to launch a massive offensive on the Western Front. They hoped the *Kaiserschlacht* (Kaiser's Battle) would turn out to be the decisive moment of the war and see them victorious. They were right on one count.

*** ★★★

For David and all Allied soldiers on the Western Front, they knew exactly what was coming. All they could do was build the best defences they could and speculate about a date and what sector the Germans were going to hit first. Politicians, generals, and soldiers alike all knew that sometime in the early months of 1918 a 'Grey Avalanche'[22] would fall upon them. During the winter months of January, February and the first two weeks in March, all was quiet. Enemy shelling continued, but it was not particularly heavy or sustained. The 19th Division, now one of the five divisions of V Corps, spent the months strengthening existing defences and building new ones.

British defensive positions on the Western Front were constructed, with the major consideration being depth with which to absorb and fend off the German Army when it attacked. Three zones – Forward, Battle and Rear – were lines of defensive positions with intermediate lines in between each of those, all of which were connected by support trenches. The V Corps area of operations had three divisions in the 'Forward' and 'Battle' line trenches, and two divisions in the 'Rear' and 'Battle' trenches. The 19th was the Rear right division.

At divisional headquarters in Neuville-Bourjonval, David felt the heightened tension. There were several false alarms emanating from reports by other divisions, of Germans massing in trenches and large columns of troops and artillery being moved from one area to

A year before graduating from Keble College. Whilst in Oxford, he also served as a private soldier with 1st (Oxford University) Volunteer Battalion. *(Railton Family Archives)*

Gordon Road, Margate, 1907. The Railtons moved into No. 42 (two doors to the right) around 1888. During the war David's mother and sister lived in Broadstairs, moving back to Margate in 1920. She sold the house and moved to Hastings in 1925. *(By kind permission of Anthony Lee)*

The Ashford Mission, 1910. Canon Peter Francis Tindall (centre) would have a huge influence on David Railton (far left). David followed Canon Tindall when he moved to Folkestone at the outbreak of war in 1914. *(Railton Family Archives)*

Portrait of the newly ordained curate in Liverpool, 1910. *(Railton Family Archives)*

Top left: Chaplain to the Forces, Folkestone, January 1916. Just 72 hours after being commissioned in London, David joined his new battalion in Southampton. But he still had time for the obligatory portrait before leaving for France. *(Railton Family Archives)*

Top right: A competent rider, David travelled on horseback to the front line whenever a horse was available. But their important role with ambulances and pulling artillery pieces meant they were taken away from most padres early in the war. *(Railton Family Archives)*

Left: Lieutenant-Colonel A. P. Hamilton (Queen's), Commanding Officer, 1/19th (County of London) Battalion, London Regiment (St Pancras). Killed in action at High Wood on 15 September 1916. *(Railton Family Archives)*

Above left: Chaplain to the Forces Class 4 (Captain) Revd David Railton. Photograph taken before November 1916, when he was awarded the Military Cross. *(Railton Family Archives)*

Above right: A destroyed German bunker on the banks of the River Scarpe, used by David and some of his padres as a billet during the final advance to victory in 1918. *(Railton Family Archives)*

Right: The wooden candle holders used by David Railton during the war. Whether it was a regimental church parade or communion inside a trench dugout for just a few men, they were always used. *(By kind permission of David Blake, the Army Museum of Chaplaincy)*

CHRISTMAS GREETINGS
FROM THE 19th DIVISION :·: :·:

Christmas card sent by David to his family – December 1918. Inside he wrote, 'My Dear Family, This is to wish you all a joyful Christmas and a bright New Year. Our divisional call sign is a butterfly, as we are always chasing the Hun. What victory is, peace will be, and brighter progress for mankind. God bless you and keep you the brave merry little people that you are. Your Daddie'. *(Railton Family Archives)*

The vicarage, St Peters Road, Margate. The Railton family moved into the house in November 1920. The building was badly damaged by German bombs in the Second World War and although rebuilt, it looks nothing like it did in the 1920s. *(By kind permission of Anthony Lee)*

St John the Baptist Church, Margate, in the 1920s. *(By kind permission of Anthony Lee)*

The drumhead and replacement flag. Meant to be a farewell gift for Lt-Col Hamilton, the drumhead, signed by all of 19th Londons' officers and NCOs, is a poignant reminder of the cost of the battalion's attack on High Wood. *(Author's collection)*

Above: Drums of the 19th Londons – many of these men would find themselves in the trenches of High Wood trying to help consolidate the positions taken on 15 September at such a high cost. *(Railton Family Archives)*

Left: David Railton, his mother and wife at Buckingham Palace on the morning of 11 November 1920. They arrived in the fog-covered capital that morning at Victoria Station. *(Railton Family Archives)*

The funeral procession of the Unknown Warrior before arriving at the Cenotaph. The bearers, from the 3rd Battalion, Coldstream Guards are behind, while the distinguished pallbearers flank the gun-carriage. Field Marshal Douglas Haig is marching next to the right wheel. (© *Imperial War Museums Q 47639*)

King George V placed a wreath of red roses and bay leaves upon the coffin after it arrived at the Cenotaph. (© *Imperial War Museums Q 47637*)

Waiting for the chimes of Big Ben. At the eleventh hour, of the eleventh day, of the eleventh month, the King unveils the Cenotaph. *(© Imperial War Museums Q 14965)*

Held aloft by the bearers, the Unknown Warrior enters Westminster Abbey's North door. *(© Imperial War Museums Q 47636)*

Because of the sheer number of people wanting to pay their respects, the grave of the Unknown Warrior was not sealed until 18 November 1920. A slab of York stone was placed over it, and David's flag was laid at the foot of the grave for the next 12 months. *(Image by Wildt and Kray, London)*

The vicar of Bradford, 1927–31. *(Railton Family Archives)*

Above: Blessing Margate's new lifeboat – September 1925. One of David's last acts as vicar of Margate was to bless the town's new lifeboat. The *Lord Southborough* would take part in the 1940 evacuation of the British Expeditionary Force from Dunkirk. *(Railton Family Archives)*

Revd Geoffrey Studdert Kennedy (Woodbine Willie). *(Railton Family Archives)*

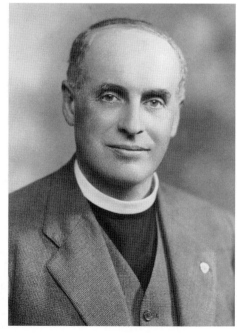

The vicar of Shalford, 1931–35. *(Railton Family Archives)*

Above: David in the 'Children's Corner' the morning after German bombers had destroyed large parts of St Nick's. *(Railton Family Archives)*

Below: Despite David's bravery in rushing into the burning church to save some artefacts, St Nick's was so badly damaged that it would not reopen until October 1952. *(Railton Family Archives)*

Above left: Notes written on the back of the photo: 'RMR & DR – 1945. In the lovely garden of Ard Rhu. Look at the lovely gardening attire. Trews – bags indeed.' *(Railton Family Archives)*

Above right: Revd David Railton in his vestments – 1950. David remained very active, although officially retired in 1945. *(Railton Family Archives)*

Right: Taken shortly before David's accident in 1955, both he and Ruby seemed to have an idyllic life at Ard Rhu. *(Railton Family Archives)*

The Padre's Flag was dedicated and hung above the grave of the Unknown Warrior on Armistice Day 1921. It remained there until 1953, when it was moved to St George's Chapel prior to the Coronation of Queen Elizabeth II. *(Photo by Walter Scott)*

another. Writing the war history of the 19th Division, Everard Wyrall summarises how most men on the Western Front felt while they sat and waited for the inevitable hammer blow to fall: 'No words can give an accurate picture of the tense feeling existing in the Fifth and Third Armies between the 1st and 21st March 1918. The Great German Offensive was expected – but when? The question held everyone, from GOC to private, in a constant state of anxious suspense.'[23]

The attack came on the morning of 21 March 1918. The German plan was simple. They would break through the British lines on the Somme, splitting the French and British armies apart. Haig would be forced back to the Channel ports and the French towards Paris. By taking on the British first, Ludendorff figured that the French Army would fold once a decisive blow had been dealt against their allies. But the clock was ticking, and the Germans needed a quick knockout blow before American divisions arrived.

The 19th Division was not contacted by the enemy until 22 March. Then, for four straight days until it was relieved by the 2nd Anzac Division on the evening of 26 March, the 19th Division fought a brave rearguard action against overwhelming enemy numbers. During this time, David was ready to move at a moment's notice. Where he had situated the padres under his command is not known, but the speed at which the advance happened probably meant they would not have been any further forward than the division's ADS and probably much further back at the MDS. His views on padres becoming casualties themselves was clear, so he probably had them all well to the rear, out of harm's way while the German advance continued.

Divisional HQ was moved almost daily: from Neuville-Bourjonval to Bancourt on 22 March; to Grévillers on 24 March; to Achiet-le-Petit on 25 March; and to Souastre on 26 March. But because there were no buildings left standing there, they soon moved to Pommier. Today, each of these villages has a cemetery now maintained by the Commonwealth War Graves Commission, in which lay soldiers who were killed and hastily buried by David's padres while the 19th Division kept fighting back the German onslaught. The division was relieved sometime late on 26 March, with divisional headquarters moving to La Cauchie. Although casualties were extremely high, the division had performed gallantly. Between 22 and 26 March 1918, the 19th division lost a total of 154 officers and 3,719 other ranks.[24] The divisional history continues: 'If ever a divisional commander had reason to be proud of his men, General Jeffreys must have felt pride in having under him officers and men who so willingly and gallantly responded to every call made upon them.'[25]

On 29 April, the 19th Division was moved north to familiar territory. A day later it took over a 6,000-yard sector of the line at the Messines Ridge. If the depleted troops under General Jeffreys' command thought themselves lucky to be away from the Somme and they would be left alone at Messines, then they were in for a surprise.

During the attacks on the Somme, codenamed Operation *Michael*, the Germans had made large gains, overrunning many divisions in the process. But they had not broken through and were held in check by the sacrifice of divisions such as the 19th. Although the British endured about 75,000 casualties, the German offensive was now running into trouble. German losses started to mount; their artillery could not keep up with the pace of its infantry, and its communication lines and supply routes were getting stretched longer and longer.

The pace of Operation *Michael* slowed down so much that for the German High Command it looked like it was coming to an unsatisfactory end. Ludendorff needed to break through. So he struck again on 28 March by launching Operation *Mars,* an attack either side of the River Scarpe. Once again German infantry fell upon British defences, but this time they only made small gains. Troops in well-prepared British defensive lines beat back the enemy. Seeing that Operation *Mars* was a failure, Ludendorff attacked for a third time at Amiens, but this too failed.

While the 19th Division quickly tried to improve its trenches at Messines, Ludendorff prepared for what was becoming an act of desperation. Despite having gained large tracts of land, his army was in need of a rest. But he knew he had to attack again – Germany's future depended upon them being able to win a quick and decisive victory. Ludendorff now decided to attack in Flanders along the length of the Messines Ridge. The battered remnants of the 19th Division would again feel the full force of the German Army in the form of

Operation *Georgette*. The aim was the same – to knock the British out of the war. They would attempt to bludgeon their way through British defences on a line from Ypres to Armentières, then turn north to encircle and cut off the troops on the Ypres Salient.

At 5:00 A.M. on the morning of 10 April, David and the rest of the men at 19th Division Headquarters at Westhof Farm, just south-west of Neuve-Église, awoke to the sound of a massive artillery bombardment along the entire length of the Messines Ridge. David quickly got word to all his padres to fall back to the various dressing stations. The thick mist that hung above the ground that morning created perfect conditions for a German attack, which commenced at 6:00 A.M. Outnumbered five or six to one, the infantry battalions stood and fought the best they could. According to the divisional history, 'The 57th Brigade were completely overrun. Practically none of the garrison were seen again. In one instance the enemy was observed all around a British post, killing off the garrison.'[26]

All along the Messines Ridge, the German infantry swarmed forward – the situation was desperate. From platoon, company, and battalion, up to Corps, Army, and GHQ, everyone knew that this was the make or break moment that might decide the war. That evening Field Marshal Haig wrote what became known as 'The Backs to the Wall' order. The next morning it was hastily printed and sent to all troops of the British Expeditionary Force:

> Three weeks ago today the enemy began his terrific attacks against us on a fifty-mile front. His objects are to separate us from the French, to take the Channel Ports and destroy the British Army. In spite of throwing already 106 Divisions into the battle and enduring the most reckless sacrifice of human life, he has as yet made little progress towards his goals. We owe this to the determined fighting and self-sacrifice of our troops. Words fail me to express the admiration which I feel for the splendid resistance offered by all ranks of our Army under the most trying circumstances. Many amongst us now are tired. To those I would say that Victory will belong to the side which holds out the longest. The French Army is moving rapidly and in great force to our support. There is no other course open to us but to fight it out. Every position must be held to the last man: there must be no retirement. With our backs to the wall and believing in the justice of our cause each one of us must fight on to the end. The safety of our homes and the Freedom of mankind alike depend upon the conduct of each one of us at this critical moment.[27]

Some might say that this was just theatrics from Field Marshal Haig. But this really was the most decisive moment of the war; its outcome still hung in the balance, and Haig knew it.

Over the course of the next three weeks at Messines Ridge, Bailleul, and Mont Kemmel, the 19th Division and the rest of the British Army fought desperately to stop the German Army from breaking through their lines. At Mont Kemmel, David witnessed the destruction of the hill where he had spent the last night of Private Blakemore's life before his execution. The ground was churned up by millions of rounds of artillery, its trees ripped apart or laid flat. The division was finally withdrawn 11–12 May, as the offensive in Flanders came to an end.

On 30 April, Field Marshal Haig sent a 'wire' to the headquarters of 19th Division:

> I wish to thank General Jeffreys and all officers and men under his command for the very gallant service rendered by them both on the battle front south of Arras and in the recent fighting south of Ypres. The great effort which the enemy is making to break down the resistance of the British Army will undoubtedly fail if all ranks of our Army continue to show the same resolve and determined courage which has characterised the action of the 19th Division.[28]

David's men of the 19th Division had fought gallantly but had sacrificed terribly, with another 3,774 casualties on top of the 3,873 they had lost on the Somme. If ever a division deserved to be rewarded by being sent south to the Champagne region to a 'Quiet Sector', then it was the 19th Division.

★★★

At about 4:00 P.M. on 27 May 1918, David sat at a table outside his makeshift office and billet with a beautiful view of the River Marne. He was enjoying afternoon tea in the spring sunshine. He had not got over the disappointment of losing his flag but he was starting to enjoy this delightful part of France. Suddenly, he heard the sound of running feet on the cobblestones. He turned around to see that it was one of the division's staff officers.

'Padre, we just got word that the Germans have attacked on the Aisne,' he said, breathing heavily.

'Attacked?' David replied, stunned and not really knowing what else he could say.

'Yes,' the staff officer repeated, 'about 30 miles from here. They've launched a very heavy attack on a wide front between Reims and Soissons, and they've penetrated the IX Corps line to a considerable depth. The GOC has ordered all dismounted personnel to be ready to move within the hour. We're going to set up headquarters at Chaumuzy.'[29]

David sat there with his mouth agape; he had nothing to say.

'Sorry to be the bearer of bad news, Padre.' The staff officer hurried off back in the direction from which he had come.

CHAPTER 9

Back to Blighty

'Only the dead have seen the end of war.'

PLATO

Monday, 13 January 1919, Folkestone, England

David looked out the window of his study. Sleet mixed with heavy rain splattered noisily upon the window panes in the gale force winds. He had only just arrived back in Folkestone after a rough crossing from France. The cold, wet start to the new year was unpleasant but expected for that time of year. At least he was home, far away from the mud and the cold and the death of the trenches. What he had been through made him appreciate being home more than ever. But back in Folkestone he felt the same as he had those first few days after the guns fell silent on Armistice Day, just two months earlier. There was now a huge void where before every part of his being was focused on winning the war, making sure he did all he could for the fighting men. He was happy for it to be over, but he knew nothing would ever be the same again.

His release from duty as Senior Chaplain of the slowly disbanding 19th Division occurred almost to the day that he had been enlisted for service three years earlier. His contract termination date of 10 January 1919[1] was deemed the right time for him to head home, even though there was still work to do. He felt torn leaving many thousands of men still in France. But he was being discharged, so there was nothing he could do. He would return to his parish in Folkestone as an 'Honorary Chaplain Third Class'.[2]

After the Armistice was signed and the cessation in hostilities started at 11:00 A.M. on Monday, 11 November 1918, the 19th Division remained in place for a few days until it was moved to the Candas-Canaples-Naours area 15 miles north of Amiens, where it remained whilst de-mobilisation took place. Like every soldier who had served on the Western Front, David was relieved and happy that the war was finally over. But during those first few days and weeks, everyone struggled to cope with this sudden change in their lives. The victory they had all strived so hard to obtain, and sacrificed so much for, had been won. But millions of men, scarred and traumatised, both physically and mentally, were left asking, *What now?*

Since the German advance was halted on the Marne, everyone knew that Germany was a spent force and it was just a matter of time before the fighting stopped. After the best part of three years at war, David did not appear to have lost his respect for the men who fought and had defeated the hated Boche. He had the deepest respect for men such as Field Marshal Haig who had led the Army to victory. But even for David, the losses had taken their toll, and in the aftermath of it all, his tolerance of some who would put their own self-interest over the interests of the men was at an all-time low.

Two days after the Armistice, David held a 'Thanksgiving Service' in the town of Maresches, where the 56th Brigade was now billeted. Handwriting on a copy of routine orders next to the announcement of the service that he kept reveals what appear to be subtle barbs aimed at some of the staff officers of the brigade: 'HQ 56th Brigade attended fully. They had shelled the Huns out of Maresches a few days earlier. Now they required the best remaining house for their mess!'[3]

This comment could be considered from several viewpoints. On its own, it really does not reveal anything. But when we read accounts written by others describing the same people, and we fully understand David Railton's values, then you may interpret his meaning differently.

David was still looking out of the window, thinking of those final months in 1918, before the Armistice, when there was a knock at the study door.

'Come in,' said David.

'Lunch will be ready in about five minutes, Mr Railton,' the housekeeper said, in her thick north-east accent.

'Thank you, Mrs Murdoch. I'll be through shortly.' He smiled at the thought of home-cooked food.

Three meals a day; he would soon put the weight back on that he had lost over the past three years.

★★★

After the shock of being told that for a third time in as many months, the 19th Division was going to have to face another massed German assault, the men started to deploy further forward in the IX Corps area of responsibility. One can only wonder as to their state of mind. Fear was probably the overriding emotion – fear of the unknown for new recruits who had recently joined the division, and fear of what *was* known for men who had survived March and April. But what they were to face dulled in comparison to what was already being inflicted upon the four divisions that were in the front line when the German attack, code-named Operation *Blucher*, was launched. Intelligence had been gleaned by both French and British troops that an attack was imminent. The news came just hours before the attack started at midnight, 26–27 May. It shattered morale. Captain Sidney Rogerson was with his men of the 8th Division when he heard of the attack,

> For a second we looked at each other in silence. In a flash the whole world had changed. The landscape around us smiled no longer. It was all a grinning reality, a mockery designed to raise our hopes so that they could be shattered the more pitilessly. The sun still blazed down but it had lost its heat.[4]

That evening British artillery fired at possible assembly points in a vain attempt to disrupt or possibly deter German intentions, but the lack of any response by the enemy proved that intentions were set.

The initial German bombardment was devastating – General Hamilton-Gordon's worst fears had come true. The troops massed in the forward trenches (on French orders) were bombarded so heavily that when the German infantry attacked, they did so almost unopposed, taking large tracts of territory very quickly. The 8th and 50th divisions were nearly wiped out. What was left of the 21st Division was pulled back over the River Aisne where they joined the 25th Division in reserve. They would then try to hold a line further back. Rogerson writes, 'As regards the 8th, it is doubtful if the total strength of all ranks who succeeded in getting back across the river was more than a few hundred.'[5]

By the morning of 29 May, only the 57th and 58th brigades of the 19th Division had arrived. The 56th had been delayed, but they would arrive with the machine-gun battalion within two to three hours. Both available brigades were then ordered forward to establish a line between Faverolles and Lhéry. In front of them, the remnants of the other four IX Corps divisions were doing everything they could to slow down the German advance.

David arrived in Chaumuzy on the morning of 29 May.[6] By then, word of the German attack had spread. In small towns and villages throughout the Champagne region, panic had taken hold. Captain Sidney Rogerson of the 8th Division would experience Chaumuzy the next day, after survivors of his division were ordered to withdraw back to the River Marne. He painted a vivid picture of what David and the 19th Division HQ staff in Chaumuzy faced:

> It was an ugly scene that met me. Chaos was king. The narrow, cobbled streets were blocked from end to end with transport and guns; with farm carts piled high with chairs, mattresses, fodder, fowls in crates, and all the pathetic impedimenta of the peasant refugee; and with drunken French infantry. They had apparently looted the wine shops and a big canteen and, demoralised as they were drunken, were in a state bordering on hysteria. All semblance of discipline had gone.[7]

The evening of 29–30 May, before Rogerson and his men passed through Chaumuzy, several changes were made regarding command and control of some British units. The 56th Brigade had finally arrived at the village of Sarcy and was placed under temporary command of the 8th Division. They were immediately tasked with relieving what was left of the 8th Division's 23rd Brigade.

On the morning of 30 May, Sidney Rogerson arrived under new orders at HQ 56th Brigade:

> The brigadier and two of his staff had just come down to breakfast and, after our experiences of the past three days, it was a surprise to see a table laid out with tea and bread and marmalade. I had not broken my fast, but the officers appeared so concerned that their usual eggs and bacon were not forthcoming that they omitted to offer me any refreshment. Nor was their attitude particularly

congenial, although I realise that against their neat uniforms and polished belts and buttons I must have looked dirty, ragged, and unsoldierly and no agreeable decoration for a breakfast-room. At the time I was furious; furious because I was hungry; furious because they should presume to have a breakfast room; and furious to think that those who were to take over our responsibilities should be so out of touch with reality as to complain because a hot meal was not punctual. I was as polite as discipline demanded, and no more.[8]

The GOC 56th Brigade was Brigadier-General Ronald Macclesfield Heath. He was newly promoted having previously commanded 10th Battalion, The Royal Warwicks. The 19th Division war history describes him as a 'thoroughly sound and most popular officer' but also goes on to describe an odd idiosyncrasy of his: 'When advancing to the attack with the battalion he had a deck chair carried behind him by an orderly, whilst a long cigar was seldom absent from his mouth.'[9] Reading these and Captain Rogerson's comments might bring some clarity to David's note about the 56th Brigade staff officers' 'Mess House' and put his comments in context.

Later that afternoon, 56th Brigade would have a dose of reality when the German attack continued with added impetus through to the next morning. Although the division was holding most of the line despite heavy fighting, it was under pressure in some places where the enemy broke through. On the right of the 57th Brigade, French troops had withdrawn (without telling the two British battalions there). This created a gap between the 9th Royal Welch Fusiliers and the 9th Welch. The 9th Welch was completely surrounded – the entire battalion was either killed or captured.[10]

French troops were still proving to be very unreliable. Rogerson's eyewitness account of the drunken, looting soldiers in Chaumuzy seems not to be an isolated case. It can be added to an incident he writes about earlier in the offensive when he found French soldiers unwilling to fight, preferring to be 'comfortably ensconced in a cellar, very much at their ease'.[11] And it was not only French soldiers who were causing problems. As British soldiers were withdrawing, there were reports of some local inhabitants spitting at them. The locals refused to leave, saying they had been through the occupations of 1914, and some could even remember Bismarck's invasion of 1870. "'The Germans were better than the British!" they declared, and rushing to the road side, they spat at us in their rage.'[12]

This moment marked a real low point in the *Entente Cordiale*. Signed in 1904, the agreement brought an end to nearly a thousand years of intermittent conflict between the two countries. But since the disaster of the Nivelle offensive and the mutiny that followed, French commanders had struggled to rebuild its army into a viable fighting force. And although many French units were to fight bravely, amongst British troops in the Champagne region, there was not a lot of goodwill towards their Gallic ally. Rogerson adds, 'The observations of our men were equally bitter. At this point the conviction among rank and file that "we were fighting on the wrong side", a conviction I had heard expressed many times since 1917, but never before with such feeling.'[13]

On the evening of 30 May, General Jeffreys took over complete control of the British portion of the line from IX Corps. The remnants of its four divisions were withdrawn, and the 19th Division came under the command of General Pellé and the French V Corps.[14] Over the next few days, the 19th Division and its French allies tried to stop the seemingly relentless German advance. General Jeffreys ordered several successful counter-attacks that slowed down the enemy and, in another action, prevented a German advance up the valley of the River Ardre, stopping them from enveloping Reims in the process.[15]

By 3 June, the German advance brought them to within 56 miles of Paris. But with its forward troops now outstretching its supply columns, and with French reinforcements arriving on the Marne, Ludendorff brought the offensive to a halt. There was an attack launched on 6 June to take the strategically important Montagne de Bligny, a feature that overlooked the River Marne, but it was limited to just that area. The 56th Brigade was ordered to launch an immediate counter-attack, which it did, and on a second attempt, the enemy was forced from the high ground.[16] Later that night the division was relieved, and although it was subjected to shelling that included gas shells over the next few days, the division saw no further action in the Champagne region. On 19 June, the division was moved further south to rest and refit before being moved by train north back to the British zone on 1 July. The division was then held in the Fauquembergues area, about 30 miles west of Étaples on the Channel coast. On 11 July, the division was transferred to XIII Corps and moved to the Bomy–Auchel area, where it spent the rest of the month.[17]

While the 19th Division was out of the line training and rebuilding its shattered battalions, the German offensive had finally ground to a halt. Although the Germans again attacked at the River Matz on 9 June, and then threw 52 divisions at the French on 15 July in one last desperate attempt to take Paris, Ludendorff could not replace the men or equipment that had been lost. The great German spring offensive of 1918 was over. In pugilistic terms, Germany had punched itself to a standstill.

The French had detected Ludendorff's final attack. Learning from past mistakes, they cleared the front-line trenches before the obligatory artillery bombardment prior to an assault, which allowed them to soak up the initial attack. Just three days later on 18 July, they launched a massive counter-attack in the Champagne region. By the time the 19th Division was again manning a section of the front line at Hinges on 7 August, German forces were pushed back over the River Aisne, losing all the territory gained during Operation *Blucher*. The next day – 8 August 1918 – was described by General Ludendorff as 'the black day of the German Army'. British and French forces attacked at Amiens in a battle that broke and completely demoralised the German Army. It marked the beginning of the end of the war.

★★★

Since losing his flag on the train journey south to the Champagne region, David used the replacement flag sent to him by his mother-in-law. Only a handful of people knew what had happened to the original flag. He was saddened by its loss – it had been through so much and covered the bodies of so many fallen comrades. But he resigned himself to the fact that the pack, the sack of letters, and his flag were lost forever. Some weeks later, he received a note from a Cavalry APM (Assistant Provost Marshal).

Writing in the voice of the Flag, David describes what happened when he received the message:

> A pack has been found with the padre's name on it, and a sack with some letters; did he want these? The padre nearly upset the table in the mess and sent off a wire followed by a letter of gratitude. How I ever got into the hands of an APM of a Cavalry Division I do not know, but thanks are due, for I was soon in my old home and the padre and many others welcomed me as if I was the one Bairn in the family that mattered.[18]

Many months before the flag was lost, David had an idea of what he was going to do with the flag after the war was over. On several occasions after church services while soldiers folded the flag for him, David said, 'When this terrible business is over, I am going to offer the flag to a cathedral in London.'[19] After he lost the flag, he must have thought his plan was over. He could have used the replacement, but it had not seen the service the original had. When it was returned, he was determined to ensure that it would not go missing again, so that after the war had ended he would be able to fulfil the promise he had made to those soldiers:

> The padre decided that I was to go back to Blighty and that my place would be taken by my brother flag who had done duty when I was missing after the journey on the troop train. He was determined that no misfortune should result in the loss of the flag that had done real duty in modern warfare.[20]

The first time that David was granted leave after he had recovered the flag, he carefully placed it in his pack and took it home with him:

> When the padre's next leave came I found myself aboard a ship… When we got to Folkestone a kind porter offered to take the pack with a valise that the Padre had with him. But the padre said, 'No, thanks old lad, I wouldn't let that pack out of my sight for a thousand pounds,' where upon the porter laughed and wanted to know if he had French paper money or rations in it. The valise was sent up and the padre slung the pack on his back and walked up the slope that goes up to the Lees. For a good while I had a rest in some cupboard in the Padre's house. I felt most lazy and wondered whenever he was coming back again from France. But his wife kept on cheering me up saying that my day of usefulness was not yet done, but that I must wait my chance in patience.[21]

As soon as the 19th Division took over its section of the line in the Lys Salient, east of Locon, they received orders to make sure that those in the front-line trenches continually harassed the enemy, every chance they got.[22] Allied commanders knew the Germans were on the ropes, and they did not want to give them any chance to recover and regroup. Although the division would not officially fight a battle until the Battle of the Selle in October, from August 7 they were involved continuously with patrolling its sector of the front and several large attacks as the Germans withdrew back towards the Belgian frontier.

★★★

During this time, David continued serving as Senior Chaplain. He worked hard to help and guide the padres under his control as the division advanced. By this time, it seems that he had a hard-working and effective team providing spiritual help to the fighting men of the division as they advanced towards victory. However, David was also not afraid to discipline or even recommend that a padre be sent home if he was not up to the task. In September 1917, he wrote one such report to the Chaplain-General. But even when recommending that a padre should be removed from his division, because his colonel had described him as unreliable and lazy, David still emphasised the good: 'The Colonel is very anxious to have a chaplain but he says that Mr "Smith" is not the right man... I have tried to report as fairly as possible ... he has been friendly and loyal to me in every way.'[23]

One of his padres who at first appeared to struggle but later became an asset to the division and the battalion he was assigned to was the Revd J. J. Wallace. It was Wallace's battalion, 8th Bn N. Staffs, that David had worked with when Private Blakemore was executed. After his attendance at the 'Padre's School', Wallace appears to have returned to his battalion and worked with them throughout 1917 and 1918, and he was with them in 1918 when it looked like victory was finally at hand.

Amongst the items collected by David that have been kept by his family for almost a century is the partial remains of a copy of a 'Certificate of Marriage':

> Registration District – BEF, Marriage solemnised at Hinges, Nord-pas-de-Calais. Date – 20th September 1918.
> John James Wallace, 38, widower, Clerk in Holy Orders, Eltham Park, London.
> Mary Jane Dubois, 50, Twice widow, No fixed abode.

The service was conducted by David in the 'Parish Church', 'according to the Rites and Ceremonies of the Church of England', and it was witnessed by H. Reeves and T. Harris.[24] From this marriage certificate we can speculate that Wallace met a French woman (considerably older than him) who had no home and had been twice widowed (presumably by the war) and assume that his intention was to take care of her in England after the war. Nothing else is known.

For David to have consented to marry them, the situation and circumstances must have been exceptional. David had very strong views about wartime marriages, and he expressed these in letters to his wife. Earlier, in October 1916, he made the decision that he would not marry anyone, especially front-line soldiers:

> Up until recently I encouraged and urged marriage during the war; never, never, never again. No, I would rather make a man, if I could, break off his engagement and never write again, than that he be married till this war is over. Even if a man has been engaged for years, let them wait or break it off. On no account marry. It is more than cruel to the wives and children, it is an agony to the men, and often they have told me so. Half the men do not fear death or wounds. I don't fear death as death, but I dread even a wound for the anxiety that it may give to you... I promised to marry several of our officers, if they liked during the war. Now I shall refuse to do it, and I hope every Vicar they meet will do his best to prevent it... At the end of the war, if he lives, they will receive their reward in the joy-life of marriage.[25]

A few months later, writing from the Ypres Salient during the deep winter freeze of February 1917, David reiterated his stance:

> The lot of the married man – is indescribably worse than that of a single man if he is out there. That is why I will marry no front-line man during this war – with a glad heart. The other night I went round the Line with a young officer who had recently married. Nothing used to affect him... Now, he is a two-in-one soul with all his love and thoughts around a little wife. So he has changed in the two months.[26]

★★★

On 1 and 2 October, the 19th Division was relieved and started to move south to the Cambrai area. By 5 October, the division was centred on the town of Hénu where 19th Division HQ was situated.[27] Now a part of XVII Corps when the final phase of the British advance started on

8 October, the 19th Division was initially in corps reserve. Everyone knew that the end of the war was close – there had been rumours that German allies, Turkey and Bulgaria, were negotiating an armistice, and with the current rate of the German withdrawal, most of the territory taken by the Germans since 1914 had been won back.

As they advanced into parts of France and Belgium that had been under German occupation for over four years, hatred of the 'Boche' intensified. Stories were told describing the way German soldiers had conducted themselves – torture, rape, and summary executions were all said to be commonplace. Some of the stories were undoubtedly exaggerated by the Allies for propaganda purposes, but evidence of the wanton destruction of property during the withdrawal to the Hindenburg Line in 1917 was everywhere. There was no doubt that the civilian population had to live and endure terrible conditions whilst under German occupation. Amongst the documents David brought back after the war is a thin paper leaflet that was widely distributed to the population under German occupation. 'Verboten' is written in bold letters across the top. Translated, it reveals the realities of what most French and Belgian civilians had endured under German occupation: 'It is forbidden to … purchase milk, cream, butter, eggs, livestock, poultry, and wine … and the removal of hay/straw or fruits and plants from community reserves … without the approval of the sector commander.'[28] At the bottom of the leaflet there was a threat that disobedience would be punished accordingly.

The 19th Division took part in the Battle of the Selle (19–25 October) and the Battle of the Sambre (4–10 November); then the division finished its fighting days just five to six miles south of Mons, where four years earlier, in August 1914, it had all begun for the British Army. Right up until the eleventh hour of the eleventh day of the eleventh month, the fighting continued. Even after an armistice had been agreed, and the clock moved slowly towards the agreed hour of the ceasefire, soldiers continued to die.

For David, the war would end not far from Malplaquet, the site of the famous battlefield where the Duke of Marlborough won a decisive bloody battle in the War of Spanish Succession in 1709. The irony that Marlborough was fighting alongside Prussians against the French and

Spanish would not have been lost on him. The tragedy of war had scarred these lands before, and he must have hoped that H. G. Wells was right when he wrote that this was 'The War That Will End War'.[29] Whether Wells was right or not, only time would tell. But for David Railton, this war, in which he had seen so much tragedy, was not yet done.

On 5 November 1918, the 8th Bn N. Staffs advanced on the outskirts of La Flamengrie while still taking heavy fire from German artillery and machine guns on high ground to the west.[30] The battalion's war diary lists their casualties as 'Captain & Adjutant EC Good, and the Rev. JJ Wallace and a few other ranks'.[31]

The exact circumstances surrounding Wallace being injured are not known, and there is no burial record for Captain Good, so he looks to have survived whatever happened. But three days later, on 8 November 1918, Revd J. J. Wallace died of his wounds and was buried just a few miles south of Cambrai. The Awoingt British Cemetery[32] was started in 1918, and the majority of the 653 British and Commonwealth soldiers buried there came from nearby casualty clearing stations. It is likely that Wallace went to a CCS near Cambrai after he had been through the divisional dressing stations.

As the CCS was some distance from the 19th Division's position on the Belgian border, it is unlikely David presided over Wallace's funeral. Amongst items he kept after the war is a double-sided memorial card from the Wallace Family on which, in the left-hand corner, he has written, 'Keep':

In Loving Memory of
JOHN JAMES WALLACE,
Priest,
Chaplain to the Forces,
Attached 8th North Stafford Regiment,
Died of wounds received while helping a wounded comrade,
November 8th 1918,
R.I.P.
'Greater love hath no man than this, that a man lay down his life for his friends.'

On the reverse side is printed: 'Mrs Wallace and family return sincere thanks for kind sympathy in their great sorrow.' And on the card there is also a handwritten note: 'Mrs Wallace is exceedingly grateful to Mr Railton for his very kind letter.'[33] No details have surfaced as to what happened to Wallace's bride, Mary Jane Dubois, now three-times widowed, whom he married less than two months before he died, just three days before the end of the war.

★★★

David looked up from his desk and rubbed his eyes. He was working on a sermon he was to deliver the next Sunday; however, he was finding it hard to concentrate. On a bookshelf across the room, folded and stacked neatly side by side, were the two Union Jacks he had used during the war. He could tell them apart, so there would be no problem ensuring the original was used when the time came. Even so, he wondered what the future would be for them. He had used those flags to help his men in France, and now he wanted to make sure that they didn't just sit there in his study collecting dust. He had used them to bury hundreds of his fellow countrymen – now he was determined they would be suitably used to commemorate the lives of those whom they had covered.

CHAPTER 10

Now or Never

'A noble man compares himself by an idea which is higher than himself.'
MARCUS AURELIUS

Wednesday, 10 November 1920, Margate, England

David was sat at his desk in the study of their new home. There were still a few things that needed to be put away. Several wooden tea chests cluttered up his study, full of books and papers that needed to be unpacked. But for now, he was resting, letting his supper digest. The rest of the house was busy. His wife was upstairs with the nanny putting the children to bed, and Mrs Murdock and the cook were tidying up, getting everything ready for an early start in the morning. The big day had finally arrived.

He loved their new home. It was everything he could have hoped for, and he was looking forward to living there with his family in the community where he had grown up. There was plenty of room; the house sat on the edge of town with open farmland opposite the driveway entrance. It was also close enough for him to walk to St John's.

Although there is still a building on the site where the vicarage stood during the time the Railton family resided there, it looks much different today. During the Second World War, the vicarage was hit by Luftwaffe bombs and mostly destroyed.[1] Although rebuilt after the war, it had nothing of the beauty of the original building. Today it is rental apartments – the manicured gardens and gravel driveway now swallowed up in Margate's urban expansion. The town was hit by German bombs from Zeppelin and Gotha bombers during the First World War as well. A total of 88 bombs were dropped between 1914 and 1918. On 13 September 1915, the vacant Railton family home on Gordon Road had a near miss when the house at 26 Gordon Road was hit. Miss Agnes Robbins was killed by splinters and shrapnel from the bomb.[2]

***

It was almost two years since the Armistice, and David had been back in England one year and 10 months. It had been hard for him to adjust; the three years he had spent in Belgium and France had taken their toll. At some stage during the last year of the war, David was caught in a gas attack that had affected his eyes.[3] Both the Allies and Germans had used mustard gas in the 1918 offensive, and although deadly in large enough amounts, most casualties suffered damage to their eyes and blisters to their skin. The 19th Division was bombarded with gas before the 21 March offensive began,[4] but because he was not evacuated, he probably did not get the worse of it. The support of his family and being immersed back into parish work helped him through these difficult days.

Now that the war was over, David was keen to move ahead with his idea. But these were difficult days for Great Britain, too. Because of constant industrial unrest at home and political struggles throughout the world, David felt that the time was not right. In an article for *Our Empire*, David writes, 'Do you recall that dreadful year of reaction? Men and nations stumbled back … the endless shedding of blood ceased, but there was no real peace in the souls of men or nations. The mind of the world was in a fever.'[5]

Back in England, he continued his habit of using the flag as a central part of his services. Many times when he was preaching the flag would be draped over the pulpit. And because of the publicity surrounding the announcement of his Military Cross and his natural skills as an orator, every time he was due to speak, people would line up outside the church long before the doors were opened.[6]

Despite this, David was restless – he knew that there was something he needed to do before he would feel like he was back home again and could throw himself into his work. The misery, suffering, and pain felt by millions of families whose sons, husbands, fathers and brothers had not returned home was still eating away at him. He hoped the idea, which he had been keeping to himself for so long, would bring some relief, a small crumb of comfort to those families whose loved ones had died.

How David came upon the idea is now well known because of the 1931 article 'The Origin of the Unknown Warrior's Grave', written for the magazine *Our Empire* and quoted many times. In it he lays out precisely how 'it came to him' in the garden of the billet at Erquinghem Lys near Armentières that he had shared with his friend, Revd Edward Duncan MC, in early 1916. He explained how the sight of the white cross of an 'Unknown British Soldier' inspired him to try to get the body of an unknown soldier brought back home to be buried in Westminster Abbey.[7]

In his unpublished work, *The Story of a Padre's Flag,* written in the early 1920s, David tells a slightly different version of how the idea came to him. It happened while he was thinking of ways of comforting families whose loved ones had died with no known grave:

> Sometimes on the way back the padre would think out what he should write in response to a particular letter. I do not know and I do not think he is sure himself as to the time when an idea came to him by which he thought all those longings and desires could be more fully satisfied. As a matter of fact, he was not thinking of any particular letter when the idea first came. He had been speaking at a Church Parade one day in praise of certain fallen comrades. When he was riding from that parade to another he was wondering how the 'unknown' as well as the known could be sufficiently honoured in the minds of Englishmen. The idea that came brought great joy to him. But war is war and there is no time for what some people call the luxury of idealism. Life is as cheap as a blade of grass and no Army, Navy or Government could carry out such an idea as came to him in the middle of the war. In truth he felt that most people would simply laugh at the notion of taking the mortal remains of an Unknown Soldier or Sailor back to Blighty to be enshrined in the heart of London.[8]

Although he says he 'nearly wrote to Sir Douglas Haig' during the war,[9] he kept his idea about the repatriation of a body of an unknown soldier to himself until he came back home. During 1919 and much of 1920, he still kept the idea private, telling only his wife and a friend. In the *Our Empire* article, he describes this friend as 'an artist in Folkestone'.[10] In *The Story of a Padre's Flag: Told by the Flag*, he calls this friend, 'Mr H. Evans'.[11] There are two possibilities as to the identity of this friend. The first is well-known photographer and artist Mr Frederick H. Evans, who specialised in church and cathedral photography and who retired in 1915. The second is Company Sergeant Major (CSM) H. Evans of the 17th Londons. He was the soldier who, on Armistice Day 1921, had the honour of climbing the ladder in Westminster Abbey to place the 'Padre's Flag' on a column close to the grave of the Unknown Warrior.

David's wife and friend agreed that he should wait a little longer, but Mr Evans encouraged him to 'decide soon which of the men in authority'[12] he would approach when the time came to write. He had considered the King, Field Marshal Haig and the Prime Minister. But for varying reasons, he decided against all of these. So David made his choice and waited for the right moment, during which time there were several changes that took place in his life.

In April 1920, he was made aware of the vacant position of vicar of Margate. The Revd Thomas Harrison had resigned a month earlier.[13] He discussed the opening with Canon Tindall who had already recommended him for the position. In June, he received word from Canterbury that he had been appointed vicar of Margate and his 'induction' would take place on 25 September 1920.[14] Also, on 1 August 1920, his wife gave birth to twins, Andrew Scott and Freda.

It was now 13 August 1920. Despite being busy with a newborn son and fourth daughter, and with the prospects of starting a new living as vicar in Margate, all in just over a month, David was still determined to see through his idea. He was not absolutely sure about the timing, but the 'noise of peace quarrels'[15] after the signing of the Treaty of Versailles seemed to be dying down. Still not convinced, he posed the same question to his wife that he had been asking himself for weeks: 'Was this a good time?' Reassuringly, his wife, still recovering from delivering twins said, 'Now or never!'[16]

That evening, sat at his desk in the family home at 16 Millfield, Folkestone, he finally wrote the letter he had been thinking about for almost four years:

> So I wrote to the Right Rev. Bishop Herbert Ryle, then Dean of Westminster. I had never written or spoken to the Dean. I asked him if he would consider the possibility of burying in the Abbey the body of one of our unknown comrades. I also made bold to suggest that a real 'war' flag in my possession be used at such a burial, rather than a new flag of no service experience.[17]

Three days later, on 16 August, the Dean of Westminster replied to David's letter from his holiday residence in Harrogate:

> I have read your letter of the 13th, which has reached me at the above address, with deep interest and sympathy. At a distance from the Abbey and in the middle of a needed holiday, I am perhaps not altogether in a position to give you a final decision on either of your two suggestions. But they make a strong appeal to me. On first consideration of them I find myself warmly inclined to favour them – would it be all the same to you if I defer decision until I have the opportunity both of seeing you and of consulting my chapter?
> 1. The fact that the flag was not a regimental flag might be against it being hung in some parts of the Abbey. But I should contemplate the possibility of hanging it in St Faiths Chapel.
> 2. The suggestion of commemorating the Unknown Dead, has indeed, been made in different quarters. But your suggestion strikes me as the best I have received. If I could obtain the War Office permission, I think I could carry out the rest of the proposal – the interment etc. And the idea occurs to me that it would be appropriate as a wonderful way of commemorating the Armistice. However, I must not move, or talk, too fast. The idea shall germinate. On my return at the beginning of September or beginning of October, I would see you if possible; discuss it with my chapter; approach the government; and try and find a vacant and suitable spot on the floor of the nave… These ideas of which you have spoken to me and to which I am now responding, had better not be talked about; or they may get prematurely into the newspapers and do harm instead of good.[18]

Although the Dean had set David's expectations as to when he might hear back from him, he was still anxious, believing that his idea had not been accepted by the authorities in London. Despite the positive tone of Dean Ryle's letter, 'he doubted very much as to whether the great scheme would ever be carried out'.[19] As time passed, these doubts must have increased. 'August went by and September. No further news! The first two weeks in October brought nothing.'[20] Even though David always thought of himself as an optimist, he admitted that even he 'began to despair of a favourable reply'.[21] As he waited, preparations for Armistice Day 1920 were already becoming public knowledge.

On 19 July 1919, a 'peace parade' took place in London. With the Treaty of Versailles now signed, the Prime Minister, David Lloyd George, convinced the Cabinet and His Majesty King George V to sanction a pageant and victory march. He thought that it would be a fitting end to the devastation that had deprived the nation of so many young men. He also decided that the parade needed a centrepiece or focal point. The architect Sir Edwin Lutyens was given the task to come up with a design and have it ready in just two weeks. Aptly named the Cenotaph, his striking design and wooden construction was so moving that when the thousands of soldiers marched past it on that damp London-summer's day, many did so with tears in their eyes. The word 'Cenotaph' was taken from two Greek words – *kenos*, meaning 'empty', and *taphos*, meaning 'tomb'. Lutyens' instructions were that it was to be non-denominational, with no Christian symbols that might offend other religious beliefs. This did not sit well with Anglican Church authorities; however, the public took it to their hearts and wanted the Cenotaph to become a permanent symbol of the sacrifice the country had made.

For the first anniversary of the Armistice, 11 November 1919, Buckingham Palace announced there would be a two-minute silence to commemorate the moment the Armistice had come into effect a year earlier. The palace statement, which was published in all the major newspapers on Friday, 7 November, explained how it would be observed: 'No elaborate organisation appears to be required. At a given signal, which can be easily arranged to suit the circumstances of the locality. I believe that we shall interrupt our business and pleasure, whatever it may be, and unite in this simple service of Silence and Remembrance.'[22]

To develop the protocol, both the King and the Prime Minister met to discuss the proposal of a universal observance of five minutes' silence. The Prime Minister was enthusiastic about the idea; however, the King was not. He immediately rejected the length of five minutes and even suggested that three minutes was probably too long for the British public to remain silent.[23] As David Lloyd-George would go on to do so well again in less than a year, he persuaded the King to change his mind. He finally acquiesced when the Prime Minister explained that large maroons would be fired above London and other major cities at the start and end of the silence.

The idea of a silence itself can be traced back three or four centuries, to the Quaker tradition of a shared silence designed to bring the community together. During the war, a brief moment of silence was observed each day in Cape Town to commemorate the dead. This practice was reported by a *Reuters* newspaper correspondent and became known throughout Commonwealth countries. But the idea for the silence to be observed on Armistice Day 1919 looks to have come from Australian journalist Edward Honey, who wrote to the *London Evening News* in 1919 suggesting the first anniversary of the end of the war 'should be greeted with a moment of silence'.[24]

For the rest of his life, David thought the 'Great Silence' that came into being on Armistice Day 1919, and was observed so universally by the nation that day, should forever be observed, along with a service and day of remembrance. In 1935, while he was the Rector of Liverpool, he wrote an article as a counter-argument to the growing calls to abandon the two-minute silence and service of remembrance on Armistice Day. In the opinion of some, all the observed silence did was to 'open old wounds', but David disagreed:

> If you remove the service of Remembrance Day you will add another wound. The true mourner can never forget… These wounded mourners deserve their brief hour of justifiable pride and consolation. There is for them this thought: I am not alone in my grief… If you who read this only knew the pain that is caused to a relative and comrade if, by chance, one name is omitted from a war memorial, or if the padre should fail to read it when the Roll of Honour is read aloud, you would know how sacred is the service for those who mourn.[25]

While David waited for news from the Dean of Westminster, he was preoccupied. In September 1920, they moved from their house in Folkestone. They said farewell to the parish and their friends and moved to Margate where he became vicar. As the vicarage was not ready to be occupied, they moved into temporary accommodation in Sussex Avenue.[26] It was there that a letter dated 19 October 1920 finally arrived from the Dean of Westminster:

> The idea which you suggested to me in August I have kept steadily in view ever since. I have been occupied actively upon it for the last 2 or 3 weeks. It necessitated communications with the War Office, Prime Minister, Cabinet and Buckingham Palace. The announcement which the Prime Minister will, or intends to, make this afternoon, will show how the government is ready to cooperate. Once more I express my warm acknowledgement and thanks for your letter.[27]

After reading the letter, David 'was overwhelmed with joy'.[28] His fears had been unfounded and now he waited to hear what arrangements were being made and if his offer of the flag had been accepted too.

News of the repatriation of an unknown soldier from the battlefields of the Western Front to be buried in Westminster Abbey was warmly received both by the public and the newspapers. *The Times,* in its typically understated way, mentioned it in a small column on 22 October, entitled 'Cenotaph':

> We understand that all the arrangements made for the unveiling of the Cenotaph on Armistice Day are now in abeyance. They were to have been finally settled yesterday, but Lord Curzon's Committee, which is now considering the details of the ceremony of re-interring the body of an unknown warrior in the Abbey, will also be responsible for the arrangements in connexion with the Cenotaph, the two ceremonies being inter-dependent.[29]

While the details for Armistice Day were being finalised, David did not have long to wait to hear of his flag. On 25 October Dean Ryle once again wrote to David with more good news:

> The War Office will be quite willing to accept the Flag for use at the service on the 11th of November – provided that it is in a condition not unsuitable for the occasion. Perhaps you may be able to bring it up to Town in the course of the next week or so.
>
> In any case, if it is used, I should like to have a short description of it, so that I could let the press have full information – it would add further interest (not that such is needed) to the ceremony.
>
> The grave at my request is to be filled in with French earth which the War Office consents to have brought over.

> When will you come & preach to our evening (popular) congregation in Westminster Abbey? Would Dec 12th (6.30pm) suit you, or a Sunday evening next Lent? Stay at the Deanery for the occasion Saturday & Sunday nights; or Sunday night only, as suits you best.[30]

It is difficult to understand exactly what David must have been feeling at this time. His 'great idea' was happening, his flag would also be used during the entire ceremony, and now here he was, the newly installed vicar of Margate who until recently had been just a humble curate, being asked to preach in Westminster Abbey.

David wrote back to the Dean that evening accepting the honour to preach at Westminster Abbey and confirmed he could travel to London next week with his flag. On 28 October, he received another letter from the Dean, confirming when David would deliver a sermon in the Abbey, and he also asked, 'Could you bring your flag on Wednesday next? We could give you lunch at 1.15.'[31]

Before the flag could be taken to London, David knew it had to be in top condition to be used for the burial of the repatriated unknown comrade. Several holes had to be patched in the centre of the flag, and the letters '141 Inf Brig' had to be removed from one of the corners. David noted on a postcard that 'RMR [his wife] removed the letters'.[32] She did a good job, as the neat stitching is still visible today and has held the flag together for almost a century. In 1992, a worried 'Keeper of the Muniments' wrote an internal memorandum to the Dean about a possible issue with the flag. They had read in David's 1931 article in *Our Empire,* kept in the Abbey archive, that the Padre's Flag had been used to cover bodies and was described as being 'literally tinged with the life-blood of fellow Britons'.[33]

> There must therefore be a strong possibility that there is blood on the flag, and if so it would present a conservation problem – like any organic material. It might attract insects or mold. The question of cleaning it would then become a rather delicate one. Perhaps a report on its condition by the conservators, with recommendations, would be in order before a decision is made on what action to take.[34]

It is not known whether Mrs Murdock or the nannies had washed it before David took it to London. A handwritten note on the memorandum held in the Abbey archive simply indicates, 'None found'.[35]

On Wednesday, 3 November 1920, David boarded a train in Margate and travelled to London. In the voice of his flag, he describes his last journey with the padre and the last time the flag was tucked into the padre's pack:

> A week before Armistice Day 1920 I was once more put into the same dear old pack to go to London to be inspected... During the journey to London the padre was scribbling away all the time writing a summary of my history for the Dean of Westminster. This summary subsequently appeared in *The Times*[36] in a leading article... When we got to the Deanery they spread me out for measurement. The Dean and Mrs Ryle were delighted to find that I should suffice for the purpose of the burial of the Unknown.[37]

★★★

That evening David made sure his uniform was ready. Although he was now no longer a serving chaplain to the forces, his status as an 'Honorary Chaplain' allowed him to wear the uniform on an occasion such as this. And before David went to bed that night, on the eve of the second anniversary of Armistice Day, he would have seen and taken a certain pride reading the article on page 14 of *The Times* entitled, 'The Story of the Padre's Flag'.[38] It outlined the notes he had written for the Dean of Westminster a week earlier when he took the flag to London. The newspaper also honoured his request to remain anonymous.

In the same paper, on page 13, appeared an editorial article to the Unknown Warrior. Had David read the editor's closing remarks before going to sleep that night, he would have been pleased with the way this great day and the repatriation were being presented by the papers, and it might have prepared him for what he was to witness the next day:

> Thus, the Unknown Soldier returns to-day to English shores bearing with him the banner of a victory greater than any victory of the sword. All that man can do to honour the dead the nation will do for him tomorrow; for he, dead, returning in the name of all who died as he did honours his country more than we, living, can honour him.[39]

CHAPTER 11

The Unknown Warrior

'The corner of the Foreign Field is here.'

ALAN BENNETT

Friday, 12 November 1920, Margate, England

David pushed hard against the solid oak door and stepped into St John's. After turning on the lights, he walked down the main aisle, paused at the altar, and bowed. It was cold outside, but he felt the heat coming from the newly installed boiler as soon as he entered the vestry, so he propped open the door. The morning service was due to start in 30 minutes – more than enough time for most parts of the church to warm up.

For the first time in months, David had slept all the way through the night. The length of the previous day and the emotion of the occasion meant that by the time the train pulled into Margate the evening before, David, Ruby and his mother were all quite exhausted. He'd woken up the next day feeling rested and revitalised. He was sure that many sleepless nights might lie ahead, but for now he felt content at having had a full night's sleep.

Armistice Day 1920 had been a wonderful success – even the weather had cooperated. The prolonged spell of calm conditions across southern England meant London was prone to morning fog. Arriving early at Victoria Station, the thick mist that hung over the capital matched the sombre mood of the occasion and was enhanced by most women and men (not in uniform) wearing black mourning clothes. But even though it was exacerbated by the city's pollution, the fog had mostly cleared by the time Big Ben sounded out 11 times across Whitehall. *The Times* commented on the weather, saying, 'The morning was beautiful, as November can be.'[1] Mr L. Barbor-Might, the civil servant at the Ministry of Works who had supervised the delivery of the French soil used to bury the Unknown Warrior, added to *The Times'* description of the day. In a memoir that he wrote some time later, he said, 'On that eventful day, the weather conditions were the best and the most fitting.'[2]

The crowds, the emotion, and the reverence with which the burial and the unveiling of the Cenotaph were treated by the entire nation was everything David had hoped for. Being able to attend with his mother and wife made him very happy. Not being one to boast of his achievements, David always downplayed his role in what happened that day. But there is no doubt that he was extremely pleased with what had been achieved and proud of the small part he felt he had played.

***

The Dean of Westminster received David's letter whilst he was in Harrogate at his holiday residence. This was the first time he had spent any length of time away from London since the war had begun six years earlier. Both the Dean and his wife were enjoying their time in the quiet Yorkshire market town, relaxing in their Victorian home on Valley Drive.

During his time in Harrogate, the Dean thought long and hard about David's idea of burying an unknown soldier from the Western Front in Westminster Abbey. No letters remain to confirm that he contacted members of his chapter, trying to gauge their opinion on the matter. But it is likely that he did so. In a letter to David Railton after Armistice Day, he wrote, describing how he presented the idea, 'As you know I took four or five weeks to think about it and to consult with friends.'[3] One of these friends was the Chief of the Imperial General Staff, Sir Henry Wilson, from whom he got a positive response. Encouraged by what he had heard and having returned to London, on 4 October 1920 Dean Ryle wrote to King George V's private secretary, Lord Stamfordham.

In his letter he said, 'I am desirous to approach the King upon a matter… There are thousands of graves, I am told, of English "Tommies" who fell at the front – names not known. My idea is that one such body (name not known) should be exhumed and interred in Westminster Abbey.'[4]

The Anglican Church had been opposed to the construction of a non-denominational, secular monument in the centre of Whitehall with no Christian symbol upon it. Instead of the Cenotaph, they would have preferred a large stone cross. Worse still, because the public had taken it to their hearts as the nation's focal point for its grief, Lutyens' temporary wood and plaster structure was being rebuilt in granite to become a permanent memorial. Dwindling attendance and a general ambivalence towards the church all over Britain added to this perceived assault. In her book, *The Great Silence*, Juliet Nicholson does not share the church's view that the Cenotaph lacked any religious meaning: 'For a Christian, the very emptiness of the Cenotaph held a symbolism like that of Christ's tomb after the Resurrection.'[5]

But leading figures within the Anglican Church didn't see it that way. In an editorial for the *Church Times* just after the first anniversary of Armistice Day, they saw fit to vent their distaste. They saw public and media calls for the Cenotaph to become permanent as nothing more than a 'cult', with its members practising 'Cenotaphology'.[6] No one admitted it publicly, but many in the church were looking for a way to wrestle back the national symbol of mourning, placing the church at the heart of it. So when David Railton's letter landed on Dean Ryle's desk, with the idea being suggested 'in a perfectly definitive form',[7] it seemed like manna from heaven. Here was an opportunity for the Church of England to build its own national shrine inside the heart of Britain's most prominent place of worship in a new way that might help revive the church's relevance.

The reply Dean Ryle received on 8 October from Lord Stamfordham was not all he had hoped for:

> For the moment the king is doubtful about the proposal contained in your letter of the 4th. Nearly two years after the last shot fired in the battlefields of France and Flanders is so long that a funeral now might be regarded as belated, and almost, as it were, re-open war wounds, which time is generally healing.[8]

But there was still hope. The letter continues:

> On the other hand, the king recognises the force of your argument, and notes what you say of Sir Henry Wilson's view upon the proposal. His majesty would like you to speak to the Prime Minister on the subject, and let him know how Mr Lloyd George regards the suggestion.[9]

Dean Ryle was enthused by this response and seemed determined to see it implemented despite the King's initial reluctance. Although he did not send an official memorandum to the Prime Minister until a week later, on 15 October, the speed of the response (the same day) and the detailed information it contained showed quite clearly that the Dean had been in touch with the Prime Minister during that week with all the details already in place. The memorandum and response look like a formality: 'I am directed by the Prime Minister to inform you that your memorandum of the 15th October, suggesting that the remains of one of the unknown men who fell and were buried in France should be exhumed and buried in Westminster Abbey, has been accepted. The Prime Minister has already notified the King.'[10] The letter contained details of the committee to be led by the Foreign Secretary, Lord George Curzon, and a polite reminder of how the news was to be made public: 'I should add that the Cabinet would prefer that the first announcement of the adoption of this proposal should be made in Parliament... The Prime Minister asks me to thank you for this impressive suggestion.'[11]

During the period 8–15 October, the week before the Dean's official memorandum was sent to the Prime Minister, David Lloyd George had been busy persuading the King and gaining the support of the Cabinet to approve the addition of the burial of an unknown soldier in Westminster Abbey on Armistice Day at the same time as the unveiling of the permanent Cenotaph.

David Lloyd George considered persuading the King a simple task. He had managed to convince the reluctant monarch that the 'Great Silence' was something the British people would willingly observe (and been proven right). Lloyd George didn't really see the King as an equal intellect. In 1910, he wrote about King George V in a letter to his wife that revealed how he felt about the royal family: 'The King is a very jolly chap but thank God there is not much in his head. They're simple, very, very ordinary people, and perhaps on the whole that's how it should be.'[12]

After the victory parade in July 1919, it became obvious that the nation wanted Lutyens' temporary Cenotaph to be replaced with a permanent structure. Having convinced the King, despite objections from his bishops, Lloyd George then used press and public opinion to pressure the Cabinet regarding a permanent Cenotaph. There was no doubt what the media thought. *The Times* led the way:

> Simple, grave and beautiful in design, [the Cenotaph] has been universally recognised as a just and fitting memorial of those who have made the greatest sacrifice; and the flowers which have daily been laid upon it since the march, show the strength of its appeal to the imagination. It ought undoubtedly be retained, in a more permanent form among the monuments of London.[13]

The article fell short of calling for it to be in the same location. But others felt strongly that the Cenotaph should not be moved. *The Daily Mail* said the site, 'had been consecrated by the tears of many mothers'.[14]

With finishing touches being made to the permanent Cenotaph out of public view – covered with scaffolding and boards – and with the full support of all branches of the armed forces, the Cabinet agreed to the Dean's proposal. With just three weeks until Armistice Day, the Cabinet appointed a committee to be led by the Foreign Secretary, Lord Curzon. As well as the Foreign Secretary in the chair, it was comprised of Lord Lee of Fareham, Mr Winston Churchill, Mr Walter Long, Mr Edward Shortt, and Sir Alfred Mond. Lt-Col L. Storr of the Cabinet office was the committee's secretary.

The 'Interim Report of the Committee' was written after its first meeting took place on 19 October at the Foreign Office and marked 'Secret'.[15] Considering the date – just 22 days before Armistice Day – the report is striking. It not only shows to what extent so many details needed to be organised beforehand, but also how many details had changed from the 'provisional recommendations'[16] made by the Cabinet. Sir Lionel Earle, First Commissioner of Works, who was already tasked with forming a committee to discuss the Cenotaph ceremony, was now re-tasked as the chair of a sub-committee. Its job was 'to act under the committee's instructions, and to consider the working out of such recommendations in respect of the proposed combined ceremony'.[17]

Historians have always credited the Foreign Secretary – 'The arrangements for Armistice Day were almost entirely of Curzon's devising'[18] – praising his 'unrivalled skill and imagination as a master of ceremonies … inventor of traditions'.[19] Curzon captured the mood of the country perfectly, and what he was able to achieve in such a short time scale is remarkable. The traditions Curzon was able to create have lasted almost a century. Neil Hanson writes, 'His vision would ever after dictate the form of public remembrance of the war dead.'[20]

There is no doubt that Curzon was the driving force behind the events of Armistice Day 1920, but it also has to be said that a huge amount of credit must be given to Sir Lionel Earle and members of his sub-committee. They were instrumental in taking care of the details to make sure the occasion went off without a hitch. The list of questions and pages of details from the 'Agenda'[21] that had to be answered would have been acted upon by many more men than Lord Curzon and his committee of distinguished politicians.

One of the major differences between the Cabinet's proposals and the events of the day was with regard to the railway station in London where the body of the Unknown Warrior would arrive and be placed onto the gun carriage. The initial proposal said 'that the coffin be conveyed by train, without ceremony, on the morning of the 11th November, so that it shall be at Charing Cross Station not later than 10 a.m. that morning'.[22]

Why the station was changed to Victoria from Charing Cross, or who suggested it, is not known. It may have been because Victoria had a larger capacity for the guard that was to watch over the carriage. It may have been because the body would arrive the evening of 10 November, or it may have been to give more members of the public a chance to pay their respects. The route from Victoria to the Cenotaph was over two miles in length as opposed to less than half a mile from Charing Cross. And when we take into account the size of the crowds that gathered in London that day, the change to Victoria Station makes perfect sense.

One of the men on Sir Lionel Earle's sub-committee was Major-General G. D. Jeffreys. Wartime GOC of 19th Division when David was

Senior Chaplain, General Jeffreys was now the GOC Brigade of Guards and London District. With his staff at Horse Guards Parade, General Jeffreys would be the one to make sure this unprecedented and solemn occasion was conducted to the highest standards and traditions of the British military. Although London had seen similar occasions, with large-scale state funerals of monarchs and politicians, such as King Edward VII in 1910 and Prime Minister William Gladstone in 1895, there really was no precedent for anything like the burial of the Unknown Warrior. If Lord Curzon is to be credited for how the country commemorated its war dead after 1920, then General Jeffreys and his staff should also be mentioned for the way such ceremonies and state occasions in London are conducted today. The orders issued by London District and signed by Lieutenant-Colonel R. Luker[23] cover every detail of the occasion from the arrival of the body at Victoria Station the night before, until it was finally laid to rest in Westminster Abbey. The orders even have detailed diagrams. They show where each military unit's mourners would stand at the Cenotaph, those marching behind the Unknown Warrior, and details of the start of the procession from Victoria Station.[24] Great Britain had never witnessed anything like this before.

***

It is almost a hundred years since the Unknown Warrior was laid to rest in Westminster Abbey, and many aspects of how it all happened remain shrouded in mystery, with conflicting opinions and stories from many different sources. There is still doubt surrounding many things: Whose idea was it? What flags were actually used? How many bodies were exhumed? Where were those bodies not selected actually reburied? And now, there is even doubt surrounding the timeline of the journey of the Unknown Warrior on its way home.

In light of the few days Lord Curzon, his committee and the sub-committee had to prepare for Armistice Day, it is remarkable that they were actually able to pull off such an unprecedented occasion, almost without a hitch. But in the rush it appears that many of the details were not recorded for posterity, and sadly, a lot has been lost to time. Rather than quoting official documents as evidence, historians and writers have had to use newspaper articles and subjective accounts, sometimes written many years later. Also, because it was vitally important that the selection of the Unknown Warrior was carried out in a meticulously secretive fashion, we have to rely on the testimony of only a few people. For families of men who died and had no known grave, to imagine that their son, husband, father, brother, or friend could be the Unknown Warrior, there had to be a thorough process to select a body whose identity would remain unknown for all time.

Until recently, most official accounts of how the body was selected have originated from Brigadier General L. J. Wyatt, GOC British Forces in France and Belgium. In a 1939 letter to the editor of the *Daily Telegraph*,[25] he describes the recovery of a number of unidentified corpses from various battlefields in France and Flanders and the events leading up to the departure of the selected Unknown Warrior for Boulogne.

In the letter, General Wyatt describes how four separate digging parties were despatched to the Somme, Aisne, Ypres, and Arras battlefields, where they were tasked to exhume the bodies of unknown British soldiers. Their remit was to choose the corpse of a soldier who had died early in the war to ensure it could not be identified. They were told to ensure that there was nothing on the body that could be used to recognise it, and as a final check, the body must have been wearing a British uniform when it was exhumed. Once they had carried out this grisly task, the exhumed body was placed in a sack, laid on a stretcher, and taken to a building that had been converted to a temporary chapel at General Wyatt's HQ at St-Pol-sur-Ternoise, 21 miles north-west of Arras. He says that they even went to great lengths to ensure the four parties never met and each returned to its own area before the selection was made, so that there was no chance that they would know if their exhumed body was selected.

There have been different claims regarding the number of bodies that were actually exhumed that day, 7 November 1920. General Wyatt is adamant it was four. Neil Hanson acknowledges the varying accounts but says, 'There seems no reason to doubt the version of events given by Brigadier General L. J. Wyatt himself.'[26] The only caveat that should really be added is that General Wyatt wrote his letter to the editor of the *Daily Telegraph* in 1939, almost 20 years after the event.

In April 2014, Tim Kendall, the grandson of Revd George Kendall, OBE, Senior Chaplain at St Pol in November 1920, produced an auto-biographical account written by his grandfather, stating six bodies were exhumed, not four. His autobiography, which Padre Kendall did not want to be published or made public until after his death in 1961, has now been published.[27] It confirms most of General Wyatt's version of events except the number of bodies exhumed and the exact time the Unknown Warrior was selected. Padre Kendall wrote his testimony in 1961, so the same caveat used for General Wyatt's letter must also be applied here. However, Padre Kendall's claim is supported by several other articles that say the number of bodies exhumed was six.

In June 1933, writing for the FIDAC (*Federation Interalliee des Anciens Combattants*) magazine, Major P. F. Anderson says, 'a total of six shell-torn and unrecognisable bodies of British Warriors were disinterred'.[28] In the November 1939 edition of *The British Legion Journal*, E. E. P. Tisdall states that parties of soldiers, each led by a subaltern, 'set out across the six famous battlefields, Ypres, Marne, Cambrai, Arras, Somme and Aisne'.[29] And in 1955, writing in *The Legionary* about David's idea, John Hundevad, says, 'The remains of six bodies were taken.'[30]

In his book, *The Final Betrayal*, first published in 1989, Richard Garrett adds more confusion to the debate when he writes, 'Eight unmarked graves containing unrecognisable bodies from eight different battlefields were dug up.'[31] He doesn't cite a source for this information, so there is no way of knowing how he came up with this number. In 1929, writing in *The British Legion Journal*, Herbert Jeans suggests that only one body was dug up, 'somewhere in the vicinity of Ypres'.[32]

Was it four, six, or eight bodies, or just one? Until new evidence – such as a set of orders or instructions written by General Wyatt's headquarters – comes to light, we will probably never know for sure. For the sake of neutrality, with no way of knowing who was right, the exhumed soldiers will now just be referred to as 'the bodies'.

After the bodies were placed in the hut, Padre Kendall inspected them for a final time, checking that there was no way any of the remains could be identified other than that they were British. As a chaplain with the Imperial War Graves Commission (IWGC), he was used to examining decomposed remains whilst trying to establish an identity. After he was done, each of the bodies, which were lying on canvas stretchers, was covered with a Union Jack. He says that after he left, 'The door of the hut was locked and sentries were posted outside.'[33] General Wyatt recalls that at midnight on 7 November he was accompanied into the chapel by Lieutenant-Colonel E. A. S. Gell. General Wyatt selected a body at random (Garrett and some others say he was blindfolded), which they then placed into a plain pine coffin that had been placed in front of the altar. General Wyatt goes on to say, 'I selected one and, with the assistance of Col. Gell placed it in the shell and screwed down the lid.'[34]

The seriousness with which they undertook this task and the need for secrecy is obvious. In normal circumstances, two senior officers carrying out such a task was unheard of. British Army protocol of the time would have been for soldiers or NCOs to carry out the work with officers watching on from the side. Padre Kendall recalls a slightly different story, saying, 'In the morning a general entered the hut. He placed his hand on one of the flag-shrouded coffins, and the body therein became the Unknown Warrior.'[35] The confusion surrounding when General Wyatt selected the Unknown Warrior becomes even more relevant when we start to discuss the timeline of the journey taken by the Unknown Warrior to Boulogne, Dover, and London.

General Wyatt says that after the selection, the other bodies were reburied in a nearby military cemetery. But a conflicting account written in a 1978 letter to the Dean of Westminster by Major-General Sir Cecil Smith says that the bodies had a rather less reverent re-burial. As a young subaltern, he recalls what happened to the remaining exhumed unknown soldiers: 'The bodies were buried in a shell-hole on the road to Albert, to which the chaplain added a simple prayer.'[36]

Why the bodies were taken nearly 50 miles to the south to be buried in 'old trenches' on the Somme battlefield, when General Wyatt stated otherwise, is not known. Again, the fact that Sir Cecil wrote this letter 58 years after it happened needs to be taken into account, in the same way as the accounts of General Wyatt and Padre Kendall.

Whose version of events is right will probably never be known, always shrouded in mystery. The problem is that historians, writers, officials at

Westminster Abbey, the Imperial War Museum, and anyone who has ever written about the Unknown Warrior have always used General Wyatt's letter as the *de facto* timeline of events. Even if we accept Padre Kendall's version that the selection took place 'in the morning' instead of midnight, the date of 7–8 November as given by General Wyatt still does not hold up to close scrutiny. We know that the ambulance carrying the Unknown Warrior arrived in Boulogne, mid-afternoon, 9 November 1920. Thousands witnessed the arrival and accounts appeared in newspapers the next day.[37] On the morning of 10 November the Unknown Warrior was transported on board HMS *Verdun* to Dover, then went by train to London and was buried in Westminster Abbey on 11 November 1920.

According to General Wyatt's version of events, the digging parties returned to St Pol with their exhumed corpses on 7 November, with the Unknown Warrior being selected at midnight. The next morning there was a service held in the chapel, then at midday an ambulance and a military escort drove the 50 miles with the Unknown Warrior to Boulogne, arriving at 3:30 P.M. The problem with this version of the account is that we are missing a whole day, and there is no evidence to suggest the body was kept somewhere else or spent two nights at St Pol or in Boulogne.

Using Occam's Razor, the theory that says the simplest solution is usually the correct one, it would appear to be cut and dry – General Wyatt simply got his dates wrong. But the problem is that since 1939, General Wyatt's version of events has been used as an 'official source'. Even the inscribed memorial stone at St Pol says the body was selected the night of 7–8 November. As historians, we contemplate that if he got the date wrong, then perhaps he was mistaken with regards to the number of bodies, where those bodies were reinterred, and maybe some other details, too.

In 1954, an interesting story appeared in the *Daily Telegraph*[38] regarding Major S. G. Hammack, the second-in-command at St Pol. While the Unknown Warrior lay in the temporary chapel, according to Mrs Hammack (the widow of Major Hammack, Royal Warwickshire Regiment, who died in 1950), a second and more clandestine service was held. Realising that the Unknown Warrior might have been a Catholic, Major Hammack, a Catholic himself, found a priest. Alone in the chapel, a Requiem Mass was said over the body of the Unknown Warrior.[39]

David was unaware of all of this, and as this is an account of him and his flag, we will leave any further discussion of the events at St Pol to others eminently more qualified. But I like to think that David, with his pluralistic views where faith was concerned, would have smiled at the thought of a Roman Catholic priest being sneaked into the chapel to say a Requiem Mass over the body of the Unknown Warrior, just in case he happened to be a Catholic.

★★★

David knew very little of the meticulous preparations that were being put in place, both in London and in France. Letters he received from the Dean were brief and void of many details, and the Dean appears to have been the only person involved with whom David had been corresponding. All he would have known was what he had read in the papers the previous day: 'The Union Jack with which the coffin, and later, the tomb will be covered has an extraordinary history, of which the Dean of Westminster has received the following account from the Chaplain to the Forces, who presented it for the great occasion...'[40]

As they boarded the early morning train from Margate on Armistice Day, David would have picked up a copy of The Times and read with interest how the Unknown Warrior had travelled home across the English Channel from Boulogne.

★★★

The morning after the selection of the Unknown Warrior, an 'official' service was held in the chapel at St Pol by Church of England, Roman Catholic and Non-Conformist chaplains. At midday, the body was taken by ambulance with a military escort to Boulogne. The 50-mile journey over rough country roads took about three hours. A Times correspondent wrote, 'The body arrived here at 3.30 P.M. this afternoon, and was conveyed in a motor ambulance to the historic 13th century chateau.'[41]

As the ambulance entered the city, which had been fought over and captured several times during the Anglo-French wars of years gone by, it passed hundreds of French soldiers and citizens who had come out to line the route. The ambulance passed slowly through the city before climbing the hill to the French Army HQ, which was situated in the Château de Boulogne-sur-Mer. Once it had come to a halt in the sand- and dirt-covered courtyard, eight soldiers from different British and Commonwealth regiments, whose rank ranged from that of sergeant-major to private, carried the coffin down narrow corridors lined with French soldiers, to the castle's library which had been converted especially for the occasion. The *chapelle ardente,* usually only afforded to heads of state and dignitaries, was decorated with flags and palms. The French 8th Regiment, a highly decorated unit with a war record that had recently won them the *Légion d'Honneur,* would stand guard over the *Tommy Anonyme*[42] during his last night on French soil.

Waiting inside the castle when the ambulance arrived were two British undertakers, Mr Noades and Mr Sowerbutts. They brought an English oak casket provided by the British Undertakers Association. The wood came from an oak tree on the grounds of Hampton Court Palace. With wrought iron bands and handles and a crusader's sword (provided by King George V) mounted on top, the coffin weighed over 225 pounds. Bolted over the sword was an iron shield inscribed, 'A British Warrior who fell in the Great War 1914–18 for King and Country'. Before it was brought to France, the coffin was taken to Westminster Abbey, where it was placed on the chosen spot so that the exact size grave could be dug without having to excavate more of the ancient soil underneath the Abbey than necessary. The two undertakers lifted the plain pine shell containing the exhumed body, placed it into the oak casket, and closed the lid of the coffin for all time. They then left the French soldiers to their overnight vigil.

The next morning, a French Army wagon drawn by six horses waited in the courtyard of the chateau. Standing with Marshal Ferdinand Foch was the King's representative, the Adjutant General, Lieutenant-General George MacDonogh. A guard of French soldiers presented arms as the same eight soldiers who had carried the Unknown Warrior the day before now gently loaded the significantly heavier coffin onto the wagon. Two soldiers then climbed up and covered the coffin with a single Union Jack.[43]

No effort or expense was spared by a grateful nation to send back over the English Channel the remains of a warrior who they believed had given up his life for France and Belgium. At 10:30 A.M. on 9 November 1920:

> after a salute from the trumpets of the French Cavalry, the procession moved off as the tender melancholy of Chopin's Funeral March filled the air. Children and representatives of local associations were at the head, followed by seemingly endless ranks of cavalry and with marines and infantry next. Then came the coffin followed by a number of wreaths.[44]

The long procession slowly made its way to the quayside, the grey sky and heavy mist befitting the mood felt by thousands of respectful Boulogne citizens who lined the route. 'Along streets bordered with be-flagged Venetian masts, past the silent watching crowd, the cortege passed through the town to the Quai Gambretta, where the *Verdun*, with her motto *On ne passe pas*, was moored, her crew mustered on deck.'[45]

After the procession had halted beside HMS *Verdun*, Marshal Foch gave an eloquent speech in which he praised British bravery and 'pleaded that the sacrifice symbolised by the body of the Unknown Soldier should serve to keep the two countries united in victory as they were in war'.[46]

After General MacDonogh responded, the band played the 'Marseillaise' and 'God Save the King'. HMS *Verdun*'s white ensign was lowered to half-mast as the eight bearers carried the Unknown Warrior on board. Marshal Foch, visibly moved by the whole occasion, stood alone by the gangway staring at the coffin as huge French wreaths were placed on board. Four seamen moved into place at each corner and stood guard, heads bowed and with rifles reversed.

At about 11:45 A.M., the *Times* correspondent stood with thousands of other silent onlookers and watched HMS *Verdun* cast off its lines as 'God Save the King' played again. 'As the destroyer slipped into the mist, the 19 rounds of the Field-Marshal's salute boomed out. The Unknown Warrior was on his way home to the island whence he came.'[47]

HMS *Verdun* was escorted to mid-Channel by French torpedo boats and aircraft flying above. As the *Verdun* came into sight, it was signalled to identify itself. Reporters aboard HMS *Vendetta* saw it flash back the response, 'Verdun and escort, with Unknown Warrior'.[48] Six Royal Navy destroyers lowered their ensigns and formed an escort, three ships in line ahead, the *Verdun* alone, then came three ships in line astern. Once they were underway, it soon became obvious that the flat conditions had put them ahead of time. So, when HMS *Verdun* came close to the western approaches of Dover, it laid up in the mist for two hours.

At 3:00 P.M., the flotilla started to move towards the port. HMS *Verdun* slowly entered the western entrance, while its escort ships left it alone and entered Dover through the eastern entrance. Dover had turned out in force; its shops and businesses closed so workers could see the Unknown Warrior return home. With thousands of people taking up every possible vantage point along the docks and surrounding coastline, another 19-gun salute was fired from Dover Castle's lofty perch on top of the white cliffs. A *Times* reporter wrote, 'After this salute there was an extraordinary quiet. There was not a ripple on the water in the harbour. All the troops who were waiting on the Admiralty Pier to greet the Unknown Warrior had been called to attention and were standing with arms reversed. The Verdun bore down on them without a sound.'[49]

After HMS *Verdun* had tied off, the coffin was carried off the ship by six warrant officers who were veterans of the war and had been drawn from all branches of the military. With the Adjutant General now standing behind the coffin, a procession which consisted of officers and civilians from both the garrison and town followed slowly as the bearers made the short journey along the quayside to Dover's Marine Station. 'The body was placed inside the car – really a travelling chapel – which brought the bodies of Nurse Cavell and Captain Fryatt to London.'[50]

Edith Cavell and Charles Fryatt were two civilians who had been executed by the Germans during the war. Cavell was a nurse in Brussels who was accused by the Germans of helping hundreds of Allied prisoners escape. She was executed on 12 October 1915. Fryatt was a steamer captain who had rammed a U-Boat in the North Sea. He was praised as a hero and given an engraved cigarette case in honour of his actions. But when his ship was captured and the engraving was read, he was tried and executed on 27 July 1917. Their deaths caused outrage around the world, with both their funerals providing huge propaganda opportunities.

About an hour later, when the wreaths that had come from France were loaded, the carriage (with a white painted roof so it could be easily identified) and a connected passenger car were hooked up to the 5:50 P.M. Dover to Victoria boat train. As luggage van SECR 132 and its precious cargo pulled away, a Guard of Honour from the Connaught Rangers presented arms. When it passed through Dover's Harbour Station a few minutes later, the Royal Irish Fusiliers did the same. As the train traversed the Kent countryside, people crowded on bridges, embankments, station platforms, and every available vantage point they could find. They braved the dark and cold to see the train as it went by, hoping to catch a glimpse of the coffin inside the dimly lit carriage. At Gillingham and Chatham, honour guards presented arms on the stations' platforms, and throughout the journey to London, civilians crowded the route.

A little after 8:30 P.M. a *Times* correspondent, along with thousands of others at Victoria Station, waited silently for the Unknown Warrior to arrive:

> Men wept as they saw the double railway carriage, with its one compartment full of soldiers and its other compartment, as it seemed, full of flowers. They knew not why they wept. But the great gloomy arches of the station and the rows on rows of white faces pressed to the barriers were a setting which might not be denied. The carriage, with its small shunting engine, came in very slowly.[51]

As the train arrived, officers on the platform saluted, and the few civilians present removed their hats. A very simple handover took place between the Connaught Rangers and the King's Company, Grenadier Guards, who were now responsible for guarding the Unknown Warrior. Guardsmen would stand either side of the luggage car door with their heads bowed, or as it is described officially in orders, 'The 2 sentries will Rest on their Arms Reversed and be relieved every half hour.'[52]

Platform 8, which was next to the Buckingham Palace Road entrance and where the gun-carriage would come the next morning, remained busy for a while. But as it cleared, leaving only the guardsmen to their vigil, thoughts turned to the morning, as *The Times* relates: 'Other women in the crowd were crying bitterly, and yet others held their heads high and smiled. Today they will bury our Unknown with great honour; but the wonder of this swift hour will scarcely come again.'[53]

★★★

David left very little to posterity regarding his experience in London on Armistice Day 1920. No evidence exists to suggest that he wrote or talked about the day in detail, and there are only a few published references that mention him that day. Neil Hanson placed David at the Cenotaph. He wrote, 'Among them stood David Railton, the ribbon of the Military Cross upon his cassock.'[54] But information in the Railton family Archive indicates that David was, in fact, inside Westminster Abbey, not by the Cenotaph, and that he was wearing his uniform and not a cassock.

It is not known for certain how David, his wife, and his mother travelled to London on Armistice Day. David preached late in the evening on 10 November and early in the morning on 12 November at St John's,[55] so they must have travelled up early to London on 11 November and returned home later the same day. The Dean's wife wrote to David on 7 November with tickets for the Abbey: 'When you get into the Dean's Yard, don't let them try to send you into the Abbey – tell them you are coming to the Deanery.'[56]

In order to avoid getting caught in the crowds that were expected, she advised them to approach from the south, entering the Dean's Yard from Tufton Street. She also warned them 'to keep an eye on the traffic instructions in *The Times*',[57] which seems to suggest that they might have travelled by car. But photographs taken by a press photographer of them outside Buckingham Palace, in the heavy fog that hung over London early that morning, suggest that they had travelled by train. Both of Margate's stations were just a short distance from the vicarage, and the first train from Margate would have arrived at Victoria Station (close to Buckingham Palace where the photographs were taken), leaving more than enough time to walk to the Abbey. Whether they went into the Dean's Yard before the Abbey is not known, but a line written in the voice of the Flag gives a clear indication that David Railton was in Westminster Abbey that day: 'The Dean had the courtesy to give him a special place on Armistice Day close to the grave.'[58]

In 1961, in a *British Legion Journal*, a Mrs M. Sparrow, who says her husband was related to David, said that at the service for the burial of the Unknown Warrior, David 'sat beside King George V and Queen Mary in the Abbey'.[59]

★★★

As David, his wife, and his mother headed to London through the Kent countryside along the same tracks that the train carrying the Unknown Warrior had passed just hours before, the carefully ordered plan of General Jeffreys' staff was being acted upon. By first light crowds had started to gather along the route to be taken by the procession carrying the Unknown Warrior. The night had been cold and a heavy fog now covered central London. Even though trains came and went and almost a thousand soldiers and ex-servicemen started to form up around platform 8 or on the approaches along the Buckingham Palace Road entrance, a strange silence hung over Victoria Station.

Grenadier Guardsmen maintained their vigil until the bearer and firing parties furnished by the 3rd Battalion, Coldstream Guards, arrived on the platform. At 9:20 A.M., the sergeant commanding the bearer party entered the luggage van. On top of the Union Jack he placed a steel helmet and side arms. The bearer party, who did not carry arms, then marched into the van, lifted the coffin, and carried the Unknown Warrior to the waiting gun-carriage which had been pulled adjacent to the luggage van facing Eccleston Bridge. Before the bearer party re-appeared, the officer commanding the parade barked his orders for the firing party to come to attention and present arms. Once the coffin was secured, the bearers took their position behind the carriage, and the distinguished pallbearers marched forward, saluted, and took up their positions either side of the gun-carriage. Pallbearers for the Unknown Warrior consisted of the highest-ranking officers in the British forces. They included the Admiral of the Fleet, Earl Beatty, and Field Marshals Sir Henry Wilson, Viscount French, and Earl Haig.

At precisely 9:40 A.M., the order was given for the firing party to turn to its right, reverse arms, and slow march. The firing party marched forwards underneath Eccleston Bridge as the massed bands started to play Chopin's 'Funeral March'. As the firing party came level with the bands that were formed up in four ranks either side of the road on the other side of the bridge, the bands started to wheel inwards behind the firing party, forming a rank of musicians eight wide. As the bands were wheeling in front of them, the gun-carriage, pallbearers, and bearers moved forward so it came up behind the rear of the bands. The Unknown Warrior then passed through the ranks of mourners from the Navy, Army and Air Force. Once the carriage had passed through the final ranks of sailors close to the station entrance on to Buckingham Palace Road, the mourners turned towards the entrance and marched behind the bearers. Finally, behind the service mourners came 400 ex-servicemen who had been waiting on the platform. Some were in uniform but most wore civilian clothes. They brought up the rear of the procession.

At the same time as the order was given for the procession to move, N Battery, Royal Horse Artillery, commenced a 19-gun salute from Hyde Park. The booms that echoed around the buildings could still be heard as the cortege emerged from the entrance of the station on to Buckingham Palace Road. Standing on the side of the roads behind the thousands of soldiers lining the route, arms reversed with heads bowed, were many more hundreds of thousands of mourners dressed in black, many carrying wreaths and flowers. Some women quietly cried. The sound of horses' hooves and some rattling from the carriage could be heard easily above the silent crowds. As the procession moved along the route, men removed their hats, and children were totally silent stood next to their black-clad parents.

All along the 2½-mile route between Victoria Station and the Cenotaph, the crowds were 10–20 deep. At Hyde Park Corner, the sound of the Scots Guards' pipes could be heard bouncing off the tall buildings along Grosvenor Place. As the Unknown Warrior passed, the crowd appeared to be in a trance. The lines of black, bareheaded mourners stood silent and 'spellbound'.[60] Even after the procession had gone by, those who did speak to one another did so 'in low tones'.[61] The *Times* correspondent standing in the crowd tried to explain this raw, public display of emotion: 'For the people were silent, and they conveyed mystery because they had come out to do homage, not to satisfy curiosity. Their hearts were speaking; therefore their tongues were still.'[62]

The procession moved on through the Wellington Arch and up to Buckingham Palace, along the Mall towards Admiralty Arch, and turned right on to Whitehall. So long was the procession that it took over five minutes from when the firing party with rifles reversed went by to the arrival of the final rank of ex-servicemen.

At the Cenotaph, everyone, including King George V, was in place before the arrival of the gun-carriage. Access to Whitehall was by ticket only, chosen at random from the millions of bereaved parents and wives. All were still, standing silently as the procession approached. The King, dressed in the uniform of a field marshal, stood alone on the north side of the Cenotaph looking towards Trafalgar Square.

The firing party passed the Cenotaph to its east, immediately wheeled right, halted, turned to its right, then rested on its reversed arms. The massed bands, which were still playing, followed on past the Cenotaph as far as King Charles Street, counter-marched, then halted behind the firing party facing the Cenotaph. As the gun-carriage approached, it moved to the west of the traffic island opposite Downing Street and just before the Cenotaph it swung left across Whitehall, 'halting with the Coffin on the crown of the street opposite His Majesty'.[63] The mourners split into ranks, three either side of the road, as they passed Downing Street. At points marked by military policemen wearing redcaps, the mourners halted and turned inwards, facing the Cenotaph from their respective sides of the road. The ex-servicemen halted by Downing Street. This very intricate sequence of events was controlled by a single officer under the command of General Jeffreys, whose orders had stated categorically that 'all movement will have been completed by 10.50 Hours'.[64]

Right on time, as the gun-carriage came to a halt, the King moved forward and placed a wreath of bay leaves and red roses upon the coffin. Once he was back in place, the hymn 'Oh God, Our Help in Ages Past' was played by the massed bands and sung by the Abbey choirs. Although General Jeffreys' orders had stated the hymn was to be 'sung by all those present', it appeared that no one but the choristers were singing. After the hymn, the Archbishop of Canterbury recited the Lord's Prayer. As with the hymn, very few people joined in, preferring to remain still and silent.

After the Archbishop said, 'Amen', the assembled gathering waited for precisely the eleventh hour of the eleventh day of the eleventh month. At that very moment, the sound of Big Ben, whose chimes were used to synchronise all watches,[65] could be heard clearly across the silent streets of central London. On the first stroke of 11, the King turned towards the Cenotaph and pressed a button that released the two massive Union Jacks that had been covering the 35-foot memorial. Two officials had been placed specifically to gather up the flags quickly after they had fallen – the one on the north side had to rush forward and give his flag a gentle tug to bring it down as it had briefly hung up. With the flags down and the stark grey granite of Luytens' impressive monument now revealed, the final stroke of eleven marked the start of the two-minute silence.

Across London, the entire country, and even most of the Empire, there was a complete suspension of all normal activities. People working in factories, those driving cars and buses, and even prisoners in their cells – everyone stopped what they were doing and remained silent for two minutes, as one newspaper reported: 'Nobody who stood in Whitehall during the two minutes in which the Metropolis stilled the beating of its mighty heart, will ever forget the scene or the sensation it evoked.'[66]

The silence was broken by eight buglers of the Brigade of Guards playing the 'Last Post'. As the final notes died away, the King, followed by leaders of the government, including Prime Minister David Lloyd George, laid wreaths at the foot of the Cenotaph. When the Coldstream Guards' sergeant commanding the firing party saw the last official wreath laid, he gave the order for his men to come to attention, turn to the left, and reverse arms. As he gave the order to slow march, the massed bands resumed playing Chopin's 'Funeral March'. The firing party marched through the massed bands that counter-marched then followed behind the firing party. Whilst the official wreaths were being rearranged by officials, the Archbishop of Canterbury's party followed behind the bands. With the pallbearers in place either side of the coffin, the gun-carriage moved forward behind the Archbishop of Canterbury.

General Jeffreys' orders stated that the carriage would be followed by the bearers,[67] but film of the ceremony clearly shows the bearers following behind the firing party.[68] Behind the carriage marched the King; behind him came five members of the royal family, including the two princes, the Prince of Wales and the Duke of York. Then came the 130 'Distinguished Personages' who had been standing on the west side of the Cenotaph in front of the Members of Parliament. Once they were clear, the three ranks of mourners from each of the armed services, on either side of the street, stepped off together towards Parliament Square. Bringing up the rear of the procession came the ex-servicemen – some walking with a limp and some using a cane, obviously struggling through the march and being on their feet for so long but determined to pay their respects to those who had not returned home after the war. Once the ex-servicemen passed the Cenotaph, four sentries, one from each of the four branches of the forces, were posted, 'at each corner of the Cenotaph, facing outwards, and Resting on their Arms Reversed'.[69]

In the Abbey, every seat had been taken long before the gun-carriage arrived at the Cenotaph. Unlike any event held in the Abbey since its consecration in 1065, the congregation for such a momentous event was drawn from all classes, not just the elite. Lord Curzon, anxious that the ceremony should not become a society event, excluded all but Lloyd George and his Cabinet ministers, turning over the majority of seats to mothers and widows who had lost men during the war. Seats were decided by ballot, with priority given to those who had lost the most. Of the 8,000 tickets issued, a small group of about a hundred women were the top priority for Lord Curzon and his committee – they had lost both their husband and all their sons.

David kept the Order of Service from that day,[70] described by *The Times* as 'the most beautiful, the most touching and the most impressive that in all its long eventful story, this island has ever seen'.[71] It began at 10:00 A.M. with the band of the Grenadier Guards playing music by Sullivan, Giulmant, César Franck and Somervell. At 10:45 A.M., the choir and clergy, headed by the Beadle and the Cross of Westminster, moved from the Nave to the High Altar.

While this took place, the choir sang a hymn entitled 'The Supreme Sacrifice'. Taken from a book of poems of the same name[72] by Sir John Stanhope Arkwright, an MP from Herefordshire, and set to music by Dr Charles Harris, this was the first major occasion where it had been sung. Known now simply as 'O Valiant Hearts', it is one of the most well-known and widely sung hymns at remembrance services every November.

After singing 'O God, Our Help in Ages Past' and reciting the Lord's Prayer came the chiming of Big Ben and the two-minute silence. As the final notes of the bugles playing the 'Last Post' at the Cenotaph died away, 'The Contakion of the Faithful Departed' was sung. The Dean then read three collects before the choir sang, and he moved in procession to the North Porch.

Outside, the Unknown Warrior arrived at the gates opposite the North door. The firing party marched through the gates, opened up the distance between the ranks to six paces, halted, turned inwards, and were once again ordered to be 'Resting on their Arms Reversed'.[73] The massed bands wheeled into Broad Street, counter-marched, halted and stopped playing. The bearers stood to attention on the kerb, waiting for the gun-carriage to pull up. Once it arrived, they moved into position and carried the coffin feet first through the line of soldiers and the firing party to the entrance where the Dean and Chapter of Westminster were waiting. Inside the Abbey, standing each side of the aisle from the North door to the grave, was a Guard of Honour consisting of 96 men who had won awards for gallantry; 75 of these had been awarded the Victoria Cross during the war. Commanded by Lt-Col Freyberg, VC, Grenadier Guards, this was probably the most prestigious Guard of Honour ever mounted for a funeral.

196 • THE FLAG

As the bearers entered the church, every eye of the congregation was fixed upon the coffin. With the distinguished pallbearers immediately behind, David caught the first glimpse of his flag since he had left it with Dean Ryle a week earlier. The sound of women sobbing could be heard despite the choir singing Croft and Purcell's, 'I Am the Resurrection and the Life'. The bearers carefully laid the coffin, which they had carried with great care, upon bars over the grave. The pallbearers took up positions either side of the coffin. With the King at the head of the grave and his two sons behind him, the Dean of Westminster with the Archbishop of Canterbury and the Bishop of London facing him, and 'row upon row of cabinet ministers'[74] now in place, the burial of the Unknown Warrior could begin.

Beethoven's 'Equale for Trombones' played by the band of the Grenadier Guards was followed by the 23rd Psalm, 'The Lord is My Shepherd'. Dean Ryle read a lesson taken from Revelation 7:9. During the singing of 'Lead, Kindly Light', the bearers removed the helmet, the side arm and David's flag. Then, with the bars removed, the Coldstream Guardsmen lowered the iron-clad oak coffin into the grave. As the Dean started the committal, 'For as much as it hath pleased Almighty God...', the King was handed a silver shell case that contained some of the soil brought in 100 sandbags from France. As the Dean said, 'Earth to earth, ashes to ashes, dust to dust', the King sprinkled soil from the shell onto the coffin. The service continued with the hymn, 'Abide with Me', followed by the reading of two collects.

The singing of Kipling's 'Recessional' seemed to evoke much emotion in the Abbey. Originally written for Queen Victoria's Diamond Jubilee in 1897, the words 'Lest we forget' would forever be associated with remembrance of the war dead. An article in *The Times* noted, 'The great wave of feeling which that hymn always arouses could be felt surging through the whole congregation, and seen in many a woman, and even some men, finding expression in tears.'[75]

After the hymn, the Dean gave the blessing followed by a lengthy pause. The article continues:

> For a moment, to those at the West end of the Abbey it seemed as if this perfect ceremony were not, after all, to pass without a hitch. In a moment the keener ears amongst us realised the truth. From somewhere far away in the great church

a scarcely audible whisper began to steal upon us. It swelled, with absolute smoothness, until we knew it for the roll of drums. Then the whole Abbey was full of the reverberating roar; and then it began to die away, and died into a whisper so soft that no one could say for certain when it stopped.[76]

Into the silence came the sound of the service buglers playing 'The Reveille'. After the last notes died away, the band of the Grenadier Guards played 'Miller's Grand Solemn March' and the Great West door was opened. The King, members of the royal family, and other dignitaries left the Abbey's dark confines into autumnal sunlight that now basked the nation's capital.

Outside the Abbey, the gun-carriage, firing party, massed bands, and service mourners had all marched back to barracks once the service had started. In their place were now thousands of members of the public who lined up outside the North door. The line, four deep, already stretched back as far as the Cenotaph. After the royal family, Lloyd-George and his ministers were clear of the door, Lt-Col Freyberg, VC, and the other members of the Guard of Honour started to slowly file past the grave of the Unknown Warrior on their way out of the Abbey through the West door. After the last members of the congregation had left, both the North and West doors were closed, and policemen stood by to make sure no one could enter.

Inside the Abbey, the grave was covered by the 'Actors Pall', given by the Actor's Union in honour of their members who had died during the war. David's flag was spread over it, the steel helmet and side arms placed upon it, along with wreaths from the Dean and Chapter of Westminster and the War Graves Inquiry Bureau. Finally, four large candles were lit, and a prepared wooden barrier was put in place around the grave. Just before the doors were re-opened at 12:40 P.M., as had happened at the Cenotaph, four sentries, one from each of the services, was posted on each corner of the grave.

★★★

There is no evidence David wrote or discussed how he felt about the service in Westminster Abbey. In fact, he was so unwilling to talk about it, the Railton family has never been quite sure exactly where David was on Armistice Day 1920. His reluctance to accept credit for anything and the difficulties he faced after he had returned from France masked what he must have felt that day. But the sight of his flag on the coffin as it entered the Abbey, and to see the completion of his idea, must have filled him with joy. *The Times* summed up what David and everyone who was in the Abbey for the burial of the Unknown Warrior must have been feeling: 'The ceremony was bound to be a moving one. Few could have foreseen how strangely and intensely moving it was. Of all the great ceremonies of which Westminster Abbey has been the scene of recent years, this was the most beautiful and the most affecting.'[77]

★★★

After the service was over and David had shaken hands with the few parishioners who had braved the early morning cold, he went back to the vestry, took off his surplice and made sure all was tidied away. Then he walked back along St Peter's Road to the vicarage where Mrs Murdoch's hearty breakfast awaited him.

'One egg or two this morning, Mr Railton?' she asked, as David poured himself a cup of tea and opened the papers.

'Two, I think, Mrs Murdoch. Thank you,' he replied. 'The walk back has made me rather hungry this morning.'

Mrs Murdoch went back to the kitchen and left David to read *The Times* and the 12-page supplement that came with it that day.

★★★

As already noted, we cannot be certain about David's movements that day. Mrs Ryle's letter and his *Story of the Flag* place them in the Abbey for the burial. The press photographs of him, his wife, and his mother outside Buckingham Palace lead us to believe that they travelled by train to and from Victoria Station. After they left the Abbey, they may have been invited into the Deanery, but regardless, sometime that afternoon or evening they would have made their way from the Abbey back to Victoria Station.

Being ticketholders for the Abbey, they were allowed inside the barriers that were put in place by the police early that morning. So they probably would have been able to walk through Whitehall. But even by the time the service in the Abbey had finished, there were already lengthy columns of people quietly waiting to file past the Cenotaph and past the grave. One line wound its way down Northumberland Avenue to the Victoria Embankment on the River Thames and then back up the same way, with people joining at the Strand. A second line on the other side of Trafalgar Square stretched from Admiralty Arch to Piccadilly Circus; and another, of many more thousands of mourners, waited on Horse Guards Parade. Whatever route the Railtons took to get back to Victoria Station, they would have witnessed the unprecedented sight of many hundreds of thousands of people waiting in line. They also would have seen the start of what *The Times* described as many people's 'test of endurance',[78] waiting for many hours to pay their respect. The Cenotaph, which had only a few wreaths placed on it during the unveiling ceremony, quickly became covered with wreaths and flowers. Soon, only its grey granite sides were visible.

There is no doubt that the authorities underestimated the size of the crowds that would be in London on Armistice Day. They also underestimated how many people would travel from all over the country that weekend and into the following week. The organisation of mourners and speed at which the lines moved did improve on Friday and over the weekend. *The Times* published details of where mourners should join the queues either at Horse Guards or Parliament Square.[79] But the sheer numbers of people wanting to pay their respects in the Abbey caused the Dean to postpone the sealing of the grave to 18 November. The *Daily Mirror* reported over the weekend that there had been a 'seven-mile queue of pilgrims at the Cenotaph'.[80]

There is no way to say for sure, but by the time the grave was filled in with the soil brought over from France and the temporary stone placed upon it, an estimated one million people had paid their respects to the Unknown Warrior, with another two million having done so at the Cenotaph. Neil Hanson describes it perfectly:

> There had never been an outpouring of public emotion on this scale and nothing like it has ever been seen again – the great state funeral of Queen Victoria, the later burials of George V and Winston Churchill, and even the public displays of grief at the death of Diana, Princess of Wales, were modest in comparison to the overwhelming emotional response to the burial of the Unknown Warrior.[81]

For the next 12 months, every time the Abbey was open to the public, thousands of mourners continued to visit the grave. As they did so, they read the simple inscription, written in gold on the slab of York stone:

> A BRITISH WARRIOR WHO FELL IN THE GREAT WAR 1914–1918 FOR KING AND COUNTRY. GREATER LOVE HATH NO MAN THAN THIS.

At the foot of the stone, spread out immaculately was David's flag. There it would lie until Armistice Day 1921.

CHAPTER 12

Hanging the Flag

'To-day we honour the dead. Let us not forget the living.'

EARL HAIG

Monday, 21 November 1921, Margate, England

'Morning vicar,' said Sergeant Palmer, as David pushed open the front door to the police station.

'Good morning, Sergeant. Are you up for some company?' he asked, already taking off his hat and scarf.

'Yes, of course, sir,' replied Palmer. 'And as it happens, we've been really quiet through the night, so after Constable Fleet has made a fresh pot of tea, we'll go down to my office.'

Constable Bruce Fleet had already gone to the muster room once he'd seen it was the vicar who had come through the door.

★★★

David awoke a little after midnight. Unable to go back to sleep, he quietly got dressed, left the vicarage and walked through the town to Dane Park, then along King Street to Trinity Square where he sat on a bench opposite Trinity Church for a short while. The night was mild with just a hint of dampness in the air coming off the sea. He often came across homeless people in Dane Park, sleeping on the benches, but tonight he hadn't seen anyone. Throughout 1921 he'd continued to try to help the homeless and unemployed people of the town. With the Church

House open to the unemployed, at least they could get a hot meal most times of the day. But he knew that the situation had got worse all over the country, with hundreds of thousands of people without jobs or roofs over their heads. For those out of work and on the streets, with another winter beckoning, there seemed to be no light at the end of the tunnel.

Through the dark, from where he sat, he looked over towards Trinity Church. There was talk amongst members of the town council about the erection of a war memorial there on the small patch of ground. Public opinion had been so strong there was no doubt there would be a memorial to commemorate those who died; even if money was tight, it was going to be built. The only question was, where would it go? David was very much in favour of it being placed close to the town's most prominent place of worship. The most visible point in Margate, Trinity Church could be seen for miles around. It seemed to be an obvious choice. Unlike the Cenotaph, memorials being constructed in the largest cities and the smallest villages were in the form of a cross.

David was a strong advocate of a central monument that memorialised all who died as equals. His wish to have the Unknown Warrior called the 'Unknown Comrade', because it seemed more 'homely and friendly',[1] shows that he believed there should be no distinction because of someone's class or social standing when commemorating the dead. But the use of the word 'comrade' was rejected immediately. Almost a century later, comrade might seem to be more appropriate. But at that time, the word's link to communism, the Bolshevik Revolution in Russia, and the murder of the King's cousin, Tsar Nicholas II, and his entire family, ruled out its use.

The issue of individual and collective memorials would arise as soon as David became vicar of Margate. In April 1920, a month after Thomas Harrison had resigned and before David was inducted, the Parochial Church Council (PCC) approved the installation of two memorial plaques that were placed inside St John's to commemorate the loss of two sons from two of the town's eminent families.[2] The Doughty family who were builders in Margate had lost two sons, George and Robert, in 1917 and 1918 respectively. Their father, Mr F. J. Doughty, had served on the PCC in the early 1920s. Their mother also died in 1918. The Wanstall family who owned several butcher's shops in the town had also lost two sons, in 1915 and 1916. Mr Percy Wanstall, father to Elton and Bloye Wanstall, never recovered from the loss of his sons, and he himself died in 1918. Thomas Harrison was a close friend to both families. Added to the other families he had to comfort, the stress of all these tragedies led to his ill health. An urgent need for complete rest was the main reason for his resignation.[3]

The losses suffered by the Doughty and Wanstall families were tragic and had torn both families apart. But while David had great sympathy and pathos for all families who had been through such a terrible time, he was against the idea of allowing memorials for individual families in the church, regardless of their losses or status in the town or church community. Whenever the subject came up, he would always think about Mrs Topham and the letter he had to write, telling her that she had lost her sixth son.[4]

During his five-year tenure as vicar at St John's, no other individual family memorial was approved; David became an advocate and supporter of the town memorial. In 1921, church accounts show a donation of 21 pounds and three shillings towards the memorial fund.[5] The memorial was built on the grounds of Trinity Church and unveiled on 5 November 1922. Six days later, David officiated the first Armistice Day service there. Trinity Church was bombed during the Second World War and remained a burnt-out shell until 1960, when it was demolished. There was an attempt by the vicar of Margate, Canon S. A. Odom, to keep the memorial close to one of the town's places of worship. He suggested it be moved to the upper High Street next to St John's. But this proposal was met with 'strong resistance' from the public. Today, Margate's war memorial remains where it was erected in 1922 and is part of the Trinity Memorial Gardens.[6]

★★★

'Well, you've certainly had a busy year, vicar. I read all the details of the service on Armistice Day when your flag was dedicated and hung. And now, I have just read about you disguising yourself as a tramp earlier this summer.' Sergeant Palmer talked as he sat down in his chair in the sergeant's office, pointing to a copy of the *Thanet Advertiser*[7] that lay on the desk.

'Yes, it really has been an eventful year. I was honoured to be invited to the service in the Abbey,' David replied. 'Lord Haig was there, and some of the men I served with during the war hung the flag on a pillar above the grave of the Unknown Warrior.'

Palmer nodded and smiled.

'My wife and I were lucky enough to be able to go and pay our respects at the grave this past June. It was very humbling for us, but also really special to know that it was your flag lying on the gravestone.' The sergeant paused while he picked up his cup and took a sip. 'I couldn't believe that so many people were still trying to visit the grave. They were queueing up for hours. We were stood in line for about three hours,' he continued. 'But I think the effect of seeing the grave is really helping a lot of people.' He paused again, as if deep in thought.

'There was a woman in front of us who had come down from Scotland. She told us she had lost her only son and that his body was never found. She was visibly upset and sobbed most of the time we waited in line. But once we had filed past the grave, and after she left the Abbey, she seemed transformed. I watched her walk away. She'd stopped crying and had a big smile on her face.' Sergeant Palmer smiled too as he recalled the story. 'And now your flag is hanging above the grave for all time. That's some honour.'

David lowered his head humbly. This wasn't the first time he'd heard a story like this, and he was so glad that his flag now had a permanent home in Westminster Abbey.

★★★

After talking to Sergeant Palmer for some time, David went to the muster room where he spoke to several of the constables on duty. They were discussing the weather, how hot and dry the summer had been, and the effect it was having on local farmers.

'The jobless situation was bad enough around here already without this drought. I know three farmers who have laid off all of their labourers because of crop failures this summer,' said one of the constables.

Most of the country had been in the vice-like grip of a drought since the start of the year.[8] Kent was at the epicentre, with Margate receiving less than 10 inches of rainfall over a year, the lowest ever recorded.[9]

The constables were aware that the vicar knew what it had been like in the countryside during the summer. They'd read the local papers and knew what he had been up to. They respected his opinion; he obviously knew what he was talking about.

'Yes, the farmers seem to be having a pretty tough time right now,' David said, 'and that will have a ripple effect on their employees.'

'But it's always ex-servicemen who seem to be laid off first. They don't seem to be able to get a break these days,' Constable Fleet added.

David nodded in agreement. He knew Fleet was right – the plight of ex-servicemen was visible for all to see. On street corners selling matches, or begging – once proud men in uniform who'd won the war, now reduced to this. His tramp had shown him just how bad things were in the country.

***

Earlier that year, David had decided he wanted to raise awareness of the plight of ex-servicemen. He knew that nothing would happen until those in power were made aware how bad it was. Apart from what he told the newspapers, and a few articles describing talks he'd given about his tramp, there are very few records left, with just one or two stories having been passed down through the Railton family. From what is available, we get a clear picture of a man desperate to help those he'd been with in the trenches, despite the hardships he might have to endure himself.

The main purpose of his tramp was to gain first-hand experience of what it was like to be an out-of-work ex-serviceman.[10] He wanted to see for himself whether things really were that bad, and if they were, he would then tell his story to the press. It is likely that David went on more than one tramp. But the only record we have is the story he told reporters on Friday, 19 November 1921. Sometime between 19 September and 23 October 1921, David travelled to his mother-in-law's house at Kirklinton, Cumberland. The *Vicar's Book*[11] shows that he took no services at St John's during this time.

David's family was intrigued, but both his mother-in-law and wife were concerned for his safety. Where he would go on the tramp was chosen because of its proximity to a family home so he could get to safety if needed. The family summer home at Kirklinton was an obvious choice and meant he could roam the Cumberland countryside near Carlisle.

The other choice would have been his mother-in-law's house, 'Eversley', 143 Enfield Rd, which was situated on the northern edge of Saltwell Park in Gateshead. 'Eversley' had been in the family for many years, and although Mrs Willson now spent most of her time, especially in the summer, at Kirklinton, she still spent a considerable amount of time in Gateshead. Being there would have allowed David to see how hard it was to get work on the banks of the River Tyne, where unemployment was rapidly increasing. But there was a chance he might be recognised – his first regiment, 19th Northumberland Fusiliers, had recruited heavily from that area, especially around the coal mines of Windy Nook. Rising tensions in both the coal and shipping industries meant there was a far greater chance of him being put in harm's way. Stories were circulating about ex-servicemen being roughed up by locals looking to protect their jobs. David was not frightened at the prospect of what he may find or the dangers he might face on his tramp, but as always, his thoughts were for his family. He wanted to see through his idea, but he also wanted to avoid any undue stress on them. Even though there was a greater perceived danger in Gateshead, it is very likely, although undocumented, that he made a tramp there as well as in Cumberland.

Before he left for Cumberland, he entered into a friendly wager with some of his family. He was to 'earn his sustenance during his tramp, and return with more money and a better coat than when he started'.[12] So, with a tramp's diguise, a shabby coat, and just a shilling in his pocket, he climbed into the family's chauffeur-driven car. He was then driven into Carlisle, 'keeping under cover, as he did not wish to arouse attention to his shabby appearance in a gorgeous car'.[13] Once he was left alone, he walked into the countryside, stopping at houses and farms along the way, asking for work.

He wrote that throughout his tramp in Cumberland he was treated kindly by most people, especially the poor or those who had experienced hard times themselves. During a talk he gave to the Rotary Club of Margate, entitled 'The Rambles of a Rotarian',[14] he described several examples of the generosity of the poor. A domestic servant at a magnificent house, where David had tried to secure a job as a gardener, offered to give him two shillings and sixpence, which he refused to take. Another domestic housemaid later made him take sixpence, which he took under protest. He went to great lengths to make sure any money he made or was given was refunded. After turning David down for work, saying he'd already laid men off, a garage owner gave David three shillings, saying, 'I have been down and out myself, and I know what it means to be out of a job.'[15]

Although he was met with kindness and sympathy, there were very few offers of a job. He was shocked to find that most people thought he didn't really want to work, preferring to beg.[16] After he asked if there was any work available, many would say, 'Oh, we know what you want, old man. You want money.'[17] At the one place he was able to find work, where he received two shillings and sixpence and a tract for cleaning out a garage, he had a really hard time convincing the owner. 'The idea seems to prevail that an ex-serviceman will only accept a certain kind of job.'[18]

The length of his tramp in Cumberland is unknown, but we do know he spent several nights sleeping rough, laying his head down wherever he could. And for at least one night he slept in a 'dosshouse', the lighted sign above the door saying, 'Good beds 4d – For Single Men Only'. When he had to write or state his name, he used the name 'Notliar' – Railton spelt backwards.[19]

At the end of his tramp, he was picked up and taken back to Kirklinton for a much needed bath. But before he left Carlisle, he witnessed yet more generosity, in a public house where 'a kindly waitress supplied him with a generous meal much below tariff rates'.[20] Although he was able to tell many positive stories about the experience of being poor, describing most people to be generous to a fault, when he spoke to members of the press in London who initially ran his story on 19 November 1921, he didn't have any good news to share, except a tip on how to approach people: 'I found that if one asks for work one gets a better reception than when asking for money, and though no job may be obtainable, one will probably get some food.'[21]

At the end of the interview, the *Evening Standard* summed up what most of the public already knew: 'His experiences induce the belief that the position of the ex-service man seeking work is well nigh hopeless.'[22]

Reaction to his tramp was mostly positive, yet there were some who seemed somewhat critical. The *Thanet Advertiser* agreed with most of David's observations, pointing out that it had said the same two weeks before, blaming a glut of casual labourers as the cause. But they also went on to point out, 'The Rev. Railton has added to our knowledge of industrial troubles, but we fear he has not been able to point a way to their lessening.'[23] Despite this response from a local paper, the story of 'Vicar Turns Tramp'[24] was carried in papers across the country, the British Empire[25] and across the globe.

It is rather odd that the release of this information by David came just eight days after his flag had been dedicated and hung above the grave of the Unknown Warrior. What significance there is in that isn't known. Of the many articles about his tramp, only in his old parish of Ashford[26] does the press mention his association with the Unknown Warrior or of his flag being hung in Westminster Abbey one week earlier. Knowing David's modesty, he certainly would not have mentioned it. And even if a journalist had made the connection, David might have asked them not to mention it in print. Despite it being a publicist's dream, he would not have wanted anything to detract from the cause he was trying to highlight. A clipping from a letter in an unknown newspaper kept by the family proves that David's efforts were appreciated by members of the public:

> Rev. Sir,
> You are a person to be admired. Taking up a challenge to go on the tramp and to find out for yourself what it meant for ex-service... Your pluck in sleeping in doss-houses, and living practically on 'what the swine did eat' during your vain search for work, proves that you are not one of those who are 'for ever blowing bubbles' from a comfortable pulpit.[27]

★★★

Calls to help ex-servicemen had come from some in society. Newspapers often carried appeals quoting politicians and people of note whenever they spoke in support of ex-servicemen. No one was more vocal or more active after the war than Earl Douglas Haig. On Armistice Day 1920, the retired Field Marshal made clear his opinion on the subject. In a lengthy interview, he pleaded with the country to honour the dead by helping those who had survived:

> A quarter of a million of the comrades of the Unknown Warrior are still seeking employment … these men are not begging; they are asking for means to earn a living. They are asking that the sacrifices that they have made for their country shall not be their ruin… We know that much has been done… But so long as any single ex-serviceman, able to work and willing to work, remains unemployed, the nation's debt of honour to its defenders will not be justly paid.[28]

Over the years, Douglas Haig has been heavily criticised, considered one of the 'donkeys'[29] responsible for the needless deaths of thousands of young British men. Whether he deserved all the criticism aimed his way is still being debated. But when it comes to trying to help ex-servicemen after the war, he was the one person who not only spoke up for the men he had sent into battle, but also backed up his words with actions. Some have suggested that he was motivated by guilt and others, by a desire for his legacy to be painted in a more favourable light. It matters not – what he helped build in the summer of 1921 has helped millions of ex-servicemen and continues to do so today.

In 1921, after months of negotiations, Earl Haig helped to bring four separate organisations together to form what became known as the British Legion. The various organisations, which were aligned to the different political and social factions of the day, all had competing aims. Haig convinced the Officers' Association, for whom he had helped raise funds,[30] that a separate organisation exclusive for officers was not appropriate.[31] It was clear that a single entity with one voice would better serve the needs of all, and so the British Legion was established on 14 May 1921. His Royal Highness, the Prince of Wales, was its patron, and Earl Haig became its first president.[32] Also in 1921, he set up a separate charity, the Haig Fund, to collect funds directly for ex-servicemen. In 1928, in memoriam after his death, 'Haig Homes' was set up to help house ex-servicemen and their families.

Despite the efforts of people such as Earl Haig and David Railton to help ex-servicemen, politics, industrial unrest and a stagnant economy along with the extreme drought of 1921 would all contrive to make matters worse, actually increasing the numbers of people who were out of work. In May 1920, unemployment was still under three per cent; however, just 12 months later, it had sky-rocketed to nearly 24 per cent.[33] Increased competition around the globe, cheaper raw materials from abroad, reluctance of industries to change, over-valuation of the pound, artificial high wages during the war, and increased unionisation in the workplace, were all to blame. The end result was that Britain was in deep trouble economically, and politically, and each side blamed the other for the mess.

During the war, the coalition government took control of industries, including coal and rail, and to ensure high productivity and to help achieve victory on the battlefield, workers' wages remained artificially high. After the war, the Prime Minister, David Lloyd George, seemed to lack the political will to do what was necessary – the threat of industrial unrest and even revolution were very real. He also feared a backlash at the ballot box from an increased electorate of many more millions of working class men and women.[34] Despite signs that the economy was sliding into a depression, the government waited three years – until 31 March 1921 – before handing back those industries into private ownership. The delay not only made matters worse, but it also meant that when wage reductions were made, the threat of a national strike was imminent.

In 1914, the three largest trade unions in the country – the National Transport Workers' Federation, the National Union of Railwaymen, and the Miners' Federation of Great Britain – had formed a powerful coalition which became known as the Triple Alliance. Although there was no official agreement between them, the Triple Alliance had a powerful voice. The threat of united action during a time of war hung heavy over a government that did everything it could to keep production at the highest possible levels. But on 15 April 1921, after mine owners had introduced sweeping wage cuts, and just when it seemed the Triple Alliance would bring the country to its knees in support of the miners, the Transport Workers and Railwaymen voted against strike action. That day became known as 'Black Friday'. Miners that went on strike were 'locked out', easily replaced by the many millions of unemployed. For trade unionists and socialists alike, Black Friday is considered one of their darkest days. A 2011 article in *The Socialist* explains, 'Because of Black Friday, the bosses were able to launch attacks against the working class. By the end of 1921, 6 million people had suffered wage cuts.'[35]

The country became bitterly divided into two camps – the bosses and the workers. One of the only organisations looking to bring both sides together was the Industrial Christian Fellowship (ICF). In 1919, the Christian Social Union and the Navvy Mission Society amalgamated under the ICF's first director, the Revd P. T. R. Kirk. Its main aims were to help the Church of England draw in more working class people, help owners avoid 'class warfare' and build a more 'socially just society'.[36]

In April 1921, a public meeting to discuss current labour disputes was held at the Theatre Royal in Margate. As well as the Mayor, members of his council and local business leaders, representatives from the Labour Party and ICF were invited. Nothing indicates David's involvement with the ICF before this date. But, after this meeting, David became a full member of and participant in ICF activities. It is likely David already knew several of the ICF's prominent figureheads, through the church and his time in the Army, but the Theatre Royal meeting seems to be the moment when he started to take an active role.

Soon after the ICF was formed, it recruited the famous wartime padre Revd Geoffrey Studdert Kennedy. He was known the world over as 'Woodbine Willie', because while at Rouen railway station during the war, he was said to wander the platform crowded with embarking soldiers, 'giving away New Testaments from one bag and handing out Woodbines [cigarettes] from another'.[37] Whether David and Studdert Kennedy met in the war is not known, nor whether Studdert Kennedy spoke at the Theatre Royal in April 1921 on behalf of the ICF. During April 1921, several of David's sermons at St John's included summaries of Studdert Kennedy's books, particularly *Food for the Fed-Up* (1921), showing the influence he had on David. Then, on 5 May 1921, Studdert Kennedy preached at St John's. The church must have been full because the collection taken was three times the amount it had been on previous weeks.[38] Studdert Kennedy also spoke sometime in the early 1920s at the Winter Gardens in Margate.[39]

David would be heavily involved with the ICF for the next decade and became good friends with Studdert Kennedy. In the Railton Family Archive are several pages of poetry written for David and his family by Studdert Kennedy. At the top of the page he wrote, 'They are private to you and yours.'[40] There is also a telegram sent to David informing him of the death of Studdert Kennedy who died from influenza in 1929: 'Studdert Kennedy died today – could you help with meetings – Stockport Monday – Manchester Tuesday – immediate reply please.'[41]

David kept a copy of 'The Torch' (the ICF newsletter) that was a tribute to the life of Studdert Kennedy. Despite his full-throated attacks from the pulpit on some aspects of modern life, which ruffled feathers within the church, everyone appeared to mourn the loss. P. T. R. Kirk described him as 'England's Prophet',[42] and Revd R. L. Shepperd said, 'The world is a great deal poorer by his death.' Attached to the poems and copy of *The Torch* was a note written by David on one of Studdert Kennedy's poems, 'They found it in his pocket'.

> Love is eternal, death does not touch it,
> Morning gleams through the dark,
> Today – with me – paradise.[43]

★★★

David sat and talked with Constable Fleet and his colleagues for over an hour before they started to get ready to go out on their patrols. Knowing he had an early service at St John's, he decided it was also time he was on his way, too. He always had an affinity for Margate's policemen. Even after he resigned as vicar in 1925, he remained friends with many of them, returning to Margate on several occasions to visit some of the men with whom he had shared a pot of tea or two. On one of those occasions in 1950, he was invited back to celebrate the '900th Anniversary of the Parish Church of Saint John the Baptist'.[44]

After saying goodbye to Sergeant Palmer, David stepped out into the dark and made his way back up the High Street to St John's. He had been in the station so long that there really was no time for him to go back home before the morning service. So, he decided to walk to the church and spend the last few hours before the service in the vestry.

As David walked through the dark streets up towards St John's, he started to think about the year just passed. With all that had happened – his decision to go on a tramp, the opening of the church house in Hawley Square to help the unemployed, his involvement with the ICF, the visit of Studdert Kennedy, and the announcement of his tramp to the press – he felt like the year had flown by. But all the while, despite how busy he had become, he could not stop thinking about the war. He remembered the horrible losses at High Wood, trying to identify the dead at Vimy Ridge, the shameful waste of life to firing squads of broken young men; he remembered the millions of dead horses and the stench of their rotting carcasses, and he could not get the image of the snapped and splintered trees out of his head. Even though his day was full of meetings and services, the war never seemed to leave him.

The one thing that would have given David great joy was the response to the burial of the Unknown Warrior, especially knowing the flag he had carried with him on the Western Front now lay upon the grave in Westminster Abbey. A year after that momentous day in November 1920, David was once again invited back to the Abbey.

★★★

When David returned from his tramp in Cumberland, he received a very welcome letter from the Dean of Westminster. The letter itself has not survived, but we know from two subsequent letters that it was written on or around 18 October 1921.[45] In it, the Dean formally invited David to a service in Westminster Abbey on Armistice Day 1921, when his flag would be dedicated and hung in the Abbey off a pillar close to the grave of the Unknown Warrior. David replied straightaway, and on 21 October the Dean responded with a few details of the occasion:

> I was very grateful for your kind acceptance of my invitation for November 11. It will be a great pleasure to Mrs Ryle and myself if you would care to come on Thursday evening, 10 November, and so be ready for the ceremony at about 10.45am... You will be glad to hear Lord Haig has kindly promised to come to

the occasion. Exactly what is to be done has not been finally fixed. But I shall
be wanting you to present the flag at the Altar and to carry it down the nave
where I hope we may have a small squad of men who will be competent to run
the flag up.[46]

David replied the same day. From the Dean's response of 24 October,
it appears that David had asked for the 'squad of men' to be provided
from the 19th Londons:

Many thanks for your note. I have seen Lord Haig, who will come to the
occasion in uniform; and you would present the flag to him, and he would hand
it to the clergy. I will inquire about a squad for the flag. But I am almost afraid
that arrangements have already been made. I will bear in mind your hint about
the 19th Londons.[47]

Official details of the Armistice Day commemoration, including the
service in the Abbey, appeared in *The Times* on 9 November 1921.[48]
Along with details of how many troops would be on parade, and where
they would be forming up, were details about the ceremony taking place
within the Abbey:

The Rev. David Railton, M.C., vicar of Margate, who will take part in the
ceremony by presenting the flag in the Abbey, served as chaplain in the war. He
was the original owner of the flag and carried it throughout the war, using it as
an altar cloth. He will hand the flag to Lord Haig, who will then present it to the
Dean. It was Mr Railton who gave the flag on the occasion of the burial of the
Unknown Warrior.[49]

Also in the article was a request from the War Office to veterans, which
started a tradition that still continues today. The sight of veterans on
Remembrance Day in dark suits or blazers wearing their medals is a
common one at the Cenotaph or one of the thousands of war memorials
scattered all over the UK. But the start of the tradition can be traced back
to Armistice Day 1921. Although the War Office said it was still allowing ex-servicemen in possession of their khaki uniforms to wear them,
it realised that there were many who no longer owned uniforms and
wanted to encourage them to commemorate Armistice Day the same
as those that did: 'A desire has already been expressed that all ex-service
officers and men attending ceremonies arranged to commemorate the

Armistice will mark the occasion by wearing with civilian dress the medals and decorations which have been awarded to them.'[50]

The wearing of medals in civilians clothes was not the only tradition to be started on Armistice Day 1921. In 1915, a Canadian medical officer named John McCrae was with the Canadian Field Artillery during the Second Battle of Ypres when he was inspired to write what became the most famous poem of the war, 'In Flanders Fields'. He had noticed that despite the destruction of all trees and most foliage on the battlefield, wild flowers, especially the poppy, would emerge from the churned-up mud. On 5 December 1915, the poem was published in *Punch* and became an instant success.[51] The poppy became an iconic symbol in Canada before the end of the war, being used on publications and posters encouraging people to buy war bonds. But it was not until the end of the war that the poppy was used as a symbol of remembrance.

On 9 November 1918, an American professor, Moina Michael, was inspired by McCrae's poem and conceived the idea to wear the red poppy. In her poem 'We Shall Keep the Faith', she pledged to always wear the red poppy of Flanders Fields in remembrance of those who had fallen. She worked tirelessly at her own expense to get the poppy accepted in the United States as a national memorial symbol. After two years, and despite having the support of the press, there seemed to be no sign of her idea being taken up by the United States government. But in September 1920, the newly formed American Legion, at their convention in Cleveland, 'agreed on the use of the Flanders Field Memorial poppy as the United States' national emblem of Remembrance'.[52]

In attendance at the conference in Cleveland was a representative of the French YMCA, a woman by the name of Anna Guerin. It is widely accepted that she was the first person to come up with the idea of selling manufactured poppies and donating the proceeds to charity. In 1921, she had the first batch of French-made poppies distibuted in America. Proceeds from the sale went to 'help with rehabilitation and resettlement of the areas of France devastated by the First World War'.[53] In July 1921, Anna Guerin met with Earl Haig in London and convinced him to adopt Moina Michael's idea of using the red poppy as a symbol of remembrance. After some discussion, the British Legion placed an initial

order. According to *The Times*, 'The first three million were manufactured across the channel'[54] and they sold out immediately. 'Eventually
rather more than 8,000,000 were made, and even with that number the
country centres did not receive all they could have disposed of.'[55]

The sales raised £106,000 for the Haig Fund that year – a considerable
sum in 1921 – with the money going directly to assist ex-servicemen
with employment and housing.[56] The poppy is now the established
symbol of remembrance in both Canada and the United Kingdom, with
large sums of money being raised each year. The poppy is also worn in
South Africa, New Zealand, and Australia. It's somewhat ironic that the
countries where the idea was first conceived and the poppies were first
manufactured do not do the same.

***

That morning, Friday, 11 November 1921, with new scarlet red poppies
and medals adorning the coats and jackets of the thousands of people in
London, David took his place in Westminster Abbey. For the last time,
he had carefully unfolded his flag and attached it to the pole on which
it would hang. At 10:45 A.M. David was standing in the Nave, behind
the procession, proudly holding his flag. 'The choir and clergy headed
by the Beadle and the Cross of Westminster'[57] moved to the High Altar
whilst singing 'The Supreme Sacrifice'. Behind the clergy came 'Field
Marshal The Earl Haig, Air Vice-Marshal Sir J. M. Salmond, Admiral
of the Fleet, Sir Henry Jackson, and the Rev. David Railton bearing the
flag which had rested at the Grave of the UNKNOWN WARRIOR'.[58]
The full length of the Nave was lined on both sides by 'sixty men drawn
from the Royal Navy, the Royal Air Force, the Brigade of Guards, and
the Territorial Army, together with 100 ex-servicemen'.[59]

At the end of the hymn, David moved forward and handed the flag
over to Earl Haig who in turn handed it to the Dean. He then carefully
placed it on the altar and commenced to dedicate it:

> In the faith of Jesus Christ, this flag, which was carried in France during the
> Great War and has rested for 12 months at the grave of the Unknown Warrior,
> having now been presented to the Dean and Chapter of St Peter, Westminster,
> for their safe custody, we herewith dedicate to the glory of God, and in perpetual

memory of all who gave their lives fighting on land and sea and air for their King, for Great Britain and Ireland, and for the Dominions beyond the seas; In the name of the Father, and of the Son, and of the Holy Ghost. Amen.[60]

With these words, David must have a felt a huge sense of accomplishment. Standing there in the Abbey in his uniform, waiting for the bang of the maroon outside to signify the start of the two-minute silence, David thought of all the men he had buried, of all the thousands more who attended communion in the trenches, in orchards, barns and abandoned buildings. This moment must have meant so much to him.

***

Outside at the Cenotaph, thousands of people were squeezed into Whitehall, when after the second stroke of Big Ben, the 'dull roar'[61] of a maroon signified the start of the silence. If anyone thought that the passing of a year would lessen emotions raised by the silence, then they were mistaken. The press reported:

> The hush that ensued was profound, and for the first minute the world seemed soundless… Strong men standing bareheaded allowed tears to course unchecked down their cheeks. Their womenfolk, bending before the rush of affectionate memories, could not withhold the sobs that racked them… Mercifully when the tension became more than could humanly be borne the crackling of a maroon signaled the end of the period of silent prayer.[62]

After the silence, as the Guards' band played 'O God, Our Help in Ages Past', the Prime Minister and other members of his Cabinet laid wreaths, then withdrew into the entrance to the Home Office off Whitehall. Each of the High Commissioners from Canada, South Africa, New Zealand, Newfoundland, Australia and India now came forward and laid their country's wreaths. Then followed Earl Haig, who made it just in time – only minutes earlier he had given the Padre's Flag to Dean Ryle in the Abbey. His wreath was a large circlet of poppies with the words 'Douglas Haig' emblazoned in bay leaves across the middle.

After the troops marched away, the Cenotaph was once again covered in flowers, its base quickly disappearing under a sea of floral tributes. It seemed to the London correspondent of the *Yorkshire Post* that 'every member of the crowd carried a posy of flowers', and that 'the poppy of Flanders was everywhere'.[63] A huge line quickly formed and wound its way down Whitehall to the Abbey. People were prepared to patiently wait for hours in order to pay homage to the Unknown Warrior, view the new gravestone, and see the Padre's Flag which they knew would be hanging nearby.

★★★

In the Abbey, the silence was observed by a congregation who also felt the emotional strain, one reporter noting, 'Two minutes seemed to be prolonged into an eternity.'[64] The silence was broken by the playing of 'Contakion of the Faithful Departed'.[65]

As the procession once again moved back into the Nave to stand by the grave of the Unknown Warrior, the choir sang three Psalms, leading with 'The Lord is My Shepherd'. When the procession moved off, it 'was followed by Mrs Haig, Mrs Ryle and two other ladies'.[66] The Order of Service states that the procession would be followed by 'Representatives of the Royal Family',[67] but it is unlikely protocol would have allowed royal family members or their representatives to follow the wives of an earl and a dean. In an article written many years later about David's mother-in-law and her family's charitable work on Tyneside, the *Newcastle Chronicle* states that she was present in the Abbey that day: 'When the ceremony was held in Westminster, Mrs Willson was given a foremost place in the Abbey service.'[68] As she was the person who sent David the flag in 1916, and a replacement in 1918, it is reasonable to assume that the Dean would have made sure she was in a 'foremost place', and likely that the 'two other ladies' were in fact Mrs Mary De Lancey Willson (Dubby) and her daughter, David's wife, Mrs Ruby Marion Railton.

Stood waiting by the grave of the Unknown Warrior was a squad of soldiers. They were not from David's battalion, but from the 47th Division, the division David had been with at Vimy Ridge and High Wood, and on the Ypres Salient. It was fitting that they be the ones to hang his flag. A *Yorkshire Post* correspondent wrote, 'All eyes now turned to the grave. The flag already dedicated was handed to Company

Sergent Major H. J. Evans (17th Londons), who mounted a ladder and placed it in position on a pillar, from which it will hang over the tomb of the Unknown.'[69]

A *Times* correspondent sought a more creative and exciting way to be able to describe the occasion to their readers but admitted that the telling 'sounds prosaic':

> It is impossible to convey a sense of the dignity with which the man easily marched, as it were, from rung to rung; then, putting the staff in the prepared socket, turned over the end of the flag so that it fell free. The incident, utterly simple as it was, would have been dramatic if the soldier had not somehow been able to avoid any touch of theatricalism. As the union jack dropped to its length, the music of the Doxology marked the end of this beautiful, indescribable little ceremony.[70]

It was a simple, untheatrical, yet beautiful service.

There are no surviving records or comments from anyone within the Railton family who attended the service in Westminster Abbey that day. There are only a few comments David left regarding his flag being dedicated and hung, and they appeared in *Our Empire* in 1931. Certainly, his mother-in-law and wife were there, along with Mrs Hamilton, wife of Lt-Col Hamilton, David's CO who died at High Wood.[71] We also know that the congregation was drawn from all walks of life: 'There was a notable absence of pomp or the emphasis on rank and class. All were – and seemed to be – gathered for a common purpose which had obliterated distinctions.'[72] And this is precisely how David would have wanted it to be.

After the service had ended, the congregation had left, and the doors were closed, leaving the Abbey quiet and empty, we can imagine David standing alone in front of the grave of the Unknown Warrior. He would have read the new gold leaf inscription on the black Belgian marble. What was he thinking? We like to hope that this selfless and devout man found some solace and peace that day, now that his dream, his idea, had been fully realised. And that maybe some of the pain and anguish that he had brought back from France diminished a little, as his flag now hung above the grave of the Unknown Warrior.

BENEATH THIS STONE RESTS THE BODY
OF A BRITISH WARRIOR
UNKNOWN BY NAME OR RANK
BROUGHT BACK FROM FRANCE TO LIE AMONG
THE MOST ILLUSTRIOUS OF THE LAND
AND BURIED HERE ON ARMISTICE DAY
IN NOVEMBER: 1920, IN THE PRESENCE OF
HIS MAJESTY KING GEORGE V
HIS MINISTERS OF STATE
THE CHIEFS OF HIS FORCES
AND A VAST CONCOURSE OF THE NATION
THUS COMMEMORATED ARE THE MANY
MULTITUDES WHO DURING THE GREAT
WAR OF 1914–18 GAVE THE MOST THAT
MAN CAN GIVE LIFE ITSELF
FOR GOD
FOR KING AND COUNTRY
FOR LOVED ONES HOME AND EMPIRE
FOR THE SACRED CAUSE OF JUSTICE AND
THE FREEDOM OF THE WORLD
THEY BURIED HIM AMONG THE KINGS BECAUSE HE
HAD DONE GOOD TOWARD GOD AND TOWARD
HIS HOUSE

CHAPTER 13

Going Home

'What you leave behind is not what is engraved in stone monuments, but what is woven into the lives of others.'

PERICLES

Thursday, 30 June 1955, The West Highland Line, Scotland

Looking out over the heather-clad wilderness of Rannoch Moor, David sat back and enjoyed the scenery. Clear blue skies contrasted the gales that had lashed southern England earlier in the month. It looked like summer had finally arrived. Retired and 70 years old, David was still very active. He was returning home from Battle, Sussex, where he had stood in for the Rural Dean, The Very Revd A. T. A. Naylor, for the past three weeks.[1]

He planned to read the newspapers after he had eaten breakfast while the train made its way around the western shore of Loch Lomond, but he put them down to enjoy the view. No matter how many times he had made the same journey, the raw beauty of the Highlands always took his breath away. After Crianlarich, the train wound its way up the valley alongside the River Fillan before entering the open expanses of the Highlands beyond the Bridge of Orchy. After passing Loch Tulla, the steep-sided valley of Glen Coe came into view. Looking west into the distance, he could see the hills on the other side of Loch Linnhe, on whose shores his home stood.

David and his wife had purchased Ard Rhu, an 19th-century Scots
Baronial-style house in Onich. Built in 1891, and only accessible from
the Loch, Ard Rhu (an anglicisation of the Gaelic words *Ard Rhuba*,
meaning 'high point') is said to have been built by an Edinburgh banker
who took his entire family there each summer by boat from Oban.[2]
Located just nine miles from Fort William, nestled on the shores of
Loch Linnhe, it afforded views of the Isle of Mull and spectacular sun-
sets. Having spent many summer holidays down the coast at Lismore, the
Railtons already knew the area well. Scotland had always been David's
spiritual home, so it was only natural that he would retire there. Despite
spending most of his life in England, the lure of the *Auld* country, the
land where his father had been born, had finally called him home.

Even though he was enjoying his retirement, his rousing sermons
were still in great demand. As well as rural deaneries and parishes, invi-
tations came to preach in some of the most elevated and exclusive places
of worship in England. On at least three occasions, he was invited to
deliver a sermon for the royal family in the private chapel at Buckingham
Palace.[3] So powerful was his message, and so captivating were his oratory
skills, he was sought by monarchs and the working class alike.

Even at 70, he still took his pastoral work seriously, and it was obvious
that he intended to continue until he was no longer physically able. The
only reasons he did not preach more often were his age and his desire to
spend his remaining days at Ard Rhu with his wife. Sitting on the train,
gazing out over the majestic Scottish Highlands that morning, he was
looking forward to getting home and enjoying the summer.

★★★

The year 1922 had only just begun when David started receiving requests
for his time. As well as calls from several organisations in England, he
also received an invite from the India Committee to go on a mission to
India.[4] David considered it; however, the Archbishop of Canterbury, The
Most Revd Randall Davidson, persuaded him to decline. He thought a
prolonged absence of six months might 'cause parish work to deterio-
rate'.[5] David heeded his Archbishop's advice and remained in Margate.

Within the parish, David was in a hurry to make changes and to
champion causes he believed in. In January 1922, he continued to show

concern for the plight of ex-servicemen. In a letter to the parish he wrote, 'May it be a brighter year for the presently unemployed. Our statesmen and businessmen see more and more the need to solve this problem. But we must push them on and do all we can do to save numerous men … from going mad.'[6]

One of the major changes he wanted to make was for a paid secretary to be employed to help with everyday parish administration. But by April 1922, it was clear that not all members of the PCC agreed with his proposal. Undaunted, David assembled a 'Selection Committee' which would 'select people with suitable experience to serve on the PCC Committees'. A vote was taken and passed with a two-thirds majority.[7] One of those selected was his wife. She joined the PCC in 1922 and served the parish until September 1925.

David was never one to dodge an issue or preach a sermon that he feared might upset some of his parishioners. On Easter Sunday 1922, he acknowledged the country's problems associated with industrial and political unrest. His sermon, entitled 'Brotherhood or Revolution', would have posed a difficult question for his parishioners. Despite some of his sermons being controversial, there was rarely an empty seat when he spoke. One parishioner described one of his sermons as 'magnificent … a great intellectual treat', and went on to say, 'The literary style and eloquence have seldom been surpassed.'[8]

During the July 1922 PCC meeting, David had to respond to the charge that the new secretary employed by the church, at David's request, 'had become a barrier between the Vicar and the people'. Some members of the PCC resisted change – no matter the eventual benefits. David said that he was trying to 'counter the charge that the clergy were unbusinesslike and there was work that could be delegated to a lay person'.[9]

For years David had worked non-stop on many fronts and the strain was starting to show. After a meeting with the Archbishop of Canterbury on 31 July 1922, David received a letter the next day from Lambeth Palace. Following up the meeting in writing, the Archbishop laid out in plain language what he thought. 'At present you are attempting too much,' he wrote, stressing the need for an urgent rest, otherwise David potentially faced 'over-strain, and perhaps, a measure of collapse in effectiveness'. He urged him to take a leave of absence from the parish for at least two months. 'Spend these (I should hope with your wife and family) in some chosen place and come back a refreshed man.' The Archbishop acknowledged that some parishioners would criticise David's absence, but having seen David's predecessor retire with ill-health, he obviously did not want the same to happen to him. 'No man can give out so much as you are giving out without the need of taking in. The well must speedily be pumped dry, or if not dry, the water will become muddy.'[10] A note in the PCC Minutes Book, dated 27 September 1922, indicates Revd David Railton was absent for 'a temporary period'.[11]

Throughout 1922–24, parish records note continued resistance to changes David wanted to implement. Some members of the PCC were frightened with the pace of change despite earlier warnings from their previous vicar. Thomas Harrison 'warned the parish that it must expect a substantial outlay of money on very necessary work for the preservation of the fabric and the comfort of worshippers'.[12] There were several resignations citing fiscal irresponsibility with regards to some of David's proposed expenditures.[13] These resignations came from the vicar's secretary (December 1922), the clerk to the PCC (February 1924) and the treasurer (April 1924). They said their duties were 'difficult, if not impossible'[14] and were a 'protest against the current financial policy'.[15]

In April 1925, the new treasurer reported that because of increased giving from the various appeals organised by the church, he was able to balance the budget.[16] David's policy of increasing expenditure where it was desperately needed had been vindicated. Even though he might have felt some satisfaction, David was left exhausted. He started to look for pastures anew. Struggling with the effects of the war and dealing with parochial pettiness pushed him to move on.

He would be sad to leave the town where he had grown up; he was a well-respected member of the community and had made many friends. One of his last official acts as vicar of Margate was to dedicate and bless their newly delivered 45-foot life boat, *Lord Southborough*. During his time in Margate he had also played football for Margate Town FC and was known as a very good fullback.

David's letter of resignation appeared in the May edition of the *Margate Parish Church News*. After explaining that his decision was not attributed to 'any person, or persons in Margate', he said, 'No vicar has ever had more loyal colleagues and helpers than I have here at present.'[17] He then laid out in 'blunt terms' the reasons he was leaving:

(1) I do not feel mentally strong enough to carry out this work efficiently after the last fourteen years of what has been rather strenuous going. (2) I feel sure that the time has come when a leader of a far different type should be appointed – if I may use an Army metaphor – to consolidate and make good a position that has been attacked and bombarded with at least as much energy as I have been given strength to put into it. (3) For a good while past I have been asked again and again to take up a particular type of mission work – free of the responsibilities and parochial town calls which must of necessity be attended to by whoever is vicar here.[18]

The local papers immediately picked up the shocking news. The *Thanet Times* said the resignation had 'fallen as a bombshell amongst the people', and the *Gazette* affirmed the 'Town council were sorry to lose him'. Over the next few months, as David's final service on 24 September 1925[19] drew nearer, the newspapers and parish magazines carried several letters and articles about their soon-to-be-departed vicar. A clipping of one of these letters has been kept in the Railton Family Archive and seems to sum up what ordinary people of Margate thought of David:

The resignation of the Vicar of Margate has come as a great surprise to many townspeople, and not to a few as a shock. It will be hard for the successor to the Rev. David Railton to display similar characteristics of energy, zeal and devotion to his task and in such great measure. The vicar is a man, who, irrespective of any parochial boundary or sectional ties, has gained the respect of us all. A more cheering disposition it would be hard to find; a keener desire for open and hearty fellowship than his, never.[20]

★★★

Before David resigned as vicar of Margate in the spring of 1925, he had two offers to consider. The first was to become the vicar of a church in Roker, Sunderland. In 1907, St Andrew's Church was built with a £6,000 donation from a Sunderland shipbuilder. Sir John Priestman was Dubby's brother and known to both Ruby and David as 'Uncle Jack'.

One of the conditions of his offer to build the church was that he would provide the living for a vicar of his choice. In April 1925, he offered the living to his nephew.[21] It would have meant that Ruby and the children would be nearer her family in the north-east, and it would have provided stability. But David's missionary zeal was too strong to be tied to any parish at that time.

The second job offer came in the form of an inquiry from Revd P. T. R. Kirk, in March 1925, asking if David knew of anyone to fill a position at Christ Church, Westminster.[22] In April, the job was offered formally.[23] David would have limited responsibilities and lots of time he could dedicate to missionary work. Geoffrey Studdert Kennedy had been encouraging David for some time to 'get started' and be 'more involved'.[24] Even the Archbishop of Canterbury, who at first did not want David to leave Margate, preferred that he work for Kirk in London rather than take the 'North country plan'.[25]

For the next two years, David served as 'the assistant priest at Christ Church, Westminster at a stipend of £300 a year'.[26] Very little has been left to posterity about his time in London, except for a few newspaper cuttings and letters regarding some of his sermons and affiliations he made. David's family left the vicarage in Margate and rented a house in Wimbledon.[27]

David's reputation as a great orator soon swelled the congregation, and some of his speeches were covered by the media. In August 1926, he preached a sermon the papers called 'Stiff-necked Clergy, in which he criticised several prominent bishops' 'attempt to secure coal peace'. He went on to say, 'The Dean of St Paul and those like him were successors of the stiff-necked people who caused John Wesley to leave the church. Their predecessors had tried to stop Wilberforce interfering with slavery and the Earl of Shaftesbury with the conditions of mines and factories of those days.'[28]

David was now fully immersed in the work of the ICF. But men like the Dean of St Paul's believed members of the clergy, and anyone who considered themselves a Christian for that matter, should stay away from politics.[29] Despite David preaching to packed churches, the kind of sermons David delivered did not make him any friends in bishops' palaces.

David's association with the ICF would also bring him closer to political parties. The 1920s not only saw the rise of union power, but also the rise of the Labour Party. In 1923, David showed his support when he added his name to a memorial that was presented to the Labour Party leader, Ramsay MacDonald, commemorating the occasion of his party becoming the official party of opposition in the House of Commons, following the election of 144 new Labour Members of Parliament.[30]

Despite this, not all David's sermons were politically motivated. In September 1926, David received a heartfelt letter signed by 'a working woman' who said she was 'deeply touched' by his words in a sermon on marriage. She explained why his words had meant so much to her:

> In the earlier days of the war I looked forward to marriage and a happy home with the 'one man in the world' but like those of so many others, my hopes 'went west' and I was left with nothing but memories and a vast sense of emptiness ... thank you from the bottom of my heart ... In the name of all the lonely women whose hearts you may have touched by your words.[31]

But for reasons unknown, David would only remain there for just over two years.

★★★

In December 1927, David 'accepted the living of St James, Bolton, Bradford'.[32] Christ Church, Westminster, and St James, Bradford, were very different churches. One was in the heart of the nation's capital, and the other in the heart of the industrial north. But the message that David preached from the pulpit was the same in Bradford as it had been in London. And it was not long before David's new parishioners realised they had 'a gifted preacher, a hard worker, and a capable organiser'.[33]

If his parishioners thought they were getting a vicar from the south who had a typical 'parsonic' message, then they were in for a shock. David realised that talking from his pulpit was not the only way to reach the working people of Bradford. He regularly addressed large groups of factory workers in their workplaces. On one occasion, he was asked to speak to 1,200 textile workers. During the meeting, they asked him what they could do to prevent industrial action taking place. David responded by saying, 'there should be a systematic weekly if not daily meeting of the employers and representatives of the operatives', and 'workers should share control of the industry'.[34] These suggestions would not have made him popular with the bosses, but the working-class people of Bradford knew they had a friend.

Another way David was able to reach the working classes, albeit in a manner that 'raised eyebrows', was through his 'Bar-Parlour Talks'.[35] Once a month David spent 'the last hour of an evening, between nine and ten o'clock' in the bar of a local hotel discussing all sorts of subjects. He did not 'believe that a man who drinks drowns his soul in his pint of beer'.[36] In an article published in the *Leeds Mercury*, he described how he got the men talking: 'I lead off, and then the matter is open for discussion and questions. In my opinion there is no lecture room that could be more attentive or ready to concentrate on the subject.'[37] There is no doubt that David made many friends in the confines of the public bar, and some may have become members of his congregation, too.

On 28 April 1928, David suffered a huge blow when he received news that his mother had died.[38] She had been a massive influence in his life. In the absence of Commissioner Railton, she had virtually brought up the children on her own, and she had been instrumental in helping David through difficult times in the aftermath of the war.[39] Although the strength of his belief assured him that his mother had gone to a better place, he must have been devastated at the news of her passing. A letter he received from a friend in London describes how David must have felt: 'I have just heard of your very sad loss… I am writing to send you my deepest sympathy … the love of a mother is one of the greatest things in this life. You will know how much I feel for you at this moment.'[40]

While David was vicar of Bradford, he became involved in an organisation called The Order of Crusaders. Inspired by the Unknown Warrior, members of the order met all over the country, forming various chapters, and held Church Crusades in cities including Liverpool, Bradford, and Birmingham. At these gatherings members 'wore robes of various colours, designed to resemble the dress of medieval crusaders'[41] and looked to 'renew their vow to keep alive the spirit and comradeship of the trenches'.[42] Several former generals from the war were given masonic-sounding titles such as 'Provincial Grand Master', and even David held the office of 'Deputy Provincial Grand Abbot' while he was in Bradford.

In the summer of 1931, David was ready to move on again and accepted the living of vicar of Shalford, moving south to Surrey in early October. Once the news of his departure from Bradford had been made public, 'he received an appeal from the wardens on behalf of the parishioners asking him to stay'.[43] Although he was sorry to leave, he once again wanted to be more involved with the ICF, as he explained: 'Having been a friend of Studdert Kennedy's, and being pledged to do all I can to develop the principles of the Industrial Christian Fellowship movement, I think I might possibly have a greater opportunity of doing so when I am nearer London.'[44]

David wanted to carry on the work he had begun in London. The paper went on to suggest that David's 'forceful personality made him well liked at St James's'.[45] One additional attempt to convince him to stay came from a choirboy:

> My dear Vicar,
> I am writing to ask you not to leave us. I have prayed to ask God to keep you here with us because we need you and love you. Please do not go.
> Yours Faithfully,
> Albert Victor Ray.[46]

***

David's involvement with the Order of Crusaders necessitated that he talk openly about his association with the Unknown Warrior. From the moment the Unknown Warrior was laid to rest, and throughout the 1920s, speculation continued regarding whose idea it had been. Some have said that the only reason David had not been credited throughout the country 'was due entirely to his reticence about being acknowledged as the originator'.[47] But he did speak openly in public about the Unknown Warrior on several occasions. In 1928, he told an assembled crowd in Manchester that the idea came to him as he was standing by 'the grave of an unknown Scot'.[48]

Others would lay the blame at the feet of Dean Ryle, accusing him of taking the idea and claiming it as his own. David wanted to remain anonymous, but when he read *The Times* article on 12 November 1920 that stated 'the idea ... originated with the Dean of Westminster',[49] David wrote to the Dean the same day. In his letter, David asked for clarification of whose idea it was. The Dean did not write back until 15 November, stating he had been 'rather overwhelmed'.[50] However, a small article appeared in column 4, page 12, of *The Times*, the next day. It was underneath an article called 'The People's Homage' and looked like it was an afterthought, placed there at the last minute:

> The Rev. David Railton, M.C., now vicar of Margate, who served as a chaplain in France, was the author of the idea of the burial of an Unknown Warrior in Westminster Abbey. On Thursday the authorities invited Mr Railton to be present at the service in the Abbey. The Padre's flag, described in *The Times*, which covered the coffin was brought back from France by Mr Railton. It will now hang over the grave of the Unknown Warrior in Westminster Abbey.[51]

In his reply to David, Dean Ryle wrote:

> There are any number of claimants... Some people tell me that they originated it in 1917 and others in 1918 ... the thought never crossed my mind until the first half of this year – 1920, when a lady came to me to advocate the commemoration of the unknown dead in Westminster Abbey and I told her that I would have no statues and that the only thing would be to have a burial... Your letter in August made the suggestion in a perfectly definitive form... So far as I am concerned the decisive letter came from you in the month of August.[52]

There is no evidence that Dean Ryle took any further credit for the idea. Perhaps he was just being pragmatic. By allowing the authorities to assume the idea was his own throughout the process of approval by the government, it stood a much better chance of being approved than if the idea had come from some 'ordinary padre'. David makes it very clear in his *The Story of a Padre's Flag* that without the Dean it would have never happened, as the character of the Flag reflects: 'In any case the Padre knows quite well that no words of his can ever thank the Dean sufficiently for making an idea an accomplished fact.'[53]

During the 1920s, several other people claimed to be originators of the idea. One of these was Mr J. B. Wilson, a news editor for the

Daily Express. On 16 September 1919, a short column appeared in the paper:

> Shall an unnamed British hero be brought back from a battlefield in France and buried beneath the Cenotaph in Whitehall? France proposes to honour 1,800,000 *poilus* by burying the body of anonymous hero in the Pantheon in Paris and the suggestion is made that the British nation should similarly honour private soldiers who gave up their lives for the country. The most appropriate spot, it is suggested, is the cenotaph in Whitehall.[54]

A month later, on 29 October, the subject was raised in the House of Commons after Andrew Bonar Law, the Lord Privy Seal and Leader of the House of Commons, made a statement regarding the 'National War Monument'. Lt-Col W. W. Ashley MP asked, 'whether, in order to mark the deep and lasting gratitude of the nation to those who fell while serving in the ranks during the war, will the government transfer from overseas the body of an unknown private soldier and give it burial with due pomp and ceremony in Westminster Abbey?' Mr Bonar Law said that in his opinion the building of a permanent Cenotaph in Whitehall was what the public wanted. Then Mr H. W. Bottomley MP, former editor of the magazine *John Bull,* followed Bonar Law's comments by asking whether 'such a proposal would be a source of enormous comfort to the parents of every boy whose resting place is unknown'. Bonar Law responded by saying, 'This is a matter of opinion', and that he thought what the government was proposing, 'more truly represents British feeling on the subject'.[55]

Even weeks after the burial of the Unknown Warrior, the subject came up for discussion in the House of Commons after former journalist, Sir Harry Brittain MP, raised the question:

> In view of the fact that no commemoration has ever been held in this country which has so touched the hearts of the people as did the burial of the Unknown Warrior in Westminster Abbey, is it possible to record for future history the name of the individual who first publicly made the very beautiful and appropriate suggestion?

The Prime Minister responded, 'I feel sure that the individual, whoever he was, will be quite satisfied with the result of his suggestion.'

Mr H. W. Bottomley MP chimed in, 'Will the right Hon. Gentleman accept it from me, as the individual in question, that that is so?' And when Sir Harry Brittain MP obviously had not heard the answer he wanted, he asked more directly: 'Was not this suggestion first made publicly by Mr J. B. Wilson, the news editor of one of the great metropolitan dailies?' The Prime Minister did not respond.[56]

When we look at these claims, we have to consider that Mr Wilson, Colonel Ashley and Mr Bottomley did mention burying the body of a soldier from the war back in England before David wrote to the Dean of Westminster. The strength of their claims is based on their public statements. Mr Wilson suggested that a body be interred underneath the Cenotaph, and his idea was made public, while Colonel Ashley did mention Westminster Abbey, but his comments were restricted to the chambers of the House of Commons and turned down by the government. Why Mr Bottomley would have claimed authorship is unclear. In 1922, he was expelled from the House of Commons after being charged with 'fraud' and was subsequently jailed for seven years.[57]

Anyone can have an idea, but if that idea is not acted upon, does that person have the right to claim it as their own? When David wrote his *Story of the Padre's Flag* sometime in the 1920s, he intimates, in the voice of the Flag, that he knew of some of the claimants:

> He also tells me that all kinds of people have been coming forward since he last saw me claiming to be the originators of the idea. He has referred these to the Dean. The 'claimants' include Editors of papers and indeed, a church paper. He has told some of them that it doesn't matter a brass pin who first had the idea; any ideas that are good come from God who inspires men. So in any case there is nothing to brag about. But another time when any idea that concerns the public comes to you, first choose your time and then approach some great and sympathetic leader of the church. Don't scribble about it in the papers (not even church papers) or jabber about it in drawing-rooms or even in Parliament. But go to a man like the Dean of Westminster who will get a move on and carry things out beyond your highest hopes.[58]

Even though over a 10-year period many local papers, magazines and the British Legion credited him as the originator of the idea, there were still some, especially in government, who believed it was someone else.

On 28 November 1930, David received a letter from Major A. Nelson, Secretary of the British Legion. He had read an article in a magazine published out of the parish of Heaton, called the *Heaton Review*. Written by David, the article told of how he came upon the idea of the Unknown Warrior:

> I am particularly anxious that you should meet Major-General Sir Fabian Ware in reference to the announcement made on the subject of the origin of the 'Unknown Warrior's Grave'. General Ware has written to Lord Stopford to say that it was the Dean of Westminster who originated the idea and, therefore I want you to meet the former so that you can enlighten him about the identity of the real originator of the idea.[59]

Sir Fabian Ware (former editor of the *Morning Post*) was the Head of the Imperial War Graves Commission. On 11 December 1930, Major Nelson wrote again:

> I enclose a letter received from Sir Fabian Ware's secretary. I hope you will have occasion to come to London shortly, as I feel sure your meeting Sir Fabian will serve a very useful purpose in the matter of giving publicity to the fact that you were the *fons et origo* [source and origin] of the Unknown Warrior's grave... Let me know as soon as you can set a date for meeting Ware and Lord Stopford for luncheon.[60]

There is no record or evidence of the 'luncheon' taking place. But Sir Fabian Ware never again mentioned that he thought the idea for the Unknown Warrior had emanated from Dean Ryle. And less than a year after Major Nelson's second letter, David wrote a lengthy article 'at the request of the Editor' for the magazine *Our Empire*. From that day forward, he has been rightly recognised as the originator.

If anyone has potential to claim to be the originator of the idea of burying an unknown warrior, then it is Monsieur Binet-Valmer, a highly decorated soldier and leader amongst French war veterans. In 1919, after a long campaign, French authorities announced that they would bury a *poilu inconnu* at the Arc de Triomphe. Their ceremony took place on Armistice Day 1920, the same time as the *Tommy Anonyme* was being buried in Westminster Abbey.

★★★

David and his family spent four years in Shalford, Surrey. While he was vicar there, he played a full part in parish life, just as he had in Margate and Bradford. He was an active member of the local British Legion and vice-president of both the local football and cricket clubs. He also was the originator of the Shalford Cottage scheme, which helped find housing for the poor of the community. As he had done in Margate, he improved the fabric of the church with appeals to build a new vestry, re-cast the church bells, and restore the church organ. As in all his previous positions, he was assured 'good congregations at the Parish Church, by reason of his stimulating and thought-provoking addresses'.[61]

David continued to be heavily involved with the ICF whilst at Shalford, with his travels taking him all over the country and his speeches making the headlines wherever he went. Quoted in *The Derby Daily Telegraph*, David said:

> Jesus Christ was born and brought up in a carpenter's home. He worked as a working man. The sign of the Cross is the sign of the dignity of labour... Some feel that whatever happens the church should deal with religion, and let the great industrial organisations who exist for the purpose deal with industry... There are conditions existing today however, which are soul destroying, and that is the reason for the Industrial Christian Fellowship.[62]

But David did not always please every parishioner. Of the many letters David kept are several written by parishioners who were upset with his point of view. One such letter was from an elderly parishioner in Shalford who pleaded not to have 'anymore of those alarming sermons from Russia'. Her six-sided response ended with, 'I do not apologise for this letter because I am angry with you.'[63]

After four years at Shalford, there were some members of the ICF who felt that it was time David left his quiet country parish and went to a city where he could be more useful. In a 1933 letter exchange with Revd P. B. (Tubby) Clayton, after David had visited the Toc H in Liverpool, they discussed where David should move after his time in Surrey. Revd Clayton writes, 'I am delighted to observe that you felt Gladstone House was the right atmosphere. As for the city churches ... you must hold back for a year or two, but not I hope for long. I believe it is your kind of outlook that is needed.'[64]

For the next two years David continued his parish work in Shalford and attended ICF meetings across the country. But he may have been waiting for the right opening to return to the city where he was first ordained and where he had met his wife.

★★★

In June 1935, David was offered the job of Rector of Liverpool.[65] He was instituted later that year and welcomed by the press. 'Perhaps the long wait has been a blessing in disguise, for the new rector is a man that knows Liverpool.'[66] But the press and the bishop all knew that David would be at a disadvantage. The Our Lady and Saint Nicholas Church, known as St Nick's, had stood on the banks of the Mersey since 1257. But urbanisation of the area and the changing landscape near the Pier Head meant that the number of parishioners had decreased steadily over the years, as one newspaper article describes:

> Business houses and warehouses cover most of the parish and the dwelling-houses left are rapidly being absorbed for business purposes. The character of the parish has changed so much that the new rector, has almost a free hand, and we are hoping to see interesting innovations and developments of Church work under unique conditions.[67]

Throughout the late 1930s, David went about trying to build up the parish of St Nick's. As well as his normal church services, he got out into the community, addressing clubs, committees and groups around Liverpool, soon becoming 'a popular figure in the city and diocese'.[68] After one such meeting to the Rotary Club of Liverpool, the Chairman wrote and thanked him for his talk: 'It is sometimes alleged that the clergy are out of touch with humanity, but you have been in closer touch with most of us... I am sure you got your message over and left us all thinking a bit after we had finished chuckling – which was probably exactly what you wanted.'[69]

★★★

In Europe, it was clear that the dark clouds of war were gathering once more. Young men, like the hundreds whom David had buried during the First World War, would soon be called upon to fight. As the fascist powers of Germany and Italy grew in strength and embarked upon a seemingly ever-expanding global conquest (while most politicians seemed happy enough to placate and appease the aggressors), David voiced his opinion from the pulpit. In July 1936, after Emperor Haile Selassie had pleaded with the League of Nations to intervene against Mussolini's invasion of Abyssinia, David gave an 'outspoken sermon' which the *Liverpool Daily Post and Echo* called, 'Back to Laws of the Jungle?':

> He declared that if truth was truth, Christ to-day would say to the Italians: 'I taught you that whatever you do to the least of my brethren you do to me.' You broke your word – as members of the league to Abyssinia. You broke your word to Great Britain, France and every other nation that signed those same agreements. Your word is a lie.[70]

While Germany started to carve up large slices of Europe and Italy tried to flex its muscles in Africa, Britain went about its business as normal, desperately trying to avoid war. Dissenting voices in parliament such as Winston Churchill's were few in number. Labelled a war-monger, his warnings went unheeded. While a few members of the clergy, such as David Railton, did the same from the pulpit, most chose to ignore what was happening.

Prime Minister Stanley Baldwin and his successor, Neville Chamberlain, hid behind 'scraps of paper' and guarantees from a man hell-bent on rolling back the Treaty of Versailles. In hindsight, it is easy to judge these men. Yet every day they passed the Cenotaph on their way to the Houses of Parliament from Downing Street. Nowhere in the country, except the nearby grave of the Unknown Warrior, was there a more a poignant reminder of the price of war and why it was so important they try to prevent another calamity.

In 1938, even though thousands were visiting the grave of the Unknown Warrior, the Dean and Chapter and Imperial War Graves Commission decided that Dean Ryle's simple black stone and inscription was 'too humble a covering for the symbol of a nation's sacrifice'. There had been complaints that 'strangers who have come from afar as pilgrims to the shrine have passed it unawares and have had to be directed to it by the vergers'. On the new and 'more worthy memorial of the tomb' to be unveiled the following year there was a 'provision for a niche wherein will burn an eternal flame – perpetually'.[71] David kept the newspaper clipping, but he did not comment on the proposed changes, and as Dean Ryle had died in 1925, it appeared that no one objected at the time. The new proposals scheduled to take place in 1939 were never completed.

In March 1939, Hitler invaded Bohemia and Moravia (all that remained of Czechoslovakia after the Munich Agreement). Neville Chamberlain felt betrayed. He had done all he could to stop Hitler through peaceful means – all he could do now was to threaten war. Britain and France drew a line in the sand, committing both countries to Poland's defence. But Hitler didn't take Chamberlain's threats seriously, doubting that Britain and France had the stomach for a fight. The Second World War began on 3 September 1939, after an ultimatum expired for Germany to withdraw from Poland, which it had invaded two days earlier.

***

The Railton family spent the summer at Lismore on the west coast of Scotland. When war broke out and the country was seized by panic, including mass evacuations from most cities, Ruby decided she would not return to Liverpool. Having survived German bombs during the First World War in Folkestone, Ruby was not ready to be subjected to what everyone knew would be much worse in Liverpool. Initially she rented a house south of Kentallen on the shores of Loch Linnhe prior to moving into Ard Rhu, where she stayed for the duration of the war.[72]

David's priority was to comfort and support his parishioners in Liverpool. But he also felt obliged to answer his country's call just as he had done 23 years earlier. On 12 September 1939, David received a letter from the War Office:

> Sir, I am directed to reply to your letter and thank you for your offer of service. I am, however, to inform you that a candidate for a commission as a temporary chaplain for service in the event of war must be under the age of 40. In the circumstances it is regretted that you cannot be considered for appointment.[73]

On the letter David scribbled some notes:

> A silly bit of 'red tape.' We did not expect, being 'old sweats' to be given the
> honour of serving with front-line battalions. In my note, we thought we could
> serve Base Depots at home and abroad, releasing younger men for front line
> work... Well, the RAF called for me in 1943! So here I am.[74]

David even spoke to a journalist about it:

> A padre in the last war, the man who conceived the idea of the Unknown
> Warrior has offered his services again to his country – but he has been told that
> he is not wanted at present. He is 55 – a reserve Army chaplain and wants to
> serve again. 'But they told me there was no chance at the moment... My age is
> against me but I am doing what I can at home – in the ARP – and I have a son
> who has already joined up.'[75]

David seeking publicity this way would seem to contradict his earlier
avoidance of the press. But, with war now declared, as one of the city's
more well-known citizens, David probably felt he was leading by example – if he was willing to join up at his age, then the younger men of
the city might follow suit.

David's family would also do their bit during the war. His only son,
Andrew Scott Railton, who was due to start at Balliol College, Oxford,
that autumn, joined the Liverpool Scottish, a regiment very close to
his father's heart. He was soon transferred to the South Staffordshire
Regiment and sent to Africa. He served with Lord Orde Wingate in
Ethiopia and on the Second Chindit Expedition to Burma. Like his
father, he was awarded the Military Cross and mentioned in dispatches
twice. After briefly being captured by the Japanese, he escaped and
rejoined his regiment in Norway, where, as a major, he stayed until the
end of the war. Two of David's daughters were also involved in the war
effort. Jean joined the Auxiliary Territorial Service (ATS), and Freda
joined the Women's Land Army.[76]

Although he was not asked to serve in the Army, David worked
harder than ever and became involved with many different organisations throughout the early years of the war. Now on his own in
Liverpool, he dedicated all his time to the parish and city. He was the
Chairman of the Liverpool Training School Association, which included

the Akbar Nautical School and the Liverpool Land School.[77] He also became Honorary Chaplain to Liverpool's Home Guard Battalion and was an air-raid warden.

On Armistice Day 1939, David held a special service at St Nick's. For the first time, he asked the congregation to remember not just 'those who had died in the last war but also the men who have already given their lives in this war'. The realisation that the country's youth were again being called upon to give up their lives was evident in the numbers of 'our regular congregation increasingly scattered on Active Service'.[78]

In June 1940, Britain stood alone. It faced the very real possibility of invasion. After France fell and what was left of the British Expeditionary Force in France had been evacuated out of Dunkirk, the country braced itself for the onslaught to come. Liverpool, with its strategically important docks, would surely be a target for German bombers. Hitler knew the vital role Liverpool would play in keeping the country supplied from the United States. The Battle of Britain was fought and won above the skies of southern England in the summer of 1940; but even after the threat of invasion had gone away, cities like Liverpool were not safe.

By Christmas 1940, Liverpool had been bombed 50 times; the city had already taken a pounding. David did his best trying to keep the morale of the city high, preaching in both the cathedral and at St Nick's. In an address to Merseyside Rover Scouts, he said, 'You have done grand work for your country and I hope you will hold on and see it through.'[79] In a sermon he preached about 'the immense task ahead', emphasising that the most important thing needed to win a war was 'morale'.[80] He stressed its importance, especially at Christmas, when he wrote a letter to his parishioners. 'Although we, too, cannot escape the terrors of the Nazi plague, we must not permit it to conquer the spirit of Christmas.'[81] Unfortunately, his resolve would be thoroughly tested during what became known as Liverpool's 'Christmas Blitz'.

On the night of 21 December 1940, St Nick's was hit and large parts of it were destroyed by fire. Nothing much was salvaged except what David could retrieve while the church burned. A newspaper article noted, 'Mr Railton distinguished himself during an air raid in December 1940, when his church was hit, by dashing into the blazing building and rescuing some of the altar vessels.'[82] The death toll reached 345 during three nights of raids, and although bombing decreased in the first few months of 1941, David was left without a church.

He immediately started an appeal to raise £300–£400 to help 'face the cost of salvaging'.[83] This was raised quickly, then he started to collect funds for the restoration. During the appeal, David received hundreds of letters and donations. Money came from many sources: soldiers serving abroad, businessmen of the city, and even the city's poorest parishioners – the community gave what they could. One elderly donor wrote to David, 'Kindly accept this small sum towards the salvaging of St Nicholas Church. I am sorry I cannot make it more. I only get my old age pension. Trusting it will be a little help. Had I been working I would have made it more. Hoping you will soon raise all you require.'[84]

Throughout 1941 and the first half of 1942, David raised £850 towards the salvage and restoration. But without a church, he felt that he was not being utilised. All the work he had done towards building up the church's congregation was undone in one night. In his resignation letter, published in the *Liverpool Daily Post*, 29 April 1942, he thanked the people of the city with 'a few words of gratitude'.[85] On 18 October 1952, the newly constructed St Nicholas Church was built, and David was invited to preach the sermon.[86]

★★★

In June 1941, as well as being Rector of Liverpool, David also became the 'Toc H padre to Liverpool'.[87] After his resignation in May 1942, it was this work that David chose to concentrate on. He was keen to be reunited with his wife in Scotland, and so it was logical that he would be 'especially keen in developing Toc H work' there.[88]

Once he got to Scotland, he applied to 'minister in the Presbyterian Establishment'. His belief that it did not matter what denomination you were, and his wish for a church 'reunion' between Scotland and England, were met with suspicion, as evidenced by an article in the *Scottish Guardian*: 'Whatever views may be held by churchpeople on the problems of reunion, such isolated action as Mr Railton proposes can only result in making the proper approaches more difficult.'[89]

There is no record of any licence granting David permission to preach in a Presbyterian church – his vision of a re-unified church was not appreciated by all.

In 1943, a severe shortage of service chaplains prompted the Archbishops of Canterbury and York to approve a plan for the appointment of seven prominent clergy to work part-time visiting RAF stations and establishments. These seven 'super chaplains' were approved to start 12 January 1943. They included two colleagues of David's, Neville Talbot and Harry Blackburne, who had also been padres in the First World War. For the remainder of the war he spent two weeks of every month visiting RAF bases all over Britain.[90] He helped the men who had beaten back Hitler and who were now winning the war. After Germany surrendered in May 1945, David went home to Scotland.

Although officially retired, he stayed busy at Ard Rhu and travelled back to England many times. Some trips were in an official capacity to help in various parishes while others were for family reasons. In 1948, his brother Gerry, the Archdeacon of Lindsey, died aged 62.[91] In March 1953, David travelled south to officiate with his old friend and ICF colleague, Revd P. T. R. Kirk, at the wedding of his son, Andrew Scott Railton, to Miss Margaret Elizabeth Arnit, in St Peter's Church, Eaton Square, London.[92]

★★★

Since David's flag was dedicated in 1921 and hung in Westminster Abbey, there had never been any question that it was his flag that had covered the coffin of the Unknown Warrior when it was brought home from France. David had always thought that his was the only flag used to cover the coffin. But during the 1950s, he was shocked to discover otherwise.

On 8 July 1954, while David was enjoying his retirement at Ard Rhu, the *Daily Telegraph* published a report claiming that a Mrs Hammack, the widow of Major S. G. Hammack, had in her possession two flags that she said covered the coffin of the Unknown Warrior.[93] In the article, Mrs Hammack claimed that her two flags were used to cover the coffin when it was transported to London. Her late husband brought the flags home, and now, four years after his death, she intended to donate them to Westminster Cathedral, where she hoped they would be used for Mass services each Remembrance Sunday.

After reading the article, David felt compelled to respond. But rather than writing to the editor of the newspaper, he sent a private, hand-written note to Westminster Abbey. He obviously was concerned that there may be some at the Abbey who might question the authenticity of his flag, so he was keen to tell his side of the story.

> Comments of the Revd David Railton in reference to the Report of the Daily Telegraph of 8th July.
>
> 1. I had taken the liberty to ask Bishop Ryle if the Union Jack – in my possession – might be used for the burial – instead of some newly-bought flag – as it had been used at all service occasions – including burials in the front line etc. After bringing it up from Margate for scrutiny it was accepted by the military authorities to be used – as I was told – as the pall of the coffin from France to the Abbey.
>
> 2. A photo (enclosed) and a statement from *The Legionary* – one of many similar statements in – as far as I know – all other journals – proves that it was so used.
>
> 3. I suggest – will request – that an enquiry at the Offices of the CO London Division would clear up the matter. If I remember rightly the CO London Division, at the time was Major General GD Jeffreys. (See note below) He is still – I think – a Member of Parliament, and also holds some high-up Guards' Command. I feel sure he would know all about it – and as he was a proper 'stickler for detail' he might get somewhat of a shock on discovering that – according to Mrs Hammack – the 'Order of the Day' requiring the use of the Union Jack – had been somehow side-tracked by the use of 'two Union Jacks' at the command or bidding of some other person or persons.*
>
> 4. So far as I know it was never the custom of the Royal Navy or Army to cover a coffin with 2 Union Jacks.
>
> 5. Query. If the two Hammack flags were used 'while it was being brought to England' – when were they removed, and by whom, from the British destroyer HMS Verdun? It would not seem to be a very well ordered affair.
>
> *Note – He commanded the 19th Division in which I served as Senior Chaplain. Do not be surprised if he 'flares up' over this! He will soon calm down![94]

From these notes we can conclude that David honestly believed his flag exclusively had been used to cover the coffin of the Unknown Warrior during the entirety of the journey to Westminster from France. This is a perfectly logical assumption, especially if it was what he had been told was going to happen. He gave his flag to the Dean of Westminster on Wednesday, 3 November, and the two undertakers, Mr Noades and Mr Sowerbutts, were at Westminster Abbey with the oak coffin on Sunday, 7 November. The Dean could have given them the flag to be taken to France with the coffin the next day so it could be used from the castle in Boulogne.

But it now does seem likely that David's flag never actually returned to France. It is more likely that David's flag was given to a London District staff officer who then handed it to the sergeant in command of the bearers from 3rd Battalion, the Coldstream Guards. His orders were clear: 'The Bearers will be on the platform to receive the Coffin, which they will then cover with the Union Jack, on which they will place the Steel Helmet and Side-arms.'[95] If David's flag was used from Victoria Station, then whose flag had been on the coffin in France on board HMS *Verdun* and during the rail journey to London?

Orders written on 6 November 1920, from the Admiralty to the captain of HMS *Verdun*, informed him that 'Their Lordships' had selected his ship to carry the body of the Unknown Warrior from Boulogne to Dover on 10 November 1920. The orders contained instructions covering every detail, including a sentence about a flag. 'A large Union Jack is to be taken to cover the coffin from Boulogne to London.'[96] So we have to assume that it was this flag we see being unfurled by the bearers in the castle courtyard at Boulogne on the horse-drawn cart,[97] and this flag travelled on the coffin until it was replaced with David's flag at Victoria Station.

As far as we can tell, the 1954 claims by Mrs Hammack that the two flags in her possession were used are genuine. The coffin was covered with at least one Union Jack after the body had been selected, and the second flag may have come from one of the bodies that was not selected, or it might be the one that covered the pine coffin when it was transported from St Pol to Boulogne. It would make sense that Major Hammack (second-in-command at St Pol) had access to the flags once the ambulance carrying the Unknown Warrior arrived at the castle in Boulogne.

Westminster Cathedral records show that several regimental colours belonging to Irish Regiments were allowed to be laid up on the memorial in St Patrick's Chapel whilst their nearby barracks was being rebuilt. In 1957, six years after they were placed in the Cathedral, they were removed and given back to the regiments. During this time, there seems to have been 'considerable ill-feeling from various quarters on the display of Union Flags in what was an "Irish" chapel'.[98] Bearing this in mind, it is unlikely that the Cardinal and Cathedral authorities would have accepted another two union flags in 1954. The whereabouts of the Hammack flags are unknown.

The whole incident clearly upset David. After 1920, doubts about him being the originator of the idea of the Unknown Warrior must have worn on him. Then, at almost 70 years old, discovering that his flag might not have been the only one used on Armistice Day 1920 when he had been told otherwise must have been hard for him to take.

★★★

After preaching to a large congregation at St Mary's Church, Battle, on Sunday, 26 June 1955,[99] he spent some time with his sister Esther, who still lived in Hastings. On Tuesday, 28 June, he travelled to Berkshire where he stayed with his son, Andrew, his daughter-in-law, Margaret, and his three-month-old granddaughter, Diana, at their home in Waltham St Lawrence. That afternoon whilst walking through the village, one of their neighbours offered them a punnet of fresh strawberries, which they ate after supper.[100]

The next day, David left to start the long journey home to Scotland. He travelled into London that afternoon and caught the sleeper train to Fort William. Leaving King's Cross Station that evening, he was seen off by his daughter, Ruth Railton. He enjoyed dinner on board and read the evening papers while the English countryside sped by before turning in. The train passed through York, Durham, and Newcastle, arriving the next morning at Edinburgh's Waverly Station before heading west to Glasgow. At Glasgow's Queen Street station, the sleeper carriages were attached to the 5.45 A.M. West Highland Line service to Mallaig.[101]

After a brief halt at Corrour Station, the Ben Nevis massif came into view. Situated at the western end of the Grampian mountains, a colossal-sized slab of granite is all that remains of a Devonian period volcano. Standing proud and resolute, defying the ravages of erosion and time, its summit is the highest point in the British Isles. Leaving Corrour and heading north, the 'Glen Class' steam engine hugged the shores of the steep-sided Loch Treig and then headed down into the wooded valley of the River Spean. Turning west along the river, the train stopped briefly at Tulloch, Roy Bridge and Spean Bridge. After the final stop, David put on his hat and coat, then got down his small travelling bag and suitcase from the overhead rack. He slid open the compartment door and stepped into the corridor.

David walked through the carriage, stopping to talk to someone he knew. Just a few hundred yards from the platform, David was standing in the narrow corridor conversing through their compartment door, when another person came down the corridor.[102] As David moved to let the man pass, the train went over points in the track. He lost his balance and fell against the door, which suddenly burst open. David tumbled backwards out of the train.[103] There was nothing the people who witnessed the accident could have done. One of the men pulled the emergency cord, but once the brakes were applied, the train had almost reached the platform. By the time the stationmaster had sent several men back along the track, David had died from his injuries.

***

Even though he had lived his life to the full, there was still a palpable sense of loss in the days after his death, not only because of the tragic manner of his passing, but also because many who knew him thought he was simply indestructible. Everywhere he had been and all who came in contact with him felt his loss deeply.

It is hard to imagine what Ruby must have been feeling. Her whole world must have come crashing down – her idyllic life at Ard Rhu now seeming empty, missing the person with whom she had shared 45 years of her life. But even in her darkest hour, when asked about events surrounding the Unknown Warrior and David's flag, she answered with dignity and grace, and in a way, that would have made him proud: "'My husband asked for the flag to cover dead soldiers,' said his wife last night. "He told me that many troops were being carried from the battle front without a covering, and he felt a flag would be the correct thing.'"[104]

Obituaries were published in most national papers. *The Times* showed that even in death David was still not receiving full recognition for his work. Referring to the Unknown Warrior, they said he was 'generally credited'[105] with the idea. But obituaries in parishes where he had ministered confirmed the high regard in which he was held. In the *Shalford Church Chronicle*, the writer of his obituary said David had 'a profound belief in human beings... The natural result of his attitude was to make anyone in his company feel himself to be a better man... He was truly an inspired disciple of Jesus Christ.'[106]

In Margate, he was remembered 'with fondness as a kind man with a common touch',[107] and his death was said to have 'created profound regret and sorrow amongst the many friends who had great reason to remember his ministry with gratitude'.[108] And in the local Argyle diocese, where he had upset church authorities when he applied for a licence to preach as a Presbyterian, there was nothing but praise for him. He was described as 'a man of great kindness of heart, with a marked capacity for making contacts with all manner of people'.[109]

But of all the kind words written about David after his death, the most comforting for his family would have been several personal letters written to the newspapers. An anonymous Onich resident wrote to *The Scotsman* in July 1955:

> I suppose many of his friends – and how many there must be – will feel an urge to put into words their sense of gratefulness for contact with a man who seemed to spend his whole life in helping others. We got to know David Railton only in his so-called retirement: but ministering to his neighbour must have been his overriding purpose in life, and few can have been so active in their profession after their term of office had officially ceased.
>
> His visits to us were generally unexpected. Sometimes he turned up with Wellington boots ready to give a hand with whatever job was being done. I certainly don't believe that he laboured at gardening for choice. It was a chance to talk to us, and he knew the job had to be done. His conversation – as full of humour as of interest in how each member of the family was getting on – made light work of it for us.

A special gift seemed to be his power to extract simple thoughts from people, enrich them with his own vast experience of human nature and human beings, and hand them back in a way which invariably made his listener feel better off. Who, after all, are the friends we cherish most? Surely those to whom the urge to converse is greatest – be it of joy or sorrow, achievement or disappointment.

Railton never allowed denominational differences to act as a barrier in his friendships… Many will have lost a dear friend. But the memory of him will long be an inspiration. Was there ever a man of whom it could be better said: he loved his fellow man and laboured for their good.[110]

A letter appeared in *The Times* on 8 July 1955:

> J. G. T. writes:
> Many will feel a sense of desolation at the news of the tragic accident which has taken David Railton from us. His brilliant idea … indicates his greatest qualities – an intense feeling for people and a vivid imagination. His great human gifts perhaps never quite fitted comfortably into high office in the church, but that was the church's loss. His heart was too big to be tied to the ecclesiastical machine over much. A great trainer of clergy once said that parsons need a double conversion: from nature to grace, and back again to nature. David Railton trod that way and so exercised a ministry that was irresistible, especially to men.
> *O si sic omnes!* [If all did thus][111]

Harold Broadbent, a former soldier who had worked with David when he was Senior Chaplain to the 19th Division, also wrote in July 1955 of his former padre and his flag:

> It was with sincere regret that I read in the *Echo* of the tragic death of Revd David Railton who was chaplain attached to the famous 19th Division… I used to prepare his portable altar and serve each Sunday. The Union Jack was always used as a frontal or covering. When the body of the Unknown Warrior was brought home for burial in the Abbey, I wrote to Padre Railton asking if the Union Jack used as a pall was the one he had used each Sunday. I had a pleasing answer to my letter, in which he said, 'I am sure you must be very proud that it is the same Union Jack you so often arranged for me.' It is one of my most treasured memories of my war service in France.[112]

★★★

David was buried at St Bride's Church in Onich, North Ballachulish, just a short distance from Ard Rhu. St Bride's, a small Scottish Episcopalian church on the shores of Loch Linnhe, was packed. Many were unable to get inside. Included with those who stood outside on the porch during the funeral service was a group of Roman Catholic priests still constrained by Canon Law from taking part in any non-Catholic service.[113] Unable to enter the church, they still wanted to pay their respects to their fellow clergyman and friend.[114] David was laid to rest in St Bride's graveyard, just a short distance from the loch, a fitting and idyllic resting place for a man who loved the Highlands.

Ruby would live at Ard Rhu with her daughter, Jean, for another 11 years before joining her husband at St Bride's. Written on the base of their simple granite cross are the words:

IN LOVING MEMORY OF DAVID RAILTON 1884–1955
ALSO HIS WIFE RUBY MARION RAILTON 1879–1966

On the other side of the gravestone is written an inscription taken from Song of Solomon 2:17:

UNTIL THE DAY BREAK AND
THE SHADOWS FLEE AWAY

Epilogue

After the television camera crews dismantled their equipment and left the Abbey, the staff began preparing everything for the doors to re-open to the public later that morning. The thousands of extra chairs they needed the day before were taken away, and the Abbey's floor was clear by the time the Dean walked down the Nave.

Wearing the distinctive red cassock and black gown of the Dean of Westminster, The Very Revd Wesley Carr now stood with his back to the Great West door. He was carrying a wreath of white roses and sweet peas that had the day before sat on top of the coffin of Queen Elizabeth, the Queen Mother.[1] At her request the wreath was being placed on the grave of the Unknown Warrior. The Dean slowly moved forward, tracing the footsteps that Lady Elizabeth Bowes-Lyons had taken 79 years prior. He gracefully knelt down and placed the wreath upon the grave.[2] The Abbey was perfectly quiet and still – the only sound came from the camera shutter of the photographer on the other side of the grave.

The Dean rose and stood quietly by the grave for a moment as Lady Elizabeth had done after placing her bouquet of flowers before her wedding service in 1923. But, unlike when Lady Elizabeth stood there and looked up at the Padre's Flag all those years ago, the Dean wasn't able to do so.

After David Railton's flag had been dedicated and hung on Armistice Day, 1921, it remained in place for almost 32 years, an integral part of the Abbey's fabric, intrinsically linked to the story of the Unknown Warrior for all to see. In 1953, approval was given for the BBC to broadcast the Coronation of Queen Elizabeth II. It was the first time that an event would be broadcast live on television from inside Westminster Abbey. The BBC was limited to where they could place their cameras; they needed an un-obstructed view down the length of the Abbey. So the Padre's Flag was removed. Sometime after the Coronation, it was hung where it still hangs today, in St George's Chapel, just inside the Great West doors.

Over the years there have been several appeals[3] and requests from different sources to have the flag replaced on the pillar where it belongs. Time has taken its toll on the fabric, and the colour has faded. But even if it hangs out of the way, it will forever be linked with the Unknown Warrior and the remarkable man who carried it.

Countries that adopted the idea of the Unknown Warrior

1920	France – Arc de Triomphe, Paris
	United Kingdom – Westminster Abbey, London
1921	Portugal – Monastery of the Dominicans, Batalha
	United States of America – Arlington Military Cemetery, Washington DC
1922	Belgium – Congress Column, Brussels
	Czech Republic – Czechoshslovak Tomb of the Unknown Soldier, Prague
	Italy – Altare della Patria, Rome
1923	Rumania – Bucharest
1925	Poland – Pilsudski Square, Warsaw
1932	Greece – Syntagma Square, Athens
1933	Austria – Heldenplatz, Vienna
1938	Serbia – Mount Avala, Belgrade
1944	Turkey – Gallipoli
1953	Japan – Ogoese, Saitama
1954	Finland – Hietaniemi Cemetery, Helsinki
1966	Russia – Kremlin Wall, Moscow
1967	Brazil – Flamengo Park, Rio de Janeiro
1971	India – India Gate, New Delhi
1973	Dominican Republic – Flag Square, Santo Domingo

1977	Chile – Unknown Sailor Monument, Iquique
1980	Iraq – Baghdad
1981	Bulgaria – Paris Street, Sofia
1982	Bangladesh – National Martyrs' Memorial, Savar
1983	Australia – Australian War Memorial, Canberra
1984	Egypt – Nasr City, Cairo
1989	Hungary – Heroes' Square, Budapest
1999	Canada – Canadian War Memorial, Ottawa
2002	Namibia – Heroes' Acre, Windhoek
2004	Israel – Mount Herzl, Jerusalem
	New Zealand – National War Memorial, Wellington

Notes

Preface

1 Michael Moynihan, *God on Our Side* (London, Leo Cooper, 1983), 75.
2 Mr. David Railton QC, conversation with author, 4 Sep 2015.
3 Mrs. Margaret Railton, conversation with author, 3 Apr 2014.

Prologue

1 'Duke of York engaged to Lady Elizabeth Bowes-Lyon', *The Times*, 16 Jan 1923.
2 'Service Index Card *Bowes-Lyon, The Hon, Claude*, Second Life Guards 1848–1854', Household Cavalry Museum, Windsor.
3 A New York – Newport Wedding Blog, 'Inspiration… British Royal Wedding Bouquets', http://newportweddings.blogspot.com/2011/03/inspiration-british-royal-wedding.htm (accessed 22 Mar 2014).

Chapter 1

1 'Statistics of Crime', Chief Constable's Report, dated 16 Apr 1915, Margate Museum Archive.
2 David Railton, letter to Ruby Railton, 9 Jan 1917, Railton Letters, Imperial War Museum 80/22/1.
3 'The People's Homage', *The Times*, 13 Nov 1920.
4 J. M. Trethowan, 'The Unknown Warrior Flag', letter to the editor of the *Daily Telegraph*, 26 Apr 1972, Railton Family Archive.
5 'Mandate for the induction of the Rev'd David Railton', induction date 25 Sep 1920, Canterbury Cathedral Archive, DCb-F/A/1920/19.
6 Kathleen Lockyer, letter to Andrew Scott Railton, 29 Apr 1972, Railton Family Archive.

7   Mrs Margaret Railton, conversation with author, 17 Aug 2014.

8   Mick Twyman, 'The Rev. David Railton, M.C., Inspiration for the Unknown Warrior', *Margate Historical Society Magazine*, Winter 2008.

9   Bernard Watson, *Soldier Saint* (London, Hodder & Stoughton, 1972), 18.

10 George Scott Railton, letter to Colonel Kitching, 29 Aug 1904. GSR 1/7, Salvation Army Heritage Centre, William Booth College, London.

11 David Railton, 'Transcript of Broadcast', Date Unknown, Railton Family Archive.

12 Watson, *Soldier Saint*, 74.

13 England & Wales Birth Index 1837–1915, 'David Railton', Hackney, London, accessed through *Ancestry.com*.

14 Watson, *Soldier Saint*, 94.

15 England & Wales Birth Index 1837–1915, 'Nathaniel Railton', Hackney, London, accessed through *Ancestry.com*.

16 England & Wales Birth Index 1837–1915, 'Esther Railton', Hackney, London, accessed through *Ancestry.com*.

17 1901 Census of England, 'Marianne Railton', Margate, Kent, England, accessed through *Ancestry.com*.

18 Mr Ian Dickie (Margate Museum), conversation with author, 20 Mar 2016.

19 Margate Local and Family History, 'Churchfields Area', https://www.facebook.com/MargateHistory/photos (accessed 23 Sep 2015).

20 Richard Holmes, *Tommy – The British Soldier on the Western Front 1914–18* (London, Harper Collins, 2004), 571.

21 Richard Garrett, *The Final Betrayal: The Armistice, 1918… and Afterwards* (Southampton, Martins, 1989), 147.

22 'The Vicar of Margate', *Thanet Gazette*, 16 Sep 1925.

23 Ibid.

24 Ibid.

25 Robin Colyer, 'Notes taken from Margate Parish News', email to author 31 Jan 2014.

26 Mr Ian Dickie (Margate Museum), conversation with author, 20 Mar 2016.

27 Chief Constable's Report, 1915, Margate Museum Archive.

28 UK War Memorials, 'Margate Borough Police Force', http://www.iwm.org.uk/memorials/item/memorial/48762 (accessed 7 Apr 2016).

29 Chief Constable's Report, 1915, Margate Museum Archive.

30 Ibid.

31 Ibid.

32 National Association of Retired Police Officers, 'Ramsgate Coke Riots of 1920', http://eastkentnarpo.org.uk/docs/Newsletter%20122%20Nov%2009.pdf (accessed 21 Mar 2014).

33 'Letter written by Rev. Railton to Parishioners', *Margate Parish News*, October 1920, Railton Family Archive.

Chapter 2

1 David Railton to Ruby Railton, dated 26 Apr 1916.
2 Marriage certificate, 'David Railton' Registry District – Longtown, Volume 10b, Page 885, accessed through *Ancestry.com*.
3 Mrs Margaret Railton, conversation with author, 14 Nov 2014.
4 The National Archive, *Army Service Record – David Railton*, WO374/56017 C597937.
5 1911 England Census, www.ancestry.co.uk (accessed 11 Mar 2015).
6 Ibid.
7 Mrs Margaret Railton, conversation with author, 5 Sep 2014.
8 'Enthronement of the new Bishop of Liverpool', *The Times*, 1 Jun 1900.
9 Certificate of Service – Private David Railton 1st (Oxford University) Volunteers, 15 Nov 1904 – 31 Mar 1908, Railton Family Archive.
10 Mrs Margaret Railton, conversation with author, 3 Apr 2014.
11 David Railton, *The Story of a Padre's Flag – Told by the Flag, 1*, Railton Family Archive.
12 Ibid., 16.
13 David Railton to Ruby Railton, dated 10 Jan 1917.
14 The Ancient Society of Elquire Leeds Youths, 'The Palmer, Alcock, Sharp & Tindal Trust', http://www.asely.org.uk/TCEA/aimsobjectives.html (accessed 30 April 2015).
15 'Commissions, Chaplains Dept of the Territorial Force', *London Gazette, 9075*, 1 Dec 1911.
16 David Blake, Museum of Army Chaplaincy, email to author, 28 Mar 2014.
17 The Ancient Society of Elquire Leeds Youths, 'The Palmer, Alcock, Sharp & Tindal Trust', http://www.asely.org.uk/TCEA/aimsobjectives.html (accessed 2 Feb 2015).
18 The National Archive, *Army Service Record – David Railton*, WO374/56017 C597937.
19 J. N. Trethowan, letter to Andrew Scott Railton, 24 Apr 1972.
20 The National Archive, *Army Service Record – David Railton*, WO374/56017 C597937.
21 David Railton to Ruby Railton, dated 11 Jan 1916.
22 Marianne Railton, letter to Commissioner Cadman, 24 Aug 1914. GSR 1/7, Salvation Army Heritage Centre, William Booth College, London.
23 Eileen Douglas and Mildred Duff, *Commissioner Railton* (London, Salvationist Publishing, 1920), 214.
24 Ibid.
25 David Railton, 'Poem for His Father', Railton Family Archive.
26 David Railton to Ruby Railton, dated 16 Jan 1916.
27 David Railton to Ruby Railton, dated 15 Jan 1916.

28 David Railton to Ruby Railton, dated 20 Jan 1916.

29 John Shakespear, *The Thirty-Fourth Division* (Naval & Military Press), 13.

30 David Blake, Museum of Army Chaplaincy, email to author, 30 Apr 2015.

31 David Railton to Ruby Railton, dated 16 Feb 1916.

32 Railton, *The Story of a Padre's Flag*, 12.

33 David Railton, 'The Origin of the Unknown Warrior's Grave', *Our Empire*, Vol VII, No 8, 1931.

34 David Railton to Ruby Railton, dated 20 Feb 1916.

35 Mrs Grace Reed, letter to David Railton, dated 15 Mar 1916, Railton Family Archive.

36 Ibid.

37 David Railton to Ruby Railton, dated 3 Mar 1916.

38 Ibid.

39 Ibid.

40 Ibid.

41 David Railton to Ruby Railton, dated 4 Mar 1916.

42 David Railton to Ruby Railton, dated 20 Jul 1916.

43 Edward Duncan letter to David Railton, dated 31 Mar 1916, Railton Family Archive.

44 David Railton to Ruby Railton, dated 27 Mar 1917.

Chapter 3

1 Alan H. Maude, *The 47th (London Division)* (London, Amalgamated Press, 1922), 60.

2 David Railton to Ruby Railton, dated 14 Aug 1916.

3 David Railton to Ruby Railton, dated 1 Aug 1916.

4 'Music Cure for Shellshock', *The Times*, 12 November 1920.

5 David Railton to Ruby Railton, dated 14 Aug 1916.

6 Maude, *The 47th (London Division)*, 51.

7 David Railton to Ruby Railton, dated 26 Apr 1916.

8 David Railton to Ruby Railton, dated 28 Apr 1916.

9 Douglas and Duff, *Commissioner Railton*, 34.

10 David Blake, Museum of Army Chaplaincy, email to author, 13 Oct 2014.

11 Peter Howson, *Muddling Through – The Organisation of British Army Chaplaincy in World War One* (Solihull, Helion, 2013), 83.

12 David Railton to Ruby Railton, dated 29 Apr 1916.

13 W. J. Bradley, letter to Andrew Scott Railton, 17 Aug 1965, Railton Family Archive.

14 John Smyth, *In This Sign Conquer* (London, Mowbray, 1968), 164.

15 Michael Snape, *The Royal Army Chaplains' Department – Clergy Under Fire* (Woodbridge, The Boydell Press, 2008), 221–222.

16 Robert Graves, *Goodbye to All That* (London, Jonathan Cape, 1929), 158.

17 David Railton to Ruby Railton, dated 25 Sep 1916.

18 Snape, *Clergy Under Fire*, 223.

19 Commonwealth War Graves Commission, 'Cabaret-Rouge British Cemetery', http://www.cwgc.org/find-a-cemetery/cemetery/64600/cabaret-rouge%20british%20cemetery,%20souchez (accessed 1 Jul 2015).

20 Hellfire Corner, 'Old Haunts Revisited – Major Charles Fair', http://hellfirecorner.co.uk/cfair/haunts.htm (accessed 15 Oct 2014).

21 David Railton's Correspondence Book (Field Service), Army Book 152, Railton Family Archive.

22 RAMC in the Great War, 'The RAMC Chain of Evacuation', http://ramcww1.com/chain_of_evacuation.php (accessed 2 Jul 2015).

23 Commonwealth War Graves Commission, 'Cabaret-Rouge British Cemetery', http://www.cwgc.org/find-a-cemetery/cemetery/64600/cabaret-rouge%20british%20cemetery,%20souchez (accessed 1 Jul 2015).

24 The Western Front Association, 'Identifying the Dead: A Short Study of the Identification Tags of 1914–18', http://westernfrontassociation.com/the-great-war/great-war-on-land/weapons-equipment-uniform/1033-identifying-dead-short-study-identification-tags-1914-1918.html (accessed 6 Jul 2015).

25 Ibid.

26 Maude, *The 47th (London Division)*, 56.

27 Ibid., 57.

Chapter 4

1 The National Archive, *War Diary of 1/19th Bn, The London Regiment (St Pancras)*, WO95/2738.

2 David Railton to Ruby Railton, dated 20 and 24 Sep 1916.

3 David Railton to Ruby Railton, dated 31 Jul 1916.

4 Maude, *The 47th (London) Division*, 61.

5 David Railton to Ruby Railton, dated 31 Jul 1916.

6 Maude, *The 47th (London) Division*, 61.

7 *The Official History of the Great War – Military Operations France & Belgium – 1916 Volume 1 Appendices* (Chippenham, CPI Anthony Rowe), 6–27.

8 Ibid., 7.

9 Ibid., 28.

10 Terry Norman, *The Hell They Called High Wood – The Somme 1916* (Barnsley, Pen & Sword, 2009), 21.

11 Ibid.

12 Malcolm Brown, *The Imperial War Museum Book of the Somme* (London, Sidgwick & Jackson, 1996), 4.

13 'For Gawd's Sake Don't Send Me', 1960 episode of BBC Documentary *The Great War* (The Sceptic Isle, YouTube, 2015).

14 Neil Hanson, *Unknown Soldiers – The Story of the Missing of the First World War* (New York, Vintage, 2007), 86.

15 Legends & Traditions of the Great War, 'The Leaning Virgin of Albert', http://www.worldwar1.com/heritage/leaningv.htm (accessed 20 Oct 2015).

16 David Railton to Ruby Railton, dated 5 Oct 1916.

17 Ibid.

18 Norman, *The Hell They Called High Wood*, 213–214.

19 Ibid., 214.

20 Ibid.

21 1911 Census of England, 'Robert Monro', Bethnal Green, London, England, accessed through *Ancestry.com*.

22 David Blake, Museum of Army Chaplaincy, email to author, 15 Oct 2014.

23 David Railton to Ruby Railton, dated 12 Sep 1916.

24 Ibid.

25 Norman, *The Hell They Called High Wood*, 217.

26 Maude, *The 47th (London) Division*, 64.

27 The National Archive, *War Diary of 1/19th Bn, The London Regiment (St Pancras)*, WO95/2738.

28 Ibid.

29 Ibid.

30 Ibid.

31 Reginald and Charles Fair, *Marjorie's War* (Brighton, Menin House, 2012), 425.

32 David Railton to Ruby Railton, dated 17 Aug 1916.

33 The National Archive, *War Diary of 1/19th Bn, The London Regiment (St Pancras)*, WO95/2738.

34 Ibid.

35 Ibid.

36 Ibid.

37 Ibid.

38 Commonwealth War Graves Commission, 'London Cemetery and Extension, Longueval', http://www.cwgc.org/find-acemetery/cemetery/2090400/london%20cemetery%20and%20extension,%20longueval (accessed 26 Oct 2015).

39 David Railton to Ruby Railton, dated 1 Oct 1916.

40 Fair, *Marjorie's War*, 428–433.

41 Commonwealth War Graves Commission, 'Flatiron Copse Cemetery, Mametz', http://www.cwgc.org/find-acemetery/cemetery/61700/flatiron%20copse%20cemetery,%20mametz (accessed 27 Oct 2015).

42 Railton, *The Story of a Padre's Flag*, 13.

43 The National Archive, *War Diary of 1/19th Bn, The London Regiment (St Pancras)*, WO95/2738.

44 Railton, *The Story of a Padre's Flag*, 13.

45 Commonwealth War Graves Commission, 'Flatiron Copse Cemetery, Mametz', http://www.cwgc.org/find-acemetery/cemetery/61700/flatiron%20copse%20cemetery,%20mametz (accessed 27 Oct 2015).

46 Fair, *Marjorie's War*, 194.
47 David Railton to Ruby Railton, dated 24 Sep 1916.
48 David Railton to Ruby Railton, dated 30 Aug 1916.
49 Fair, *Marjorie's War*, 71.
50 Ibid., 141.
51 Ibid., 192.
52 Ibid.
53 'Story of a Drum-Head', *The Journal of the 19th London Regiment*, Volume 2, No 11, Christmas 1922.
54 Ibid.
55 Ibid.
56 David Railton to Ruby Railton, dated 1 Oct 1916.
57 Mrs Lockyer to Andrew Scott Railton, dated 24 Apr 1972.
58 Fair, *Marjorie's War*, 196.
59 Norman, *The Hell They Called High Wood*, 235.
60 Ibid.
61 Ibid., 235–236.
62 Ibid., 235.
63 Holmes, *Tommy*, 217.
64 The National Archive, *War Diary of 1/19th Bn, The London Regiment (St Pancras)*, WO95/2738.
65 David Railton to Ruby Railton, dated 25 Sep 1916.
66 Fair, *Marjorie's War*, 196.
67 Ibid.
68 Officer's Roll & Next of Kin – 1/19th London Regiment, Railton Family Archive.
69 Note written by Captain L. J. Davis – 1/19th London Regiment, Railton Family Archive.
70 Officer's Roll & Next of Kin – 1/19th London Regiment, Railton Family Archive.
71 Fair, *Marjorie's War*, 195.
72 David Railton to Ruby Railton, dated 25 Sep 1916.
73 'Stocks of Shells and Guns Better Than Anticipated', *The Times*, 2 Jun 1916, 5.
74 Commonwealth War Graves Commission, 'Flatiron Copse Cemetery, Mametz', http://www.cwgc.org/find-acemetery/cemetery/61700/flatiron%20copse%20cemetery,%20mametz (accessed 27 Oct 2015).
75 William W. Henderson, letter to David Railton, dated 1 Oct 1916, Railton Family Archive.

Chapter 5

1 David Railton to Ruby Railton, dated 19 Dec 1916.
2 The Weather Network, Remembering WW1; weather in the trenches, http://www.theweathernetwork.com/uk/news/articles/remembering-ww1-weather-in-the-trenches/33267/ (accessed 10 Nov 2015).

3   David Railton to Ruby Railton, dated 15 Oct 1916.
4   Ibid.
5   Maude, *The 47th (London) Division*, 79.
6   Ibid.
7   David Railton to Ruby Railton, dated 15 Oct 1916.
8   Ibid.
9   Maude, *The 47th (London) Division*, 80.
10 Ibid.
11 Ibid.
12 Ibid., 70.
13 Ibid., 76.
14 David Railton to Ruby Railton, dated 1 Oct 1916.
15 Ibid.
16 Maude, *The 47th (London) Division*, 76.
17 Ibid.
18 *Supplement to The London Gazette*, 11543, 25 Nov 1916.
19 Maude, *The 47th (London) Division*, 76.
20 'Eaucourt L'Abbaye', *The Times*, 12 Oct 1916.
21 B. H. Liddell Hart, *The Tanks: The History of the Royal Tank Regiment and its Predecessors, Heavy Branch Machine Gun Corps 1914–45, Volume One* (London, Cassell, 1959), 85–86.
22 Maude, *The 47th (London) Division*, 76.
23 David Railton to Ruby Railton, dated 4 Oct 1916.
24 David Railton, letter to Marianne Railton, 5 Dec 1916. GSR 1/3, Salvation Army Heritage Centre, William Booth College, London.
25 David Railton to Ruby Railton, dated 5 Oct 1916.
26 David Railton to Ruby Railton, dated 4 Oct 1916.
27 David Railton to Ruby Railton, dated 14 Nov 1916.
28 'Statement as to the character of Pte S Filmer' – David Railton, Railton Family Archive.
29 *Supplement to The London Gazette*, 11543, 25 Nov 1916.
30 Ibid.
31 David Railton to Ruby Railton, dated 30 Aug 1916.
32 *Supplement to The London Gazette*, 1 Jan 1916, 68.
33 *Supplement to The London Gazette*, 14 Jan 1916, 577.
34 Selwyn Gummer, *The Chavasse Twins: A Biography of Christopher M. Chavasse, Bishop of Rochester, and Noel G. Chavasse* (1963), 55.
35 Ann Clayton, *Chavasse Double VC* (Barnsley, Leo Cooper, 1992), 134.
36 Ibid., 132.
37 *Supplement to The London Gazette*, 26 Oct 1916, 10394.
38 Ibid.
39 Noel Chavasse letter to Francis and Edith Chavasse, 7 Sep 1916, Imperial War Museum 17596.

40 *Supplement to The London Gazette*, 26 Oct 1916, 10394.
41 The National Archive, *War Diary of 1/19th Bn, The London Regiment (St Pancras)*, WO95/2738.
42 David Railton to Ruby Railton, dated 15 Oct 1916.
43 David Railton to Ruby Railton, dated 14 Nov 1916.
44 The National Archive, *War Diary of 1/19th Bn, The London Regiment (St Pancras)*, WO95/2738.
45 David Railton to Ruby Railton, dated 14 Nov 1916.
46 Ibid.
47 *Supplement to The London Gazette*, 11543, 25 Nov 1916.
48 The National Archive, *War Diary of 1/19th Bn, The London Regiment (St Pancras)*, WO95/2738.
49 'Brave Chaplain', *The Shorncliffe and Hythe Advertiser*, 2 Dec 1916, Railton Family Archive.
50 Ibid.
51 'Heroic Chaplain', *The East Kent Times*, 2 Dec 1916, Railton Family Archive.
52 'Brave Chaplain', *The Folkestone Express*, 2 Dec 1916, Railton Family Archive.
53 David Railton, to Marianne Railton, 5 Dec 1916.
54 Bishop Llewellyn Gwynne letter to David Railton, dated 5 Dec 1916, Railton Family Archive.
55 *Supplement to The London Gazette*, 14 Sep 1916, 953.
56 Michael Ashcroft, *Victoria Cross Heroes* (London, Headline, 2006), 165.
57 Clayton, *Chavasse Double VC*, 206.
58 Commonwealth War Graves Commission, 'Brandhoek New Military Cemetery' http://www.cwgc.org/find-acemetery/cemetery/4003808/brandhoek%20new%20military%20cemetery (accessed 3 Dec 2015).
59 Ashcroft, *Victoria Cross Heroes*, 167.

Chapter 6

1 David Railton to Ruby Railton, dated 21 Apr 1917.
2 David Railton to Ruby Railton, dated 29 Apr 1917.
3 David Railton to Ruby Railton, dated 14 Apr 1917.
4 Ibid.
5 Maude, *The 47th (London) Division*, 82.
6 Ibid.
7 Ibid., 80–81.
8 The National Archive, *War Diary of the 19th London Regiment*, WO 95/2738/1.
9 Ibid.
10 Maude, *The 47th (London) Division*, 82.
11 The National Archive, *War Diary of the 19th London Regiment*, WO 95/2738/1.
12 David Railton to Ruby Railton, dated 15 Nov 1916.

13 Commonwealth War Graves Commission, Lijessenthoek Military Cemetery, http://www.cwgc.org/find-acemetery/cemetery/14900/lijssenthoek%20military%20cemetery (Accessed 19 Apr 2016).

14 David Railton to Ruby Railton, dated 15 Nov 1916.

15 Ibid.

16 David Railton to Ruby Railton, dated 17 Nov 1916.

17 Ibid.

18 The National Archive, *War Diary of the 19th London Regiment*, WO 95/2738/1.

19 David Railton to Ruby Railton, dated 28 Nov 1916.

20 The National Archive, *War Diary of the 19th London Regiment*, WO 95/2738/1.

21 David Railton to Ruby Railton, dated 2 Dec 1916.

22 A. H. Hussey, *The Fifth Division in the Great War* (London, Nisbet, 1921), 60.

23 David Railton to Ruby Railton, dated 2 Dec 1916.

24 The National Archive, *War Diary of the 19th London Regiment*, WO 95/2738/1.

25 David Railton to Ruby Railton, dated 18 Dec 1916.

26 Maude, *The 47th (London) Division*, 84.

27 The National Archive, *War Diary of the 19th London Regiment*, WO 95/2738/1.

28 David Railton to Ruby Railton, dated 20 Dec 1916.

29 David Railton to Ruby Railton, dated 21 Dec 1916.

30 Maude, *The 47th (London) Division*, 84–85.

31 David Railton to Ruby Railton, dated 28 Apr 1917.

32 David Railton to Ruby Railton, dated 18 Dec 1916.

33 Winston Groom, *A Storm in Flanders* (New York, Grove Press, 2002), 83.

34 Thomas Vinciguerra, 'The Truce of Christmas 1914', *New York Times*, 25 Dec 2005.

35 'The Scots Guards' Christmas – A Piper's Impression', *The Times*, 11 Jan 1915.

36 Ibid.

37 Maude, *The 47th (London) Division*, 85.

38 Ibid., 86.

39 Ibid., 85.

40 Ibid.

41 David Railton to Ruby Railton, dated 23 Dec 1916.

42 Ibid.

43 David Railton to Ruby Railton, dated 24 Dec 1916.

44 David Railton to Ruby Railton, dated 26 Dec 1916.

45 Revd David Railton sermon, 6 Jan 1921, *Vicar's Book*, St John the Baptist, Margate, Canterbury Cathedral Archive.

46 The National Archive, *War Diary of the 19th London Regiment*, WO 95/2738/1.

47 Ibid.

48 David Railton to Ruby Railton, dated 28 Dec 1916.

49 David Railton to Ruby Railton, dated 30 Dec 1916.

50 The National Archive, *War Diary of the 19th London Regiment*, WO 95/2738/1.

51 David Railton to Ruby Railton, dated 5 Jan 1917.
52 The National Archive, *War Diary of the 19th London Regiment*, WO 95/2738/1.
53 David Railton to Ruby Railton, dated 8 Jan 1917.
54 Commonwealth War Graves Commission, 'Woods Cemetery', http://www.cwgc.org/find-acemetery/cemetery/53100/woods%20cemetery (accessed 11 Feb 2016).
55 David Railton to Ruby Railton, dated 8 Jan 1917.
56 Commonwealth War Graves Commission, 'Woods Cemetery', http://www.cwgc.org/find-acemetery/cemetery/53100/woods%20cemetery (accessed 11 Feb 2016).
57 David Railton to Ruby Railton, dated 8 Jan 1917.
58 David Railton to Ruby Railton, dated 9 Jan 1917.
59 WW1 Service Medal & Award Rolls, 'David Railton', accessed through *Ancestry.com*.
60 Railton, D., Service Record Index Card, Museum of Army Chaplaincy Archive.
61 Mr W. J. Bradley to Andrew Scott Railton, dated 17 Aug 1965.
62 The National Archive, *War Diary of the 19th London Regiment*, WO 95/2738/1.
63 David Railton to Ruby Railton, dated 13 Jan 1917.
64 David Railton to Ruby Railton, dated 17 Jan 1917.
65 David Railton to Ruby Railton, dated 19 Jan 1917.
66 David Railton to Ruby Railton, dated 6 Feb 1917.
67 David Railton to Ruby Railton, dated 31 Jan 1917.
68 David Railton to Ruby Railton, dated 11 Feb 1917.
69 David Railton to Ruby Railton, dated 11 Feb 1917.
70 David Railton to Ruby Railton, dated 23 Mar 1917.
71 Maude, *The 47th (London) Division*, 95.
72 Ibid.
73 Firstworldwar.com, 'Sir Douglas Haig's Third Despatch, 31 May 1917', http://www.firstworldwar.com/source/haighindenburgdespatch.htm (accessed 26 Feb 2016).
74 Ibid.
75 Jack Sheldon, *The German Army at Cambrai*, (Barnsley, Pen & Sword, 2009), 4–5.
76 Peter Chasseaud, *Mapping the First World War – The Great War Through Maps from 1914–18* (Collins, Glasgow, 2013), 222.
77 The National Archive, *War Diary of the 19th London Regiment*, WO 95/2738/1.
78 Ibid.
79 David Railton to Ruby Railton, dated 8 Apr 1917.
80 The National Archive, *War Diary of the 19th London Regiment*, WO 95/2738/1.
81 Order of Service, Talbot House, Easter 1917, Railton Family Archive.
82 World War One Battlefields, 'Poperinghe', http://www.ww1battlefields.co.uk/flanders/pop.html (accessed 7 Mar 2016).
83 Postcard from Poperinghe, Railton Family Archive.

84 Groom, *A Storm in Flanders*, 140.

85 World War One Battlefields, 'Poperinghe', http://www.ww1battlefields.co.uk/flanders/pop.html (accessed 11 Mar 2016).

86 David Railton to Ruby Railton, dated 17 Nov 1916.

87 The Great War 1914–1918, 'The Story of Talbot House (Toc H), Poperinghe', http://www.greatwar.co.uk/ypres-salient/museum-talbot-house-history.htm (accessed 11 Mar 2016).

88 Ibid.

89 Revd P. B. Clayton letter to David Railton, dated 6 May 1933, Railton Family Archive.

90 G. J. Meyer, *A World Undone – The Story of the Great War 1914 to 1918* (New York, Bantam, 2006), 480.

91 John Keegan, *The First World War* (New York, Vintage, 2000), 265.

92 David Railton to Ruby Railton, dated 10 Feb 1917.

93 The National Archive, *War Diary of the 19th London Regiment*, WO 95/2738/1.

94 David Railton to Ruby Railton, dated 14 Apr 1917.

95 The National Archive, *War Diary of the 19th London Regiment*, WO 95/2738/1.

96 Mr W. J. Bradley to Andrew Scott Railton, dated 17 Aug 1965.

Chapter 7

1 Everard Wyrall, *The Nineteenth Division 1914–18* (London, The Naval and Military Press), 106.

2 Peter Oldham, *Messines Ridge – Ypres* (Barnsley, Leo Cooper, 1998), 62.

3 Ibid., 55.

4 Wyrall, *The Nineteenth Division 1914–18*, 89.

5 Oldham, *Messines Ridge – Ypres*, 57–58.

6 David Railton to Ruby Railton, dated 17 Apr 1917.

7 Wyrall, *The Nineteenth Division 1914–18*, 89.

8 Ibid.

9 Oldham, *Messines Ridge – Ypres*, 73.

10 Chasseaud, *Mapping the First World War*, 231.

11 Harlan K. Ullman & James P. Wade, *Shock and Awe: Achieving Rapid Dominance* (National Defense University, 1996), XXIV.

12 Wyrall, *The Nineteenth Division 1914–18*, 90–91.

13 Ibid., 91.

14 John James Wallace, letter to David Railton, dated 28 Aug 1917, Railton Family Archive.

15 The National Archive, *Army Service Record – Wallace, Revd, JJ*, WO374/71367.

16 David Blake, Museum of Army Chaplaincy, email to author, 8 Dec 2015.

17 Ibid.

18 Ibid.

19 Ibid.
20 John James Wallace, to David Railton, dated 28 Aug 1917.
21 David Blake, 'Chaplain's Bombing School, St Omer', Research paper, Museum of Army Chaplaincy.
22 Ibid.
23 Ibid.
24 Ibid.
25 G. L. Blakemore, letter to David Railton, dated 10 Aug 1917, Railton Family Archive.
26 The National Archive, *War Diary of 1/8th Bn, The North Staffordshire Regiment (Prince of Wales's Own)*, WO95/2085/2.
27 Ibid.
28 1911 Census of England, 'Denis Jetson Blakemore', Bicton, Shrewsbury, England, accessed through *Ancestry.com*.
29 The National Archive, *Field General Court Martial – Blakemore, DJ*, WO71/569.
30 Ibid.
31 G. L. Blakemore, to David Railton, dated 25 Jul 1917.
32 G. L. Blakemore, to David Railton, dated 10 Aug 1917.
33 Julian Putowski and Julian Sykes, *Shot at Dawn* (London, Leo Cooper, 1989), 25.
34 Ibid., 26–27.
35 Ibid., 27–180.
36 Ibid., 11.
37 Anthony Babington, *For the Sake of Example – Capital Courts Martial 1914–20: The Truth* (London, Leo Cooper, 1983), Preface.
38 Ibid., Preface.
39 Wyrall, *The Nineteenth Division 1914–18*, 95–96.
40 Babington, *For the Sake of Example*, 13.
41 The National Archive, *Field General Court Martial – Blakemore, DJ*, WO71/569.
42 Ibid.
43 Ibid.
44 Ibid.
45 Ibid.
46 Ibid.
47 Ibid.
48 Ibid.
49 Peter Fiennes, *To War With God – The Army Chaplain Who Lost His Faith* (Edinburgh, Mainstream, 2011), 212–217.
50 Ibid., 214.
51 David Railton, to Ruby Railton, dated 20 Nov 1916.
52 David Railton, to Ruby Railton, dated 21 Nov 1916.
53 David Blake, Museum of Army Chaplaincy, email to author, 13 May 2015.
54 Fiennes, *To War With God*, 215.

55 Ibid., 211.

56 Ibid., 218.

57 Putowski and Sykes, *Shot at Dawn*, 68.

58 Philip Gibbs, *Now It Can Be Told* (London, Harper and Brothers, 1920).

59 'The Reverend Richard Griffiths Chaplain to the Forces 1914–18', *The Guardian*, https://witness.theguardian.com/assignment/52751e38e4b01fc33230d4aa/641932 (accessed 16 Dec 2015).

60 'Shot at Dawn; The Soldiers' Stories', *The Guardian*, http://www.theguardian.com/uk/2006/aug/16/military.samjones (accessed 17 Dec 2015).

61 David Railton, *The Story of a Padre's Flag*, 4–5.

62 David Railton, Army Book 152 – Correspondence Book (Field Service), Railton Family Archive.

63 David Railton, Message and Signal Notes – Blakemore Addresses, Railton Family Archive.

64 The Long, Long Trail, 'The Battle of the Lys, 1918', http://www.longlongtrail.co.uk/battles/battles-of-the-western-front-in-france-and-flanders/the-battles-of-the-lys-1918/ (accessed 17 Dec 2015).

65 Fiennes, *To War With God*, 214.

66 Ibid.

67 Commonwealth War Graves Commission, 'Locre Hospice British Cemetery', http://www.cwgc.org/find-a-cemetery/cemetery/2023737/locre%20hospice%20cemetery (accessed 18 Dec 2015).

68 G. L. Blakemore, to David Railton, dated 25 Jul 1917.

69 UK, Army Registers of Soldiers' Effects 1901–1929, 'Denis Jetson Blakemore', accessed through *Ancestry.com*.

70 G. L. Blakemore, to David Railton, dated 25 Jul 1917.

71 Richard Van Emden, *The Quick and the Dead – Fallen Soldiers and Their Families in the Great War* (London, Bloomsbury, 2011), 211.

72 Brigadier A. B. McPherson, *Discipline* (London, War Office, 1950), 116–117.

73 Brian Bond & Nigel Cave, eds., *Haig: A Re-Appraisal 80 Years On* (Barnsley, Pen & Sword, 2009), 213.

74 William More, *The Thin Yellow Line* (London, Lee Cooper, 1974).

75 Australian War Memorial, 'Desertion and the Death Penalty', https://www.awm.gov.au/encyclopedia/desertion/ (accessed 11 Jan 2016).

76 Ibid.

77 Babington, *For the Sake of Example*, 209.

78 'After 87 Years, Village Honours Its War Dead', *The Telegraph*, 16 May 2005.

79 Richard Van Emden, 'Why War Memorials Matter', *The Telegraph*, 30 Oct 2011.

80 Bicton Village, Holy Trinity Church Newsletter, 'David Pannett's History of Bicton Part 43', http://bictonvillage.co.uk/church.html (accessed 25 Mar 2015).

81 Peter Francis, Shropshire War Memorials, 'Shot at Dawn', 1 Feb 2009, www.shropshirewarmemorials.blogspot.com (accessed 25 Mar 2015).

82 The History Learning Site, 'World War One Executions', http://www.historylearningsite.co.uk/world-war-one/the-western-front-in-world-war-one/world-war-one-executions/ (accessed 18 Dec 2015).

83 Wyrall, *The Nineteenth Division 1914–18*, 65.

84 'Pardon for Soldiers of the Great War Bill', http://www.publications.parliament.uk/pa/cm200506/cmbills/087/2006087.pdf (accessed 18 Sep 2015).

85 The History Learning Site, 'World War One Executions', http://www.historylearningsite.co.uk/world-war-one/the-western-front-in-world-warone/world-war-one-executions/ (accessed 18 Dec 2015).

86 'Pardon for Soldiers of the Great War Bill', http://www.publications.parliament.uk/pa/cm200506/cmbills/087/2006087.pdf (accessed 18 Sep 2015).

87 The National Archive, *Field General Court Martial – Blakemore, DJ*, WO71/569.

Chapter 8

1 Wyrall, *The Nineteenth Division 1914–18*, 193.

2 Sidney Rogerson, *The Last of the Ebb – The Battle of the Aisne, 1918* (Barnsley, Frontline, 2011), xxv.

3 Ibid., xxvi.

4 Wyrall, *The Nineteenth Division 1914–18*, 193.

5 David Railton, Notes on a postcard – the Padre's Flag, Railton Family Archive.

6 Railton, *The Story of a Padre's Flag*, 10–11.

7 Ibid.

8 Railton, Notes on a postcard.

9 Railton, *The Story of a Padre's Flag*, 10–11.

10 Wyrall, *The Nineteenth Division 1914–18*, 113.

11 Major-General C. T. M. Bridges, letter to David Railton dated 22 Nov 1917, Railton Family Archive.

12 Wyrall, *The Nineteenth Division 1914–18*, 233.

13 Ibid.

14 Ibid., 121.

15 General G. D. Jeffreys, 'Preface and Foreword', *19th Division Standing Orders for Trenches*, Railton Family Archive.

16 'Comments of the Revd David Railton in reference to the report of the *Daily Telegraph* of July 8th', Westminster Abbey Muniment 63774 B.

17 Ibid.

18 Holmes, *Tommy*, 571.

19 Major-General G. D. Jeffreys, letter to David Railton dated 4 Nov 1920, Railton Family Archive.

20 Wyrall, *The Nineteenth Division 1914–18*, 123.

21 Ibid., 126.

22 Ibid., 173.

23 Ibid., 132.

24 Ibid., 173.

25 Ibid., 172.

26 Ibid., 176.

27 'Sir Douglas Haig's "Backs to the Wall" Order, 11 April 1918', firstworldwar. com, http://www.firstworldwar.com/source/backstothewall.htm (accessed 26 Oct 2016).

28 Wyrall, *The Nineteenth Division 1914–18*, 191.

29 Ibid., 193–194.

Chapter 9

1   The National Archive, *Army Service Record – David Railton*, WO374/56017 C597937.

2   Ibid.

3   Notes by David Railton written on 56th Brigade Routine Orders dated 13 Nov 1918, Railton Family Archive.

4   Rogerson, *The Last of the Ebb*, 24–25.

5   Ibid., 40.

6   Wyrall, *The Nineteenth Division 1914–18*, 194.

7   Rogerson, *The Last of the Ebb*, 85–86.

8   Ibid., 82–83.

9   Wyrall, *The Nineteenth Division 1914–18*, 235.

10 Ibid., 199.

11 Rogerson, *The Last of the Ebb*, 70.

12 Ibid., 85.

13 Ibid.

14 Wyrall, *The Nineteenth Division 1914–18*, 200–201.

15 Ibid., 209.

16 Wyrall, *The Nineteenth Division 1914–18*, 207–208.

17 Ibid., 209–210

18 Railton, *The Story of a Padre's Flag*, 11–12.

19 Ibid., 16.

20 Ibid.

21 Ibid., 16–17.

22 Wyrall, *The Nineteenth Division 1914–18*, 210.

23 'Report written by D. Railton', 25 Sep 1917, Railton Family Archive.

24 John James Wallace, Certificate of Marriage, 20 Sep 1918, Railton Family Archive.

25 David Railton to Ruby Railton, dated 5 Oct 1916.

26 David Railton to Ruby Railton, dated 24 Feb 1916.

27 19th Division Locations, 5 Oct 1918, Railton Family Archive.

28 'Verboten', German Army leaflet, Railton Family Archive.
29 H. G. Wells, *The War That Will End War* (London, Frank & Cecil Palmer, 1914).
30 Wyrall, *The Nineteenth Division 1914–18*, 227.
31 The National Archive, *War Diary of 1/8th Bn, The North Staffordshire Regiment (Prince of Wales's Own)*, WO95/2085/2.
32 Commonwealth War Graves Commission, 'Locre Hospice British Cemetery', http://www.cwgc.org/find-a-cemetery/cemetery/59900/awoingt%20british%20cemetery (accessed 14 Jun 2016).
33 John James Wallace Memorial Card, Railton Family Archive.

Chapter 10

1 Ian Dickie (Margate Museum), conversation with author, 20 Mar 2016.
2 Ibid.
3 Kathleen Lockyer to Andrew Scott Railton, dated 24 Apr 1972.
4 Wyrall, *The Nineteenth Division 1914–18*, 193.
5 Railton, *Our Empire*, 1931.
6 J. N. Trethowan to Andrew Scott Railton, dated 24 Apr 1972.
7 Railton, *Our Empire*, 1931.
8 Railton, *The Story of a Padre's Flag*, 14–15.
9 Railton, *Our Empire*, 1931.
10 Ibid.
11 Railton, *The Story of a Padre's Flag*, 18.
12 Railton, *Our Empire*, 1931.
13 Colyer, email to author 31 Jan 2014.
14 'Mandate for the induction of the Rev'd David Railton', Induction date 25 Sep 1920, Canterbury Cathedral Archive, DCb-F/A/1920/19.
15 Railton, *Our Empire*, 1931.
16 Ibid.
17 Ibid.
18 Dean Herbert Ryle letter to David Railton, 16 Aug 1920, Railton Family Archive.
19 Railton, *The Story of a Padre's Flag*, 19.
20 Railton, *Our Empire*, 1931.
21 Railton, *Transcript of Broadcast*.
22 'The Glorious Dead', *The Times*, 7 Nov. 1919.
23 Juliet Nicholson, *The Great Silence* (New York, Grove Press, 2009).
24 Eileen Shim, 'A Brief History of the Moment of Silence', News.Mic, https://mic.com/articles/98624/a-brief-history-of-the-moment-of-silence#.oCJTXRi5z (accessed 23 May 2016).
25 'Should We Observe the Silence? – YES', *Liverpool Echo*, 11 Nov 1935.
26 Colyer, email to author, 31 Jan 2014.
27 Railton, *Our Empire*, 1931.

28   Railton, *The Story of a Padre's Flag*, 19.
29   'Cenotaph', *The Times*, 22 Oct 1920.
30   Dean Herbert Ryle to David Railton, dated 25 Oct 1920.
31   Dean Herbert Ryle to David Railton, dated 28 Oct 1920.
32   'Postcard written by David Railton', Railton Family Archive.
33   Railton, *Our Empire*, 1931.
34   The Keeper of the Muniments, internal memorandum to the Dean, 'The Padre's Flag' (U/23860), dated 29 May 1992, Westminster Abbey Muniment 63774 B.
35   Ibid.
36   'The Story of the Padre's Flag', *The Times*, 10 Nov 1920.
37   Railton, *The Story of a Padre's Flag*, 20.
38   'The Story of the Padre's Flag', *The Times*, 10 Nov 1920.
39   'The Unknown Warrior', *The Times*, 10 Nov 1920.

Chapter 11

1   'A Radiant Symbol', *The Times*, 12 Nov 1920.
2   Narrative of events in connection with the burial of an Unknown Warrior in Westminster Abbey on 10 Nov 1920, 'Memoir of L. Barbor-Might (Civil Servant of Ministry of Works)', Westminster Abbey Muniment 63774 B.
3   Dean Herbert Ryle to David Railton, dated 15 Nov 1920.
4   Dean Ryle, letter to Lord Stamfordham, 4 Oct 1920, Westminster Abbey Muniment 63774 B.
5   Nicholson, *The Great Silence*, 263.
6   'Editorial', *Church Times*, 21 Nov 1919.
7   Dean Herbert Ryle to David Railton, dated 15 Nov 1920.
8   Lord Stamfordham, letter to Dean Ryle, 7 Oct 1920, Westminster Abbey Muniment 63774 B.
9   Ibid.
10   MPA Hankey, Secretary to the Cabinet, letter to Dean Ryle, 15 Oct 1920, Westminster Abbey Muniment 63774 B.
11   Ibid.
12   Kenneth O. Morgan, *Lloyd George* (London, Littlehampton Book Service Ltd, 1974), 153.
13   'The Glorious Dead', *The Times*, 26 July 1919.
14   'The Cenotaph', *The Daily Mail*, 23 Jul 1919.
15   Interim Report of the Committee, 'Memorial Services (November 11th) Committee', Westminster Abbey Muniment 63774 B.
16   Ibid.
17   Ibid.

18 Hanson, *Unknown Soldiers – The Story of the Missing of the First World War*, 302.

19 David Canandine, *Aspects of Aristocracy* (New Haven & London, Yale University Press, 1994), 78.

20 Hanson, *Unknown Soldiers – The Story of the Missing of the First World War*, 278.

21 Agenda, Unknown Warrior File, Westminster Abbey Muniment 63774 B.

22 Interim Report of the Committee, Westminster Abbey Muniment 63774 B.

23 'Orders by Major-General GD Jeffreys, CB, CMG, Commanding London District, on the occasion of The Burial in Westminster Abbey of the Body of Unknown Warrior and of The Unveiling of the Cenotaph in Whitehall by His Majesty The King on Thursday, 11th November, 1920', National Railway Museum Archive 1998-10871.

24 Ibid.

25 'Brigadier-General LJ Wyatt, Letter to the Editor', *Daily Telegraph*, 11 Nov 1939.

26 Hanson, *Unknown Soldiers – The Story of the Missing of the First World War*, 415.

27 George Kendall, *Daring All Things – The Autobiography of George Kendall (1881–1961)* (Solihull, Helion 2016), 151–155.

28 Major P. F. Anderson, 'The British Unknown Warrior', *FIDAC* IXe Annee Vol IX No 6, Jun 1933, Imperial War Museum 228349.

29 E. E. P. Tisdall, 'How they chose the Unknown Warrior', *The British Legion Journal* Vol 19 No 5 Nov 1939, Imperial War Museum 228349.

30 John Hundevad, 'The Unknown Warrior', *The Legionary* No 3 Vol 13 XXX, Aug 1955, Imperial War Museum 228349.

31 Garrett, *The Final Betrayal*, 174.

32 Herbert Jeans, 'In Death's Cathedral Palace – The Story of the Unknown Warrior', *The British Legion Journal* Vol 9 No 5, Nov 1929, Imperial War Museum 228349.

33 Kendall, *Daring All Things*, 151.

34 'Brigadier-General LJ Wyatt, Letter to the Editor', *Daily Telegraph*, 11 Nov 1939.

35 George Kendall, *Daring All Things*, 151.

36 Sir Cecil Smith, letter to the Dean of Westminster, July 1978, Westminster Abbey Muniment 63774 B.

37 'Scenes in Boulogne', *The Times*, 10 Nov 1920.

38 'Mass Was Said Over Unknown Warrior', *Daily Telegraph*, 8 Jul 1954.

39 Ibid.

40 'The Story of The Padre's Flag', *The Times*, 10 Nov 1920.

41 Ibid.

42 "Tommy Anonyme," *The Yorkshire Post*, 11 Nov 1920.

43 British Movietone, 'Unknown Warrior Returns Home', *Youtube* video, 0:47, 21 Jul 2015. https://www.youtube.com/watch?v=aAHiMTGCBuI.

44 'Boulogne', *The Times*, 11 Nov 1920.

45 'A Sword from the King', *The Times*, 11 Nov 1920.

46 'Marshal Foch's Plea', *The Times*, 11 Nov 1920.

47 Ibid.
48 'At England's Gate', *The Times*, 11 Nov 1920.
49 Ibid.
50 Ibid.
51 'The Journey's End, Simple Impressiveness', *The Times*, 11 Nov 1920.
52 'Orders by Major-General GD Jeffreys', National Railway Museum Archive.
53 'At England's Gate', *The Times*, 11 Nov 1920.
54 Hanson, *Unknown Soldiers – The Story of the Missing of the First World War*, 296.
55 Vicar's Book, St John the Baptist, Margate, Canterbury Cathedral Archive.
56 Mrs Ryle letter to David Railton, 7 Nov 1920, Railton Family Archive.
57 Ibid.
58 Railton, *The Story of a Padre's Flag*, 20.
59 'It Was His Idea', *British Legion Journal*, October 1961.
60 'Spellbound Crowd. Homage Too Great for Words', *The Times*, 12 Nov 1920.
61 Ibid.
62 Ibid.
63 'Orders by Major-General GD Jeffreys', National Railway Museum Archive.
64 Ibid.
65 Ibid.
66 *The Yorkshire Post*, 12 Nov 1920.
67 'Orders by Major-General GD Jeffreys', National Railway Museum Archive.
68 British Movietone, 'Unknown Warrior Returns Home', *Youtube* video, 0:47, 21 Jul 2015. https://www.youtube.com/watch?v=aAHiMTGCBuI.
69 'Orders by Major-General GD Jeffreys', National Railway Museum Archive.
70 Westminster Abbey, 'The Funeral Service of A British Warrior on The Second Anniversary of the signing of The Armistice, November 11th, 1920', Railton Family Archive.
71 'Armistice Day, 1920: The Burial of the Unknown Warrior', *The Times*, 12 Nov 1920.
72 John S. Arkwright, *The Supreme Sacrifice and Other Poems in Time of War* (London, Skeffington & Son Ltd, 1919), 17.
73 'Orders by Major-General GD Jeffreys', National Railway Museum Archive.
74 'Armistice Day, 1920: The Burial of the Unknown Warrior', *The Times*, 12 Nov 1920.
75 Ibid.
76 Ibid.
77 Ibid.
78 'The Great Pilgrimage: Mourners' Weary Hours of Waiting. A Test of Endurance', *The Times*, 12 Nov 1920.
79 'To-day at the Cenotaph. Traffic Arrangements', *The Times*, 12 Nov 1920.
80 'Seven Mile Queue of Pilgrims at Cenotaph', *The Daily Mirror*, 15 Nov 1920.
81 Hanson, *Unknown Soldiers – The Story of the Missing of the First World War*, 309.

Chapter 12

1 Railton, *Our Empire*, 1931.
2 Robin Colyer, 'Notes taken from St John's Vestry Book', email to author 31 Jan 2014.
3 Ibid.
4 David Railton to Ruby Railton, dated 8 Jan 1917.
5 Robin Colyer, 'Notes taken from St John's Vestry Book', email to author 31 Jan 2014.
6 Margate Civic Society, 'Margate War Memorial', http://www.margatecivicsociety.org.uk/margatewarmemorial.html (accessed 28 Sep 2016).
7 'A Vicar on Tramp', *Thanet Advertiser*, 19 Nov 1921, Railton Family Archive.
8 Jeremy Plester, 'Weatherwatch: The Great Year-long Drought of 1921', *The Guardian*, 13 Oct 2011.
9 Ibid.
10 'Vicar's Pose as Tramp', *Evening Standard*, 19 Nov 1921.
11 *Vicar's Book*, St John the Baptist, Margate, Canterbury Cathedral Archive.
12 'Vicar of Margate Goes on Tramp', *The Whitstable Times*, 26 Nov 1921.
13 Ibid.
14 'Rotary Club of Margate – A Vicar in Search of Employment', *Thanet Gazette*, date unknown, Railton Family Archive.
15 Ibid.
16 'Vicar Turns Tramp', *Nottingham Evening Post*, 21 Nov 1921.
17 'Vicar as Tramp', *Hull Daily Mail*, 21 Nov 1921.
18 'Vicar Turns Tramp', *Nottingham Evening Post*, 21 Nov 1921.
19 Mrs Margaret Railton, conversation with author, 3 Apr 2014.
20 'Rotary Club of Margate – A Vicar in Search of Employment', *Thanet Gazette*, date unknown, Railton Family Archive.
21 'Vicar Turns Tramp', *Nottingham Evening Post*, 21 Nov 1921.
22 'Vicar's Pose as Tramp', *Evening Standard*, 19 Nov 1921.
23 'A Vicar on Tramp', *Thanet Advertiser*, 19 Nov 1921, Railton Family Archive.
24 'Vicar Turns Tramp', *Nottingham Evening Post*, 21 Nov 1921.
25 'Vicar as Tramp', *Rhodesia Herald*, 29 Dec 1921.
26 'Former Ashford Curate as a Tramp', *Kent Messenger*, 23 Nov 1921, Railton Family Archive.
27 Unknown newspaper clipping, Railton Family Archive.
28 'The Quick and the Dead', *The Times*, 12 Nov 1920.
29 A. Clark, *The Donkeys* (London, Hutchinson, 1961)
30 Matt Croucher, GC, *The Royal British Legion, 90 Years of Heroes* (London, HarperCollins, 2011), 16.
31 Gerard J. De Groot, *Douglas Haig 1861–1928* (London, Unwin Hyman, 1988), 403–404.
32 Croucher, *The Royal British Legion, 90 Years of Heroes*, 16.

33 James Denman and Paul McDonald, 'Unemployment statistics from 1881 to the present day', *Labour Market Trends*, Jan 1996.

34 Harold L. Smith, *The British Women's Suffrage Campaign 1866–1928, Second Edition* (London, Routledge, 2013), 95.

35 'Anniversary: Black Friday 1921', *The Socialist*, 20 April 2011.

36 Bob Holman, *Woodbine Willie – An Unsung Hero of World War One* (Oxford, Lion Hudson, 2013), 111.

37 Ibid., 32.

38 *Vicar's Book*, St John the Baptist, Margate, Canterbury Cathedral Archive.

39 Christine Rowe letter to Andrew Scott Railton, dated 26 Apr 1972, Railton Family Archive.

40 Revd Geoffrey Studdert Kennedy, *Handwritten Poetry*, Railton Family Archive.

41 Telegram from Beverly Bowden to David Railton, 8 Mar 1929, Railton Family Archive.

42 Industrial Christian Fellowship, *The Torch*, Vol VII, No 76, Apr 1929, Railton Family Archive.

43 Revd Geoffrey Studdert Kennedy, *Handwritten Poetry*, Railton Family Archive.

44 Mick Twyman, 'The Reverend David Railton, M.M. Inspiration for the Unknown Warrior', *Margate Historical Society Magazine*, Winter 2008, Margate Historical Society.

45 Dean Herbert Ryle to David Railton, dated 21 Oct 1921.

46 Ibid.

47 Dean Herbert Ryle to David Railton, dated 24 Oct 1921.

48 'Armistice Day', *The Times*, 9 Nov 1921.

49 Ibid.

50 Ibid.

51 John F. Prescott, *In Flanders Fields: The Story of John McCrae* (Ontario, Boston Mills Press, 1985), 96.

52 The Great War 1914–18, 'The Story behind the Remembrance Poppy', http://www.greatwar.co.uk/article/remembrance-poppy.htm (accessed 4 Oct 2016).

53 Ibid.

54 'A Scarlet City', *The Times*, 11 Nov 1921.

55 Ibid.

56 The Royal British Legion, 'The Story of the Poppy', http://www.britishlegion.org.uk/remembrance/how-we-remember/the-story-of-the-poppy/ (accessed 4 Oct 2016).

57 Westminster Abbey – The Third Anniversary of the signing of The Armistice, 11 Nov 1921, Railton Family Archive.

58 Ibid.

59 'For Remembrance', *The Times*, 11 Nov 1921.

60 'The Silence and After', *The Times*, 12 Nov 1921.

61 Ibid.

62 'Remembrance Day – The Empire's Homage to the Fallen', *The Yorkshire Post*, 12 Nov 1921.

63 Ibid.

64 'The Warrior's Epitaph', *The Times*, 12 Nov 1921.

65 Westminster Abbey – The Third Anniversary of the signing of The Armistice, 11 Nov 1921, Railton Family Archive.

66 'The Warrior's Epitaph', *The Times*, 12 Nov 1921.

67 Westminster Abbey – The Third Anniversary of the signing of The Armistice, 11 Nov 1921, Railton Family Archive.

68 'The Unknown Warrior – Tyne Link with Originator of the Idea', *Newcastle Chronicle*, Date unknown, Railton Family Archive.

69 'The Westminster Abbey Service – A Wonderful Moment', *The Yorkshire Post*, 12 Nov 1921.

70 'The Warrior's Epitaph', *The Times*, 12 Nov 1921.

71 Mrs Lockyer to Andrew Scott Railton, dated 24 Apr 1972.

72 'Commemoration in the Abbey – Beauty in Simplicity – The Ypres Flag', *The Times*, 12 Nov 1921.

Chapter 13

1 The Very Revd Canon Dr J. J. W. Edmondson, Rural Dean of Battle and Bexhill, email to author, 30 Apr 2015.

2 Philip Green (current owner of Ard Rhu), email to author, 17 Apr 2015.

3 'Court Circular – Buckingham Palace', *The Times*, 24 Feb 1925, 28 Feb 1927 & 28 Jan 1929.

4 Handwritten notes by David Railton, The Most Revd Randall Davidson to David Railton, 11 Apr 1922, Railton Family Archive.

5 Ibid.

6 Robin Colyer, 'Notes from Margate Parish News', email to author 31 Jan 2014.

7 Ibid.

8 Letter to the Editor, *Margate Parish Magazine*, 20 Mar 1925, Railton Family Archive.

9 'PCC Minutes – 6 Jul 1922', St John's – Margate, Canterbury Cathedral Archive.

10 Randall Davidson to David Railton, 1 Aug 1922.

11 'PCC Minutes – 27 Sep 1922', St John's – Margate, Canterbury Cathedral Archive.

12 Charles R. Beaumont, 'Time Remembered', *Margate Parish Church News*, Jan 1956, Railton Family Archive.

13 Robin Colyer, 'Notes taken from St John's Vestry Book', email to author 31 Jan 2014.

14 'PCC Minutes – 4 Feb 1924', St John's – Margate, Canterbury Cathedral Archive.

15 'PCC Minutes – 8 Apr 1924', St John's – Margate, Canterbury Cathedral Archive.

16 'PCC Minutes – 20 Apr 1925', St John's – Margate, Canterbury Cathedral Archive.

17 David Railton, 'Letter of Resignation', *Margate Parish Church News*, Vol VI, May 1925, Railton Family Archive.
18 Ibid.
19 Rev David Railton Sermon, 24 Sep 1925, Vicar's Book, Canterbury Cathedral Archive.
20 Unknown newspaper clipping, 1925, Railton Family Archive.
21 Mrs Margaret Railton, conversation with author, 23 Mar 2016.
22 Revd P. T. R. Kirk to David Railton, 23 Mar 1925, Railton Family Archive.
23 P. T. R. Kirk to David Railton, 17 Apr 1925.
24 Handwritten notes by David Railton, Randall Davidson to David Railton, 4 Apr 1925.
25 Randall Davidson to David Railton, 4 Apr 1925.
26 P. T. R. Kirk to David Railton, 17 Apr 1925.
27 Mrs Margaret Railton, conversation with author, 24 Oct 2016.
28 'Stiff-necked Clergy – The Most Noble Order of the Study', *The Western Gazette*, 26 Aug 1926.
29 Holman, *Woodbine Willie*, 122.
30 'The Church and Labour Party Memorial to MPs from 500 Clergymen', *The Times*, 14 Mar 1923.
31 Anonymous letter to David Railton, 25 Sep 1925, Railton Family Archive.
32 'London Clergyman for a Bradford Vicariate', *The Yorkshire Post*, 19 Oct 1927.
33 'Vicar Who Gave Bar-Parlour Talks', *The Yorkshire Post*, 17 June 1931.
34 'Vicar's Suggestion – 1,200 Bradford Workers Listen to Address', Unknown newspaper clipping, Railton Family Archive.
35 'Parson's Talks in a Bar Parlour', *Leeds Mercury*, 11 Mar 1929.
36 Ibid.
37 Ibid.
38 England and Wales Death Index 1916–2007, Marianne D. L. E. Railton, Hastings, Sussex, accessed through Ancestry.com.
39 Kathleen Lockyer to Andrew Scott Railton, dated 24 Apr 1972.
40 Robert Holmes, letter to David Railton, 5 May 1928, Railton Family Archive.
41 'Crusaders' Service – Order Inspired by Unknown Warrior', *The Daily Mail*, 25 Jun 1928, Railton Family Archive.
42 'Church Crusade – Meetings in Garston District', Unknown newspaper clipping, Railton Family Archive.
43 'Rev D Railton Leaving Bradford', *The Yorkshire Evening Post*, 17 Jun 1931, Railton Family Archive.
44 Ibid.
45 Ibid.
46 Albert Victor Ray, letter to David Railton, 1935, Railton Family Archive.
47 Twyman, 'The Rev David Railton', Winter 2008.
48 'The Unknown Warrior', *Bradford Telegraph and Argus*, 5 Dec 1928, Railton Family Archive.

49 'Armistice Day 1920 – The Burial of the Unknown Warrior', *The Times*, 12 Nov 1920.

50 Dean Herbert Ryle to David Railton, 15 Nov 1920.

51 'The Idea of the Unknown Warrior's Burial', *The Times*, 13 Nov 1920.

52 Dean Herbert Ryle to David Railton, 15 Nov 1920.

53 Railton, *The Story of the Padre's Flag*, 20.

54 'The Cenotaph – Proposal to Follow France's Fine Idea', *Daily Express*, 16 Sep 1919.

55 HC Deb 9 Dec 1920, cc657-8.

56 HC Deb 9 Dec 1920, cc2405-6.

57 M. Srenton and S. Lees, eds, *Who's Who of British Members of Parliament, Vol III 1919–45* (London, Harvester, 1979), 36.

58 Railton, *The Story of the Padre's Flag*, 22–23.

59 Major A. Nelson to David Railton, 28 Nov 1930, Railton Family Archive.

60 Major A. Nelson to David Railton, 11 Dec 1930.

61 'Rev D. Railton's Appointment', *Surrey Weekly Press*, Date Unknown, Railton Family Archive.

62 'The Church and Industry', *The Derby Daily Telegraph*, 12 Mar 1933.

63 Anonymous letter to David Railton, 22 Nov 1933, Railton Family Archive.

64 P. B. Clayton to David Railton, 6 May 1933.

65 A. C. Gladstone letter to David Railton, 14 Jun 1935, Railton Family Archive.

66 'Liverpool – Our New Rector', *Liverpool Daily Post*, 12 Jul 1935, Railton Family Archive.

67 Unknown newspaper clipping, Railton Family Archive.

68 'Rev. D. Railton Resigns', Unknown newspaper clipping, 23 Jul 1942, Railton Family Archive.

69 Rex C. Cumming letter to David Railton, 17 Jun 1937, Railton Family Archive.

70 'Back to Laws of the Jungle', *Liverpool Daily Post*, July 1936, Railton Family Archive.

71 F. G. Prince-White, 'Unknown Warrior to have New Tomb-Perpetual Flame in Abbey', *Daily Mail*, 27 Oct 1938.

72 Mrs Margaret Railton, conversation with author, 24 Oct 2016.

73 The War Office, letter to David Railton, 12 Sep 1939, Railton Family Archive.

74 David Railton, handwritten notes on War Office letter, Railton Family Archive.

75 'Unknown Warrior His Idea – Wants to Serve at 55', *Daily Sketch*, 20 Sep 1955.

76 Mrs Margaret Railton, conversation with author, 24 Oct 2016.

77 Mr Trevor Holden, letter to David Railton, 20 Apr 1942, Railton Family Archive.

78 Unknown newspaper clipping, Nov 1939, Railton Family Archive.

79 'Rover Scouts in Conference – Rector's Tribute at Cathedral Service', *Liverpool Daily Post*, Railton Family Archive.

80 'Gradual Tightening of Lips', *Liverpool Daily Post*, Dec 1940, Railton Family Archive.

81 'The Rector's Letter', *Liverpool Parish Church Magazine*, December 1940, Railton Family Archive.

82 'Rev. D. Railton Resigns', Unknown newspaper clipping, 23 Jul 1942, Railton Family Archive.

83 'Letters to the Editor, Liverpool Parish Church', *Liverpool Daily Post*, 24 Jan 1941, Railton Family Archive.

84 Anonymous letter to David Railton, 12 Feb 1941, Railton Family Archive.

85 'Liverpool Rector's Thanks', *Liverpool Daily Post*, 29 Apr 1942, Railton Family Archive.

86 Revd R. Nelson, letter to David Railton, 15 May 1952, Railton Family Archive.

87 Herbert Leggate, letter to David Railton, 18 Feb 1941, Railton Family Archive.

88 'The Rector Resigns', *Liverpool Diocesan New and Notes*, May 1942, Railton Family Archive.

89 'Private Reunion – Extraordinary Proceedings in Scotland', *Scottish Guardian*, Date Unknown, Railton Family Archive.

90 Pastor Bruce Johnson, 'Revd David Railton, MC', email to author 16 Nov 2016.

91 'Obituary – The Venerable Nathaniel Gerard Railton', *The Times*, 9 Sep 1948.

92 Mrs Margaret Railton, conversation with author, 24 Oct 2016.

93 'Mass Was Said over Unknown Warrior', *Daily Telegraph*, 8 Jul 1954.

94 'Comments of the Revd David Railton in reference to the report of the *Daily Telegraph* of July 8th', Westminster Abbey Muniment 63774 B.

95 'Orders by Major-General GD Jeffreys', National Railway Museum Archive.

96 Michael Gavaghan, *The Story of the British Unknown Warrior* (Preston, M&L Publications, 1997), 80.

97 British Movietone, 'Unknown Warrior Returns Home', *Youtube* video, 0:47, 21 Jul 2015. https://www.youtube.com/watch?v=aAHiMTGCBuI (accessed 28 Sep 2016).

98 Miriam Power, 'Flags that covered the body of the Unknown Warrior 1920', email to author 29 Sep 2016.

99 The Very Revd Canon Dr J. J. W. Edmondson, Rural Dean of Battle and Bexhill, email to author, 30 Apr 2015.

100 Mrs Margaret Railton, conversation with author, 2 Sep 2015.

101 'Former Rector of Liverpool Dies in Accident', *Liverpool Echo*, 1 July 1955, Railton Family Archive.

102 The *Daily Mail*, 1 Jul 1955.

103 Mrs Margaret Railton, conversation with author, 10 Dec 2016.

104 The *Daily Mail*, 1 Jul 1955.

105 'Obituary – The Revd D. Railton', *The Times*, 1 Jul 1955.

106 'Obituary – The Revd David Railton', *Shalford Church Chronicle*, Aug 1955, Railton Family Archive.

107 Twyman, 'Revd David Railton', *Margate Historical Magazine*, 2008.

108 Beaumont, 'Time Remembered', 1956.

109 Undated clipping from the *Argyle and the Isle Diocesan Leaflet*, Railton Family Archive.
110 'Letter to the Editor', *The Scotsman*, 7 Jul 1955, Railton Family Archive.
111 'The Revd D. Railton', *The Times*, 8 Jul 1955.
112 'Letter to the Editor', *Liverpool Echo*, 13 Jul 1955, Railton Family Archive.
113 Revd Stanislaus Woywod, *The New Canon Law* (London, Herder, 1918).
114 Mrs Margaret Railton, conversation with author, 2 Sep 2015.

Epilogue

1 BBC World News Edition, 'Mourners visit Queen Mother's Vault', 10 Apr 2002, http://news.bbc.co.uk/2/hi/uk_news/1920360.stm (accessed 14 Nov 2016).
2 James Wilkinson, *The Unknown Warrior and the Field of Remembrance* (London, JW Publications, 2006), 20.
3 'Flying the Flag for the Padre Once More', *The Daily Telegraph*, 10 Nov 2006.

Bibliography

Books

Arkwright, John S. *The Supreme Sacrifice and Other Poems in Time of War.* London: Skeffington & Son Ltd, 1919.

Ashcroft, Michael. *Victoria Cross Heroes.* London: Headline, 2006.

Babington, Anthony. *For the Sake of Example – Capital Courts Martial 1914–20: The Truth.* London: Leo Cooper, 1983.

Bickersteth, John. *The Bickersteth Diaries 1914–18.* Barnsley: Leo Cooper, 1998.

Blackwell, H. Benjamin. *Ambassador Extraordinary – George Scott Railton.* London: Salvationist Publishing, 1952.

Bond, Brian and Cave, Nigel, eds. *Haig: A Re-Appraisal 80 Years On.* Barnsley: Pen & Sword.

Brown, Malcolm. *The Imperial War Museum Book of the Somme.* London: Sidgwick & Jackson, 1996.

Bull, Dr Stephen. *An Officer's Manual of the Western Front 1914–18.* London: Conway Maritime, 2008

Canandine, David. *Aspects of Aristocracy.* New Haven & London: Yale University Press, 1994

Cawthorne, Nigel. *History's Greatest Battles – Masterstrokes of War.* New York: Barnes & Noble, 2006.

Chapman, Guy. *A Passionate Prodigality.* London: MacGibbon & Kee, 1933.

Chasseaud, Peter. *Mapping the First World War – The Great War Through Maps from 1914–18.* Collins: Glasgow, 2013.

Clark, A. *The Donkeys.* London: Hutchinson, 1961.

Clayton, Ann. *Chavasse Double VC.* Barnsley: Pen & Sword, 2014.

Corns, Catherine and Hughes-Wilson, John. *Blindfold and Alone.* London: Cassell, 2001.

Croucher, Matt. *The Royal British Legion – 90 Years of Heroes.* London: Collins, 2011.

De Groot, Gerard J. *Douglas Haig 1861–1928*. London: Unwin Hyman, 1988.

Douglas, Eileen and Duff, Mildred. *Commissioner Railton*. London: Salvationist Publishing, 1920.

Dutton, John. *Korea 1950–53*. London: Lulu, 2015.

Edmonds, J. E. *History of the Great War: Military Operations, France and Belgium, 1918 Vol II*. London: McMillan & Co, 1937.

Edmonds, J. E. *A Short History of WW1*. Oxford: Oxford University Press, 1951.

Fair, Reginald and Charles. *Marjorie's War*. Brighton: Menin House, 2012.

Fiennes, Peter. *To War with God – The Army Chaplain Who Lost His Faith*. Edinburgh: Mainstream, 2011.

Fitzgerald, Revd Maurice H. *A Memoir of Herbert Edward Ryle*. London: MacMillan and Co, 1928.

Garrett, Richard. *The Final Betrayal – The Armistice, 1918 ... and Afterwards*. Southampton: Martins, 1989.

Gavaghan, Michael. *The Story of the British Unknown Warrior*. Preston: M&L Publications, 1995.

Gibbs, Philip. *Now It Can Be told*. London: Harper and Brothers, 1920.

Graves, Robert. *Goodbye to All That*. London: Johnathan Cape, 1929.

Groom, Winston. *A Storm in Flanders*. New York: Grove Press, 2002.

Gummer, Selwyn. *The Chavasse Twins: A Biography of Christopher M. Chavasse, Bishop of Rochester, and Noel G. Chavasse*. London: Hodder & Stoughton, 1963.

Halsey, A. H. *Trends in British Society since 1900: A Guide to the Changing Social Structure of Britain*. London: Macmillan St Martin's Press, 1972.

Hanson, Neil. *Unknown Soldiers – The Story of the Missing of the First World War*. New York: Vintage, 2007.

Hart, Peter. *The Great War – A Combat History of the First World War*. Oxford: Oxford University Press, 2013.

Holman, Bob. *Woodbine Willie – An Unsung Hero of World War One*. Oxford: Lion Hudson, 1998.

Holmes, Richard. *Atlas of Battle Plans*. Oxford: Helicon Publishing, 1998.

Holmes, Richard. *Tommy*. London: Harper Collins, 2004.

Howson, Peter. *Muddling Through – The Organisation of British Army Chaplaincy in World War One*. Solihull: Helion, 2013.

Hussey, A. H. *The Fifth Division in the Great War*. London: Nisbet, 1921.

Johnson, David. *Executed at Dawn – British Firing Squads on the Western Front 1914-18*. Stroud: Spellmount, 2015.

Keegan, John. *The First World War*. New York: Vintage, 2000.

Kendall, George, *Daring All Things – The Autobiography of George Kendall (1881–1961)*. Solihull: Helion, 2016.

Kennerley, Peter. *The Building of Liverpool Cathedral*. Preston: Carnegie Pub, 1991.

Kingsley Ward G., and Gibson, Major Edwin, *Courage Remembered*. London: HMSO, 1988.

Lee, Christopher. *This Sceptered Isle – Twentieth Century*. London: Penguin, 1999.

Lidell-Hart, B. H. *The Tanks, The History of the Royal Tank Regiment and its Predecessors, Volume One*. London: Cassell, 1959.

MacDonald, Alan. *A Lack of Offensive Spirit*. London: Iona, 2008.

MacDonald, John. *Great Battlefields of the World*. London: Michael Joseph, 1984.

Madigan, Edward. *Faith Under Fire*. London: Palgrave Macmillan, 2011.

Maude, Alan H. *The 47th (London) Division*. London: Amalgamated Press, 1922.

McPherson, Brigadier A. B. *Discipline*. London: War Office, 1950.

Meyer, G. J. *A World Undone – The Story of the Great War 1914 to 1918*. New York: Bantam, 2006.

More, William. *The Thin Yellow Line*. London: Leo Cooper, 1974.

Morgan, Kenneth O. *Lloyd George*. London: Littlehampton Book Services Ltd, 1974.

Morgan, Kenneth O., ed. *The Oxford Illustrated History of Britain*. Oxford: Oxford University Press, 1984.

Moynihan, Michael. *God on Our Side*. London: Leo Cooper, 1983.

Nicholson, Juliet. *The Great Silence*. New York: Grove Press, 2009.

Nicolson, Harold. *King George V*. London: Constable & Co, 1952.

Norman, Terry. *The Hell They Called High Wood – The Somme 1916*. Barnsley: Pen & Sword, 2009.

Oldham, Peter. *Messines Ridge – Ypres*. Barnsley: Leo Cooper, 1998.

Parker, Linda. *A Fool for Thy Feast – The Life and Times of Tubby Clayton, 1885–1972*. Solihull: Helion, 2015.

Parker, Linda. *Shellshocked Prophets*. Solihull: Helion, 2015.

Passingham, Ian. *Pillars of Fire – The Battle of Messines Ridge June 1917*. Stroud: Sutton, 1998.

Pegler, Martin. *British Tommy 1914-18*. Oxford: Osprey, 1996.

Persico, Joseph E. *Eleventh Month, Eleventh Day, Eleventh Hour*. New York: Random House, 2005.

Prescott, John, F. *In Flanders Fields: The Story of John McCrae*. Ontario: Boston Mills Press, 1985.

Putowski, Julian and Sykes, Julian. *Shot at Dawn*. London: Leo Cooper, 1989.

Rogerson, Sidney. *The Last of the Ebb – The Battle of the Aisne, 1918*. Barnsley: Frontline, 2011.

Rose, Kenneth. *King George V*. London: Knopf, 1984.

Roze, Anne. *Fields of Memory – A Testimony to the Great War*. London: Cassell, 1999.

Shakespear, John. *18th (Service) Bn, Northumberland Fusiliers*. Naval & Military Press.

Shakespear, John. *The Thirty-Fourth Division 1915–19*. Naval & Military Press.

Shawcross, William. *Counting One's Blessings*. London: Macmillan, 2012.

Shawcross, William. *The Queen Mother, The Official Biography*. New York: Vintage, 2010.

Sheldon, Jack. *The German Army at Cambrai*. Barnsley: Pen & Sword, 2009.

Shermer, David. *World War I*. London: Octopus Books, 1973.

Smith, Harold L. *The British Women's Suffrage Campaign 1866–1928, Second Edition*. London: Routledge, 2013.

Smith, Lorenzo. *Lingo of No Man's Land – World War 1*. London: The British Library, 2014.

Smyth, John. *In This Sign Conquer*. London: Mowbray, 1968.

Snape, Michael. *The Royal Army Chaplains' Department – Clergy Under Fire*. Woodbridge: The Boydell Press, 2008.

Srenton, M. & Lees, S., eds. *Who's Who of British Members of Parliament, Vol III 1919–45*. London: Harvester, 1979.

Taylor, A. J. P. *English History, 1914–1945*. London: Penguin, 1972.

Ullman, Harlan K. and Wade, James P. *Shock and Awe: Achieving Rapid Dominance*. Washington DC: National Defense University, 1996.

Van Emden, Richard. *The Quick and the Dead – Fallen Soldiers and Their Families in the Great War*. London: Bloomsbury, 2011.

Watson, Bernard. *Soldier Saint*. London: Hodder & Stoughton, 1972.

Wells, H. G. *The War That Will End War*. London: Frank & Cecil Palmer, 1914.

Wilkinson, James. *The Unknown Warrior and Field of Remembrance*. London: JW Publications, 2006.

Woywod, Revd Stanislaus. *The New Canon Law*. London: Herder, 1918.

Wyrall, Everard. *The Nineteenth Division 1914–18*. London: The Naval and Military Press.

The Official History of the Great War – Military Operations France & Belgium – 1916 Volume 1 Appendices. Chippenham: CPI Anthony Rowe.

The Official History of the Great War – Military Operations France & Belgium – 1914 London: MacMillan and Co, 1925.

The War Office, *The Manual of Military Law 1907*, London, HM Stationery Office, 1907

Websites

19th Century Longtown: www.longtown19.co.uk

Ancestry.com: www.ancestry.com

The Ancient Society of Elquire Leeds Youths: http://www.asely.org.uk/TCEA/aimsobjectives.html

Australian War Memorial: https://www.awm.gov.au

A New York – Newport Wedding Blog: http://newportweddings.blogspot.com

Bicton Village: http://bictonvillage.co.uk

Centers for Disease Control and Prevention: http://wwwnc.cdc.gov

Commonwealth War Graves Commission: http://www.cwgc.org

The Definitive guide to South-East & South-West London: http://www.southlondonguide.co.uk

Firstworldwar.com: http://www.firstworldwar.com

The Great War 1914–1918: http://www.greatwar.co.uk

The Guardian: https://www.theguardian.com/uk

Hellfire Corner: http://hellfirecorner.co.uk

Historic Graves of Ireland: www.historicgraves.com

The History Learning Site: http://www.historylearningsite.co.uk

Imperial War Museum: http://www.iwm.org.uk

Kilflynn Church: https://www.facebook.com/Kilflynn-Church-Ballyorgan-142339772519817/timeline/

Legends & Traditions of the Great War: http://www.worldwar1.com

The Long, Long Trail: http://www.1914-1918.net

Margate Civic Society: http://www.margatecivicsociety.org.uk

Margate Local and Family History: https://www.facebook.com/MargateHistory/photos

Margate in Maps and Pictures: www.maergatelocalhistory.co.uk

Margate Museum: https://margatemuseum.wordpress.com

National Army Museum: www.nam.ac.uk

National Association of Retired Police officers: http://eastkentnarpo.org.uk

News.mic: https://mic.com

Oxford University Archive: http://www.oua.ox.ac.uk

The Parish Church of St John the Baptist, Margate: http://www.stjohnschurchmargate.org.uk

Parliament Publications: http://www.publications.parliament.uk

The Peerage: http://www.thepeerage.com

Royal British Legion: http://www.britishlegion.org.uk

Shropshire War Memorials: http://shropshirewarmemorials.blogspot.com

Step Short – Remembering the soldiers of the Great War: www.stepshort.co.uk

The Times Archive: http://www.thetimes.co.uk/tto/archive/

Toc H: http://www.toch-uk.org.uk/About_Us.html

The Weather Network, Remembering WW1: http://www.theweathernetwork.com

The Western Front Association: http://westernfrontassociation.com

US Department of Veteran Affairs: www.ptsd.va.gov

World War One Battlefields: http://www.ww1battlefields.co.uk

Youtube: www.youtube.com

Index

A
Allenby, Sir Edmund 44
Anderson, Major P. F. 181
Arkwright, Sir John Stanhope 195
Armistice Day: 1918 150, 151
    1919 168–9, 170
    1920 173–4, 177–8, 179, 233
    1921 166, 213–15, 216–20
Arnit, Margaret Elizabeth 241, 243
Ashley, Lt-Col W. W. 231, 232
Auchinleck, General 130

B
Babington, Anthony 120
Baldwin, Stanley 236
Barbor-Might, L 174
Barter, Major-General Charles 65, 69, 75–6
Bateman, Private Joseph 125
Beatty, Earl 191
Bell, Revd Harold 47, 75
Bennett, Private John 39
Bennett, Captain Wesley 70
Binet-Valmer, Monsieur 233
Black, Private Peter 131
Blackburne, Harry 241
Blake, David 117, 124
Blakemore, Private Denis 118–30, 148, 158
Blakemore, Mr G. L. 118–19, 120, 132
Booth, William 6, 31
Bottomley, H. W. 231, 232
Bovey, Alfred and Jennie 95
Bovey, 2nd Lieutenant W. B. 95
Bowes-Lyon, Claude George xiv–xvii
Bowes-Lyon, Lady Elizabeth Angela Marguerite
    xiv–xvii, 249
Bradley, W. J. 48, 104–5, 112
Bridges, Major-General G. T. M. 137–8
British Legion 209, 215–16, 232–3, 234
Brittain, Sir Harry 231, 232

Broadbent, Harold 247
Brown, Des 133
Brown, Malcolm 62
Buckingham Palace 168, 170, 222
Byng, General Julian 141

C
Canterbury, Archbishop of 193, 194, 196, 222,
    223–4, 226
Carr, Revd Wesley 249
Cavell, Edith 187–8
Cenotaph 168
    and the Anglican Church 168, 175
    Armistice Day 1920 192
    Armistice Day 1921 214, 217
    permanent memorial 177, 193, 231
    unveiling of 170, 174, 199
Chamberlain, Neville 236, 237
Chapman, Guy 4
Chavasse, Christopher 24
Chavasse, Francis 24, 39, 89
Chavasse, Noel 24, 25, 88–9, 92
Christian, Ewan 8
Churchill, Winston 177, 199, 236
Clark, Elsie 82
Clark, Captain Sydney 82, 83, 84, 85–7, 89
Clayton, Revd Phillip 'Tubby' 110–11, 234
Commonwealth Defence Act (1903) 130–1
Commonwealth War Graves Commission 145
Crosse, Revd Ernest 26–7
Crozier, Private James 125
Curzon, Lord George 176, 177–8, 179, 194

D
Dartford, Captain R. C. G. 77
Davidson, Revd Randall 222, 223–4, 226
Davis, Captain L. J. 78
Derby, Lord 61
Dickens, Charles 99, 100–1

Doughty family 202, 203
Dubois, Mary Jane 158, 159, 162
Duchene, General 134, 135
Duncan, Revd Edward Francis 34–5, 39–40, 165

E
Earle, Sir Lionel 177, 178
Edward VII, King 179
Elizabeth, Queen Mother xiv–xvii, 249
Elizabeth II, Queen 132–3, 250
Evans, Frederick H. 166
Evans, Company Sergeant Major H. 166, 219–20

F
Fair, Major Charles 58–9, 69, 74–5, 77, 78
    David Railton's Military Cross 90
    Lieutenant-Colonel Hamilton 73–4
    Major-General Charles Barter 75–6
    1920 battlefield tour 72–3
Fair, Reginald 77
Farr, Private Harry 126
Fiennes, Peter 125
Filmer, Private S 87
Fleet, Constable Bruce 16, 18–19, 20, 21, 201,
    205, 212
Foch, Marshal Ferdinand 185, 186
Francis, Peter 132
Freeborn, Constable 10, 13, 18, 19
French, General Sir John 62, 191
Freyberg, Lt-Col 195
Friend, Major 91
Fryatt, Charles 187–8

G
Garrett, Richard 181
Gell, Lieutenant-Colonel E. A. S. 182
George V, King 74, 199
    burial of Unknown Warrior 3, 175–6, 190,
        192, 194, 196, 197
    crusader's sword 185
    Great Silence 168–9, 176
    Lloyd George's view of 176–7
Gibbs, Phillip 125
Gladstone, William 179
Good, Captain & Adjutant EC 161
Gorringe, Major-General G. F. 94
Graves, Robert 4, 49
Griffiths, Revd Richard 126
Guerin, Anna 215
Guilford, Revd Edward Montmorency 'Monty' 125
Gwynne, Bishop Llewellyn 92, 118

H
Haig, Douglas, 1st Earl 58, 134
    Armistice Day 1921 214
    attack in Flanders 114, 142
    attack on the Somme 62, 63
    'The Backs to the Wall' order 147–8

battalion inspections 33, 34, 98–9
burial of Unknown Warrior 165, 166, 191, 204
desertion within the army 119, 123
end of WWI 151
hanging of the flag 216, 217
High Wood 65, 66
Major-General Charles Barter 76
Operation Alberich 107–8
red poppy as remembrance symbol 215–16
reduces number of battalions 142
speaks up for ex-servicemen 209–10
Vimy Ridge 44
Haig, Mrs 218
Haig Fund 209, 216
Haldene, Richard 25
Hamilton, Lieutenant-Colonel A. P. 68, 72–4, 219
Hamilton, Mrs 72, 74, 219
Hamilton-Gordon, Lieutenant-General Sir 134,
    135, 152
Hammack, Major S. G. 183–4, 241, 243–4
Hammack, Mrs 183, 241, 242, 243
Hanson, Neil 178, 180, 189, 199
Harrison, Thomas 166, 202, 224
Henderson, Arthur 79
Henderson, Captain David 79
Highgate, Private Thomas 120
Hitler, Adolf 237, 239
Holmes, Richard 77, 140
Honey, Edward 169
Hundevad, John 181

I
Imperial War Graves Commission (IWGC) 181–2,
    233, 236
Industrial Christian Fellowship (ICF) 211, 226–7,
    229, 234
Ingouville-Williams, Major-General Edward
    Charles (Inky Bill) 36

J
Jackson, Sir Henry 216
Jeans, Herbert 181
Jeffreys, Major-General G. D. 138–41, 146, 148
    IX Corps 155
    Unknown Warrior's burial 178–9, 190, 192–3,
        194, 242
Joffre, General 33, 34, 62, 63, 107
Jones, PC Archibald 15

K
Kendall, Revd George 181–3
Kendall, Tim 181
Kipling, Rudyard 196
Kirk, Revd P. T. R. 211, 212, 226, 241

L
Law, Andrew Bonar 231
Lawton, Albert 11, 19

Lee, Lord 177
Lenin, Vladimir 143
Liddell Hart, Captain B. H. 85
Lloyd George, David 107–8
    Armistice Day 1921 217
    burial of Unknown Warrior 3, 170, 176, 197, 231–2
    Great Silence 168–9, 176
    1919 'peace parade' 168
    post WWI 209
    unveiling of Cenotaph (1920) 193
    view of George V 176–7
Lockyer, Mrs Kathleen 5
London, Bishop of 196
Long, Walter 177
Ludendorff, Erich 107, 145, 146–7, 155, 156
Luker, Lieutenant-Colonel R. 179
Lutyens, Sir Edwin 168, 175, 177, 193

M
Macclesfield Heath, Brigadier-General Ronald 154
McCrae, John 215
MacDonald, Ramsay 227
MacDonogh, Lieutenant-General George 185, 186
McDouall, Brigadier-General R. 65, 69
McGinn, Peter 73
MacLagan, Captain 90
McPherson, Brigadier A. B. 130
Marlborough, Duke of 160–1
Maude, Alan 81
Michael, Moina 215
Miners' Federation of Great Britain 210–11
Mond, Sir Alfred 177
Monro, Robert Edward 66–7
Montagu-Stuart-Wortley, Major-General A. R. 137
Montagu-Stuart-Wortley, Major-General E. J. 137
More, William 130

N
National Transport Workers' Federation 210–11
National Union of Railwaymen 210–11
Naylor, Revd A. T. A. 221
Nelson, Major A. 233
Nicholas II, Tsar 143, 202
Nicholson, Juliet 175
Nivelle, Robert 107–8, 142, 143, 155
Noades, Mr 185, 243
Norman, Lieutenant-Colonel 69
Norman, Terry 62, 66, 67

O
Odom, Canon S. A. 203
Oldham, Peter 115
The Order of Crusaders 228–9

P
Palmer, Sergeant 10, 12–17, 19, 20, 21, 201, 203–4, 212

Paris, Lt-Col 132
Pellé, General 155
Pétain, Philippe 143
Plumer, General Herbert 114, 115
poppies 215–16
Priestman, Sir John 225–6
Pulteney, Lieutenant-General Sir William 34, 65–6, 76, 77

R
Railton, Andrew Scott (DR's son) 5, 16, 74, 104, 166, 238, 241, 244
Railton, David: applies to be Chaplain to the Forces 27–8
    Armistice Day 1921 213–14, 216–19
    at Christ Church, Westminster 226–7
    at St James, Bolton 227–9
    at St John's, Margate 4–5, 8, 14, 163, 166, 169–70, 202–3, 222–5
    at St Mary's Church, Ashford 27–8
    at St Nicholas, Liverpool 169, 235, 237–40
    at Shalford 229, 234
    burial of Unknown Warrior 189–90, 195–9, 204
    character 46–7, 48
    death 245–7
    Denis Blakemore 118–33
    desire to help the homeless and unemployed 201–2, 204–13, 223
    early days in France 29–41
    early life 5, 6, 7, 31
    first burial in France 35–6
    goes on a tramp 203, 205–9, 213
    has idea of Unknown Warrior burial 165–8, 229–30, 232–3, 244, 246
    High Wood 63–79, 82, 83, 87, 213, 218
    legitimacy of the flag questioned 241–4
    loses the flag 136–7, 148, 156–7
    marriage and children 14, 15–16, 23–4, 166
    Mentioned in Dispatches 103–4
    Military Cross 3, 96, 82–92, 94, 104, 164
    mother's death 228
    move to Ard Rhu 222, 240–1
    plight of ex-servicemen 205, 206–10, 223
    promoted to Chaplain to the Forces Class 3 (Major) 93, 111
    receives flag 25–6
    receives new flag 136–7, 156
    recovers old flag 157
    relationship with father 30–1
    retirement 222
    Second World War 237–40
    The Story of a Padre's Flag 136, 165, 166, 172, 198, 230, 232
    takes leave of absence 224
    uses the flag in England 164
    Vimy Ridge 42–56, 87, 213, 218
    wartime marriages 159

Ypres Salient 94–116, 139, 159, 218

Railton, Esther (DR's sister) 7

Railton, Freda (DR's daughter) 16, 166, 238

Railton, George Scott (DR's father) 5–7, 30–1, 46–7

Railton, Jean (DR's daughter) 16, 238, 247

Railton, Marianne (DR's mother) 5, 6–7, 31, 91, 228

Railton, Mary (DR's daughter) 16, 24

Railton, Nathaniel (Gerry) (DR's brother) 5, 6, 7, 241

Railton, Ruby Marion (née Willson) (DR's wife) 223, 226
  at Ard Rhu 222, 245, 247
  Armistice Day 1921 218, 219
  David's death 245
  David's idea of the Unknown Warrior's Grave 166
  marriage and children 16, 23–4, 166
  Second World War 237

Railton, Ruth (DR's daughter) 16, 24, 244

Rawlinson, General Sir Henry 49, 66

Reed, Grace 38

Reed, Private James 37–8

Robbins, Miss Agnes 164

Rogerson, Captain Sidney 135, 152, 153–4, 155

Ryle, Bishop Herbert, Dean of Westminster 3, 167, 169–71, 172
  Armistice Day 1921 213–14, 216, 217
  burial of Unknown Warrior 182, 184, 195, 196, 229–30, 242, 243
  contacts Lord Stamfordham 174–6
  death 237
  as originator of Unknown Warrior idea 229–30, 232, 233

Ryle, Mrs 189, 198, 218

S

Salmond, Sir J. M. 216

The Salvation Army 6–7, 30, 46

Second World War (1939–45) 130, 237–41

Selassie, Emperor Haile 236

Shakespeare, Lieutenant-Colonel John 30

Shalford 229, 234

Shepperd, Revd R. L. 212

Shortt, Edward 177

Shute, Major-General C. D. 137

Smith, Major-General Sir Cecil 182

Sowerbutts, Mr 185, 243

Spanner, Sergeant-Drummer 74

Sparrow, Mrs M. 190

Stamfordham, Lord 174–6

Start, PC Joseph 15

Storr, Lt-Col L. 177

Studdert Kennedy, Revd Geoffrey (Woodbine Willie) 211–12, 213, 226, 229

T

Talbot, Lt Gilbert 110

Talbot, Neville 110, 241

Thompson, Constable Ernest 14, 18

Tindall, Canon Peter Francis 5, 27, 28, 91, 166

Tisdall, E. E. P 181

Topham, Private F. 103

Topham, Mary Anne 103, 203

Travis, Henry and Martha 36

Travis, Private Wallace Henry 35–6

Trinder, Major 73

U

Ullman, Harlan K. 116

Unknown Warrior: burial 179, 194–200, 233
  David Railton has the idea for 165–8, 229–30, 232–3, 244, 246
  Dean of Westminster seeks approval 167, 169–71, 172, 174–6
  hanging of the flag 213–14, 216–20
  memorial 236–7
  originator of idea questioned 229–33
  Queen Mother's tribute xvi–xvii , 249
  selection of body 179, 180–4
  travels to London 178–9, 183, 184–94, 241–2

V

Vendetta, HMS 187

Verdun, HMS 183, 186–7, 243

W

Wade, James P. 116

Wales, Prince of 194, 209

Walker, Private J. N. 37

Wallace, Revd. J. J. 117–18, 124, 158–9, 161–2

Wanstall, Percy 203

Ward, Private George 120

Ware, Major-General Sir Fabian 233

Wells, H. G. 161

Westminster Abbey: burial of Unknown Warrior 165, 170, 194–200, 233
  hanging of the flag 213–14, 216–20, 241–2

Whyall, Everard 139

Willson, Mary De Lancey (Dubby) 25, 136, 137, 205–6, 218, 219

Willson, Walter De Lancey 23

Wilson, Sir Henry 174, 176, 191

Wilson, J. B. 230–1, 232

Wilson, Woodrow 142

Wingate, Lord Orde 238

Wood, Revd C. T. T. 75

Wyatt, Brigadier General L. J. 180–3

Wyrall, Everard 113, 115, 116, 144, 145

Y

York, Duchess of xiv–xvii

York, Duke of xiv–xv, 194